Christian
Anti-Semitism
and
Paul's
Theology

Jewish Chautauqua Society

This book
was donated by

Centennial
Celebration
1893-1993

"Understanding Through Education"

Christian
Anti-Semitism
and
Paul's
Theology

Sidney G. Hall III

Fortress Press   Minneapolis

CHRISTIAN ANTI-SEMITISM AND PAUL'S THEOLOGY

Cover design: Terry W. Bentley
Cover art: sculpture from Yad Vashem, Jerusalem

Library of Congress Cataloging-in-Publication Data

Hall, Sidney G., 1958-
    Christian anti-Semitism and Paul's theology / Sidney G. Hall III.
        p.   cm.
    Includes bibliographical references and index.
    ISBN 0-8006-2654-0
    1. Bible. N.T. Epistles of Paul—Criticism, interpretation, etc.
    2. Paul, the Apostle, Saint—Views on Judaism.   3. Christianity and
    anti-Semitism.   4. Judaism—Relations—Christianity.   5. Christianity
    and other religions—Judaism.   I. Title.   II. Title: Christian
    anti-Semitism and Paul's theology.
    BS2655.J4H35   1993
    261.2'6'092—dc20   92-30395
                                                                                        CIP

The paper used in this publication meets the minimum requirements of American National Standard for Information Sciences—Permanence of Paper for Printed Library Materials, ANSI Z329.48-1984.   ∞™

Manufactured in the U.S.A.   AF 1-2654

97   96   95   94   93   1   2   3   4   5   6   7   8   9   10

No statement, theological or otherwise, should be made that would not be credible in the presence of the burning children.
—*Irving Greenberg*

Contents

Preface

> Have we really listened attentively during the
> last decades? Do we really know more today about
> the Jews and their religion? Have we become more
> attentive to the prophecy of their history of suf-
> fering? Or is the exploitation not beginning again,
> this time in more sublime fashion because placed
> under the banner of friendliness toward the
> Jews? . . . No prepared patterns exist for this di-
> alogue between Jews and Christians, patterns
> which could somehow be taken over from the fa-
> miliar repertoire of inner-Christian ecumenism.
> Everything has to be measured by Auschwitz.
> —J. B. Metz[1]

During the 1980 presidential campaign the Reverend Bailey Smith,
then president of the Southern Baptist Convention, stood before a large
crowd of evangelical Christians and stated, "With all due respect to
those dear people, God Almighty does not hear the prayer of a Jew.
For how in the world can God hear the prayer of a Jew, or how in the
world can God hear the prayer of a man who says that Jesus Christ is
not the true Messiah? That is blasphemy."[2] Many Jews, Roman Catholics,
and mainline Protestants were paralyzed with disbelief, wondering how
anyone could ever make such a claim. Yet, as Charles Silberman attests,
"What was noteworthy about Bailey Smith was not the view he expressed—it is widely shared—but the fact that he expressed it in public."[3]

Anti-Semitism in the West is not the prejudicial cloak of religious
fundamentalists alone. Racial anti-Semitism has been, and continues to
be, the armor of spiritual nakedness in Western society and Christian
tradition as a whole. For nearly two thousand years Christians have
espoused a theology of anti-Judaism. Since at least the latter half of the

first century, Christians have embraced a theology of rejection and replacement of the Jewish people. Anti-Jewish theology has been a principal doctrine of Christianity from early Gentile Christians to Irenaeus, from Augustine to Martin Luther, from Adolf von Harnack to Gerhard Kittel, Paul Tillich, and many contemporary theologians. There is unfortunately a hauntingly pervasive link between twenty centuries of Christian anti-Judaism and the explosion of racial anti-Semitism between 1933 and 1945.

Of course, one must not minimize the guilt of Adolf Hitler, the Nazi party, and a large segment of "cultured" European society in the deaths of eleven million people during the Holocaust. Yet one must also recognize that two thousand years of Christian anti-Jewish theology contributed to the crimes of the Nazis, through both theological justification and silence. The logical progression of anti-Jewish theology among Gentiles in the first century to the oven chambers of Auschwitz was from the Christian protest, "You have no right to live among us *as Jews*," to "You have no right to live *among us*," to "You have no right *to live*."[4]

Christians have been more conciliatory toward the Jewish people since the Nazis' systematic effort to rid the world of God's chosen ones. Awareness that the fiery pulpits of Christian anti-Judaism inevitably contributed to the fiery ovens of Auschwitz has thrust Christians into a crisis of theological integrity. It makes necessary an intentional Christian struggle to embrace a new theology that is at once particularly or distinctively Christian yet inclusively universal. Following such progressive religious leaders as Pope John XXIII and Rabbi Abraham Joshua Heschel, the Second Vatican Council helped launch the Christian church into this struggle by insisting that Christians no longer proselytize Jews. This was the first major Christian declaration in history in which Jews were accepted as Jews. Post-Auschwitz scholars and theologians such as Edward Flannery, Markus Barth, Johann Baptist Metz, E. P. Sanders, Robert McAfee Brown, and Clark M. Williamson have moved Christian theology closer to making the theology of Vatican II a reality.

Since the Second Vatican Council, however, scholars have begun interpreting the letters of the apostle Paul as one who embraced Jews as Jews, a development noted even in the popular press:

> A new generation of Scripture scholars is challenging many of the commonplace assumptions about who Paul was and what his teachings meant. Armed with more precise information about the historical Paul and his times, these scholars offer an arresting view of

> Paul as he saw himself: a Jewish apostle to the gentiles who did not
> envision the founding of a new religion, a pastor who was more
> concerned about communal behavior than individual salvation—
> and a counselor who never expected that his ad-hoc advice would
> become sacred Scripture.[5]

Paul was a Jewish apostle concerned with the liberation of those who
were oppressed—Gentiles, women, and slaves. Moreover, in contrast
to traditional interpretations, his theology is not now seen as one that
rejected Jews (i.e., called for them to convert to Christianity). The old
included groupings—Jews, men, and free—were still intact. Paul's primary message was that God's liberating love is impartial. To assert a
different gospel of God today is to blaspheme the God of Abraham and
Paul—the God who brings freedom to all who are broken, alienated,
and oppressed.

The purpose of this book is to gain a new, critical understanding of
Paul after Auschwitz. The fear that continues to grip Jewish survivors
of the Holocaust when they hear an unexpected knock on their door
entreats Christians to hear the silent cry of dead Jewish children—God's
beloved—who died in pyres of fury. These victims of systematic and
bureaucratic murder implore Christians to develop an inclusive yet
particular theology of the Jewish people. It is my conviction that Paul
espoused such a theology, which Christians can continue to support by
affirming Paul's theology of hope today.

After the Holocaust, a credible Christian theology must begin in and
result in a practical, *lived* theology. On the one hand, inclusive theology
develops out of praxis—actual encounters with the situation of the oppressed—and communicates a message of freedom to the particular
oppressed group or individual. The cry of suffering people is always the
starting place of God's liberating love. On the other hand, post-Holocaust
Christian theology must also result in praxis—the action of repentance
by the oppressor and respect for the inalienable freedom and self-determination of the oppressed. What occurs between the starting and
ending places is what Juan Luis Segundo calls "ideological suspicion,"
meaning a new perspective on Scripture and tradition grounded in a
critical reading of each.[6]

Such a view does not question the authority of God. But it does
challenge the authority of people who have misrepresented God. The
biblical witness is of a God who makes free all of humanity. One must

therefore suspect any theology that logically progresses to the captivity and destruction of others instead of their freedom and life.

Robert McAfee Brown asserts that the cry of the suffering Jew in the Holocaust is "an excellent starting point for a new [Christian] theology:" "When we hear the cry, 'I'm hurting,' we must take it seriously. And when we discover that the cry really means, 'You are hurting me,' we must hear it with utmost seriousness."[7]

The argument in this book progresses as a Christian theology of hope for the Jewish people. Thus, while I develop a distinctively Christian theology, the same theology results in respecting Judaism as a living, viable faith and the Jewish people as a living, viable people. I begin, however, with the ending, that is, with the destruction of Jewish people at Auschwitz. The first chapter, "Into the Fire," makes a confessional assessment of the Holocaust, both historically and theologically. Chapter 2, "A Revised Standard Version," journeys into the shadow side of Christian Scripture and tradition, a side of the church's story still widely ignored or repressed in classrooms and pulpits around the world. I explore the history of anti-Jewish theology in the church, which greatly contributed to the anti-Semitic racism buttressing the Nazi atrocities in the death camps. "In a Mirror Dimly," chapter 3, is the book's pivot, turning decisively to Paul and finding in him a theology of inclusiveness for both Jews and Gentiles. The fourth chapter, "Galatians: Before Moses Was Abraham," asserts a revisionist perspective of Paul's argument against the troublemakers in the Galatian church. "Romans: The Inclusive Promise of God," chapter 5, examines Paul's Letter to the Romans and offers a new, revolutionary understanding of Paul that I believe differs from all late twentieth-century revisionist perspectives on the apostle. Chapter 6, "Christology, Liberation, and the Jewish People," presents an understanding of Christ, developed from within the Pauline framework, that accents God's both inclusive and liberating love. That christology, I believe, is decisive and particularistic for Christians, yet it meets Irving Greenberg's haunting standard of being credible in the presence of the burning children, namely, Jewish children murdered in machines of flames and gas fewer than fifty years ago.[8] The concluding chapter, "No Chimneys!" proposes the hoped-for result of understanding Paul after Auschwitz: an affirmation of Christian identity and theology that results in people's freedom rather than destruction.

This book had its genesis from a doctoral dissertation on Paul and anti-Jewish theology. The passion undergirding the book emerged out of my own haunting realization that the Holocaust of the Jews in World War II and the credibility of the Church's ministry are intricately enmeshed. My hope is that this crisis of theological and ecclesiastical integrity might result in a new paradigm of Christian theology that is at once decisively Christian but also inclusively universal. It has been my experience that most Christian revisionist theologies seeking to be inclusive water down Christianity to a point where they lose their particularity, therefore becoming unrecognizable as "Christian"; while most Christian theologies that are not consciously on such a quest remain so particular that they are parochial and exclusive, often resulting in "them and us" actions that diminish everyone.

It would have been impossible to write this book without the innovative scholarship and ground work of Krister Stendahl, E. P. Sanders, Lloyd Gaston, John G. Gager, Ellis Rivkin and Clark M. Williamson. Although my indebtedness to their work is beyond measure, none of these or others listed should be held responsible for the views and positions I have asserted, particularly my own interpretation of Paul's theology and understanding of his gospel which I have named "the Inclusive Promise."

There are other people to whom I wish to express appreciation for their influence, either directly or indirectly, on this project—

My early mentors: Fern Theile, who refused to see a dried-up seed by always envisioning a greening plant; and William Dickison, who has remained working the plow in the field of his childhood, Russiaville, Indiana (except for his college education), but knew how to expand the capacity for others to plant in new fields like no teacher I have had since. His unique and creative style of teaching sparked in me an unquenchable fire for learning history and perhaps for learning in general.

I am also grateful for some very wise and gentle (and some not-so-gentle) faculty who provided safe passage for one narrowly-focused radical of the Jesus People vintage to emerge into a better integrated progressive activist (and still radical) of a different vintage: for professors Herbert Cassel, Alice Friman, Adolf Hansen, and Frederick Hill (the University of Indianapolis); Professor Clark M. Williamson (Christian Theological Seminary); and Professors Zan Holmes, Virgil Howard, Schubert M. Ogden, and W. J. A. Power (Perkins School of Theology at Southern Methodist University). I am particularly indebted to my college mentor, Adolf Hansen, now a vice president at Garrett-Evangelical Theological Seminary, and to my seminary mentor and graduate school advisor, Virgil Howard. Dr. Hansen and Dr. Howard exemplify the very best in teaching Biblical Studies and also take seriously their ongoing roles as mentors and friends to their students. Professors Robert Abzug of the University of Texas at Austin and John Holbert of Perkins School of Theology contributed directly by making helpful critical remarks in early editions of the project. Their capacity to cut to the quick was invaluable.

Thanks to my friend, Rev. David V. W. Owen, who by teaching and example, taught me that relevant, effective ministry is almost always on the fringe; and to my district superintendent, Dr. Gregory Robertson, who allows me, though sometimes trembling, to frequently be out on that fringe. Rev. Harold Williams's, Rev. Steve Conner's, Rev. Harold Sassman's, and the late Rev. Homer Weimer's influences on my ministry remind me that I am but an eclectic composite of other people's faithfulness. To them I am most grateful.

I have felt especially blessed by the dear people who, for the last fourteen years, have been my true spiritual teachers, even though I had been appointed to be a spiritual guide for them. These are the lay people of Edgewood United Methodist Church in Indianapolis, Tarrytown and St. John's United Methodist Churches in Austin, and to the incredible congregation where I have hung my hat as pastor for the last five years, Trinity United Methodist Church in Austin. Trinity's commitment not only to support a pastor on the fringe, but also to be a congregation dedicated to radical inclusion is a source of great strength for me.

The touchstone group for my work on this project has been the Jewish community of Austin. I appreciate the constructive feedback and interest expressed regarding this Christian's pursuit of developing a Christian theology of the Jewish people that Jews would deem credible in the presence of Jews and Judaism. I am thankful for Rabbis Marc Sack and Steven Folberg and the people of their synagogues: Congregation Agudas Achim and Congregation Beth Israel. Thanks also to Dr. Wayne Silverman and the Jewish Federation of Austin for entrusting to me the responsibility of being co-chair of the Yom HaShoah service for two consecutive years. A very special thanks to my co-chair and friend, Lucy Katz, who as a "Hidden Child" and Holocaust survivor, has been my inspiration to feel the urgency of commitment to "Never Again!" for all the children of the earth.

This book would not have been possible without the help of my close friends, Dr. Tim Bruster, Richard Hacker, and Dr. Rick Ricker. They have been constant companions of encouragement. Richard was gracious to read through the first copies of my manuscripts, make helpful editoral suggestions, and make me celebrate little victories along the way. My friends' presence has been my foundation.

A special thanks to the folks at Fortress Press: to J. Michael West, Senior Editor and Julie Odland (You're a patient soul, Julie!), Associate Editor, for believing in this book and seeing it through to publication.

I wish to thank my father, Sidney G. Hall Jr., for instilling in me the propensity for risk-taking, and my mother, Julia Ann Foster Hall, for giving to me a living example of someone who walks the talk of honoring all people.

Finally, I am thankful for my life companion and wife, Ronda, who lives out of integrity and inclusiveness in her vocation as a social worker, spouse, mother, and friend—especially in her commitment of love and encouragement toward me for the last eighteen years.

This book is dedicated to our children, Rachel Elizabeth and David Brendan, and to all the children of God's universe, that they may inherit a world of no chimneys—a world where compassion and justice are the measures of faithfulness and hope is the dance for all life.

—Sidney G. Hall III
February 1993

1

Into
the
Fire

Jesus said, "For I was hungry and you gave me
food, I was thirsty and you gave me something
to drink, I was a stranger and you welcomed
me, I was naked and you gave me clothing, I
was sick and you took care of me, I was in
prison and you visited me. . . . Truly I tell you,
just as you did it to one of the least of these who
are my sisters and brothers, you did it to me
. . . and just as you did not do it to one of the
least of these, you did not do it to me."

—Matthew 25:35-36, 40, 45, au. trans.

Mighty avalanche
    destroying all in its path
a child's tear descends.

—Mark E. Lett[1]

When I visited my grandparents' home as a child, one could often find
me huddled in a warm wool blanket in front of the fireplace. The reflection of flames dancing in the shadows of the room's hidden corners
lit up the room so brilliantly I could sense the presence of an immense
security beyond myself. The rich smell of smoldering birch, maple, and
pine wood, the crackling sound of a spark releasing itself from the log
to which it had once been lodged, are memories that rush back every
time I smell smoke rising from a chimney. The chimney, the fireplace—

gestures of warmth that represent everything from a cup of hot cinnamon-spiced apple cider at the home of my grandparents to the joyous advent of Santa Claus on Christmas morning. The chimneys! O the chimneys! Yet, how my memories differ from the memories of many people who still bear the tatoo of a number on their forearms from real-life nightmares that happened not so long ago. Such is the memory that haunts Filip Muller, an eyewitness at Auschwitz.

> The fire was lit in two of the pits in which about 2,500 dead bodies lay piled one on top of the other. Two hours later all that could be discerned in the white-hot flames were countless charred and scorched shapes, the blackish-phosphorescent hue a sign that they were in an advanced stage of cremation. . . . While in the crematorium ovens, once the corpses were thoroughly alight, it was possible to maintain a lasting red heat with the help of fans, in the pits the fire would burn only as long as the air could circulate freely in between the bodies. As the heap of bodies settled, no air was able to get in from the outside. This meant that we stokers had constantly to pour oil or wood alcohol on the burning corpses, in addition to human fat, large quantities of which had collected and was boiling in the two collecting pans on either side of the pit. The sizzling fat was scooped out with buckets on a long curved rod and poured all over the pit causing flames to leap up amid much crackling and hissing. Dense smoke and fumes rose incessantly. The air reeked of oil, fat, benzole and burnt flesh.[2]

It is bewildering to consider that millions of persons were killed at Auschwitz between 1942 and 1945. When the camp was liberated by the Russians on January 27th, 1945, only forty thousand prisoners had been registered among the millions who had died. The rest who perished there remain registered in the memories of loved ones and friends who survived—if any did survive. Even more astounding, approximately eleven million human beings were killed during the Holocaust, of whom about six million were Jews. The others were Europe's undesirables—Gypsies, homosexuals, Poles, mentally impaired, communists, and phys-ically impaired. What then is distinctive about the genocide of Jews?

According to Clark Williamson, although Hitler planned final solu-tions for other groups rendered as undesirable by the Nazis, the Jewish people were the top priority. Others could wait until after the war. The extermination of Jews even took priority over winning the war. Thus in 1945, even though railcars were in short supply to ship German troops to the front lines, Hitler guaranteed railcars to carry Jews to the death camps.[3]

Auschwitz becomes the symbolic event for all dialogue regarding the Nazis' Holocaust of the Jewish people. Consequently, Auschwitz also becomes the paradigm from which history and theology must work in a post-Holocaust world if anything one says, does, or believes is to be credible.

Initially, however, one must understand how and why such an atrocity was allowed to occur. Where were the voices of discontent? Could another Holocaust happen? These questions have risen up from the ashes of Auschwitz and persist; they concern the basic problem of human beings refusing to embrace their shadow side and how destructive that shadow can be when it is unleashed.

Understanding how and why Auschwitz transpired in the midst of an educated, technologically progressive, and basically Christian society is an issue that continues to perplex the world. Various explanations have been given from the perspectives of history, psychology, and religion, but the problem is so complex that only a comprehensive look at Auschwitz could begin to address the hows and whys.

Historical Perspectives

Adolf Hitler

As one searches the annals of history to find reasons for Auschwitz, one soon confronts Adolf Hitler. The consensus of history is that Hitler was a maniac, a madman who in only twelve years did more to disrupt that which is good and nurturing and sustaining in this world than any other person who ever lived. Yet he was also a master politician and a genius at motivating people. Perhaps this terrifying combination explains his cataclysmic impact on the world.[4]

Foundations of the Third Reich

Many have argued that the foundation was poured for Auschwitz with the Versailles treaty, which ended World War I. The deep-seated humiliation and anger among the German people may be evident in Hitler's forcing the French to surrender in the same railroad car in which the Germans surrendered at the end of World War I.

The Germans were a proud people who had only recently come under the nationalistic unification that had long been part of the heritage of other European countries such as England and France. The nineteenth century had become the period of cohesiveness and unity under the leadership of Prince Otto von Bismarck, who called himself and was recognized by the German people as the instigator and first chancellor of the German Empire. But after World War I, the German ethnocentric vision was on a collision course with military defeat, the destruction of Germany's industry, the infancy of democratic tradition, and the weakness of the Weimar Republic. Coupled with the world economic conditions of high inflation and the Great Depression (which hit Europe before it hit the United States), these factors no doubt put Germany in the position of quiet rage, ready to explode at the first provocation.

But these circumstances alone do not adequately explain Auschwitz. Other countries had experienced depressions, humiliations, nationalistic zeal, and shattered dreams without slaughtering millions of innocent victims, particularly Jews. At the base of Auschwitz amid the ashes of millions of bodies was the great sickness of anti-Semitism: hatred of the Jewish people. "For Hitler," observes George H. Stein, "the Jew was the cause and incarnation of all that he hated and feared: capitalism, Social Democracy, parliamentarianism, Bolshevism, antimilitarism, class welfare, pacifism, internationalism, modern art—and much more. There is no doubt that Hitler firmly believed what he said about the Jews."[5]

Hitler made many statements both before and after he rose to power as Reich chancellor in 1933. By the time President Hindenburg appointed him chancellor, Hitler's views regarding the Jewish people were public knowledge. In 1924, after being tried, convicted, and sentenced to five years in prison for his failed coup attempt, the "Beer-Hall Putsch" in Munich the previous year, he wrote the first volume of *Mein Kampf*. This passage illustrates his anti-Semitic rootedness:

> And so the Jew today is the great agitator for the complete destruction of Germany. Wherever in the world we read of attacks against Germany, Jews are their fabricators, just as in peacetime and during the War the press of the Jewish stock exchange and Marxists systematically stirred up hatred against Germany until state after state abandoned neutrality and, renouncing the true interests of the peoples, entered the service of the World War coalition.[6]

Unfortunately, this kind of sentiment was not unique to Hitler or to a handful of radicals at the end of the twentieth century's second decade.

It is estimated that the Nazi party had twenty thousand members in Germany by 1923; by 1930 it had secured 107 seats in the Reichstag election, polling approximately 2,500,000 votes. It is no surprise that the rise of the party in the 1920s is proportionate to the decline of Jewish status.[7] In spite of this trend most German Jews and informed outsiders did not imagine the magnitude of the tragic events that would occur in the thirties and early forties. Indeed, on the surface German Jews appeared to be faring better than their European neighbors in Poland, Rumania, and other countries where pogroms were common.

In 1933 roughly 503,000 Jews lived in Germany. Since the Great War they seemed omnipresent, involved in all aspects of culture and society. Although only one percent of the total population was Jewish, figures such as Albert Einstein excelled in the scientific community and novelists like Thomas Mann (a Gentile who was married to a Jew) arose in the literary field. Even though it was otherwise unheard-of for a Jew to hold a position of political influence, Walter Rathenau became foreign minister after World War I. The victim of portentous circumstances in 1920, he was murdered by an extremist who was at least partially motivated by anti-Semitism. Over a million people attended his funeral, a sign for the German Jews that Germany was their home.[8]

Were the Nazis extraordinarily evil, or did the root system run deep and wide, in the crevices and under the foundations? Abba Eban suggests that "not a single Nazi racial theory originated with Hitler. What Hitler did was to turn expounded theory into practice with a relentless consistency, extracting from the doctrine of racial anti-Semitism its murderous implications."[9] Indeed, one needs only to look at nineteenth-century Germany to see these frightening developments as precursors to what lay ahead.

Nineteenth-Century Germany

In 1881, about the same time he was finishing his Easter epic *Parsifal*, the great German opera composer Richard Wagner wrote to the Bavarian king Ludwig II: "I regard the Jewish race as the born enemy of pure humanity and everything that is noble in it; it is certain that we Germans will go under before them, and perhaps I am the last German who knows how to stand up as an art-loving man against the Judaism that is already getting control of everything."[10]

This letter is particularly important for understanding the German preoccupation with having a pure Aryan race that came to exemplify the creed of Hitler and the Nazi party from the 1920s through the mid-1940s; it is the first written account of anyone referring to the Jews *only* as a race. Thus the distinction of "racial Jew" superseded the ideas of Judaism as a religion and of Jews as the Jewish people and became a new form of discrimination. The former religious persecution in the fashion of anti-Judaism had developed into a full-fledged racial persecution of anti-Semitism.[11]

The Dreyfus Affair

In France anti-Semitism came out in the open during the Dreyfus affair in the late 1890s, a case that lasted twelve years and tore apart the Republic of France. In 1894 Captain Alfred Dreyfus, the only Jewish member of the French General Staff, was accused of spying for the Germans. High officials in the French government secretly tried, convicted, and sentenced him to life imprisonment on Devil's Island. The only evidence against Dreyfus was an unsigned document that was alleged to be in his handwriting.

In mid-1895 Colonel Picquart, the new head of counterespionage, reported to the French chief of staff that new evidence suggested that Dreyfus was innocent and that a Major Esterhazy was guilty of spying and of writing the forged letter. He was instructed to keep silent and sent to Tunisia, where French officials considered he was less likely to blurt his convictions to the public. At about the same time, the first public pamphlet attacking the trial was written.

By June 1897 Picquart revealed his convictions about the case to the vice president of the French Senate, and Georges Clemenceau, a French liberal statesperson, took on the cause of reopening the case. In the meantime, Picquart was arrested and Esterhazy was tried and acquitted. (In 1898 Esterhazy was dishonorably discharged and confessed to an English newspaper that he had forged the letter.) In an effort to add ten years to his sentence, in 1899 Dreyfus was accused and found guilty of forging more documents. A week after Dreyfus's conviction the French president acted quickly to pardon him and end the whole affair.

Understandably, Dreyfus was not completely satisfied, and in 1903 he asked for an official acquittal rather than a pardon, to clear his tainted record. The French court of appeals finally acquitted Alfred Dreyfus of all charges in 1906.[12]

The Dreyfus affair is similar to many cases in which a person is made the scapegoat to cover someone else's unwillingness to admit a mistake. But this was not just any case. Dreyfus was the only Jew in a high position of the French government. The press's actions, the secretive measures taken by high officials, and Dreyfus's persistence became the circumstances for a repressed anti-Semitism to explode into open confrontation not only in France but throughout Europe and America. Alfred Dreyfus was not the cause of the deep hatred that non-Jews felt for Jews; he was merely a catalyst that contributed in bringing on a very sad effect. "The Dreyfus affair has been seen as a dress-rehearsal for Hitlerism. Certainly it was the most extraordinary exhibit of modern antisemitism outside Germany."[13]

Other hotbeds of racism in the form of anti-Semitism existed outside Europe. With communication systems becoming more sophisticated and with the outbreak of World War I in 1914, the world was quickly becoming smaller. Thus it is no surprise that anti-Semitism found its way across the Atlantic onto the shores of "the land of free."

Anti-Semitism in the United States

An honest assessment of U.S. history has always revealed the United States is "the land of the free" only in relative terms. Freedom is never genuine if it is at the cost of another's freedom. Although one should not minimize the horrendous crimes of Hitler and the Nazis toward the Jews between 1933 and 1945, Americans should also acknowledge the truth that some top U.S. officials either ignored what was happening or did not make it a priority even after they learned of the atrocities in the death camps.

Charles Lindbergh, one of America's great twentieth-century heroes, made this statement in September 1941 in his efforts to discourage the country from backing the Allies in Europe: "The three most important groups who have been pressing this country toward war are the British, the Jewish, and the Roosevelt Administration."[14] His speech was poorly received by the American public, but his insensitivity is nevertheless a good example of the unconscious stream of anti-Semitism that flowed in this nation.

An underlying stream of anti-Semitism was also evident in this country. Even though its impetus proved too weak to have much influence when the Great Depression and World War II erupted, anti-Semitism in America did have a powerful influence from 1915 to 1925. Just as the Dreyfus affair lifted the veil on France in the late 1800s, many U.S. citizens' racism toward the Jewish people was unmasked in a number of tragic events about the time that World War I began.

The Case of Leo Frank   Two examples are of particular interest; the first because of what was involved, and the second because of who was involved. The first event involved George Watson, a native of Georgia who rose through the ranks of society as a teacher, a trial lawyer, a representative in the Georgia state legislature, and a U.S. congressman. By 1896 he was nominated as the vice presidential candidate for the Populist party. Eight years later he was nominated as the Populists' presidential candidate, but by this time the party had lost much of its authority.

Simultaneously with his political climb, he exerted his influence in the private sector in buying and publishing several newspapers in the Atlanta area. Watson was a bigot who used his newspapers to attack mostly Catholics and blacks; in 1913 he added a new group to his unwanted list—the Jews.

His bigotry is characterized in his printed defamation of Leo Frank, a prominent Jew in Atlanta who was arrested and charged for the rape and murder of a fourteen-year-old girl in his factory. Frank admitted to paying the girl wages on the day of the incident, but said that this had been his only contact with her. In the following months, he was tried in an open courtroom full of people who frequently yelled out slanderous anti-Semitic statements, and on the basis of only circumstantial evidence was convicted of murder. The court decision was appealed and eventually reached the U.S. Supreme Court, but the Court ruled that it lacked jurisdiction, with only Chief Justice Holmes and Justice Hughes dissenting. Frank was sentenced to life imprisonment. With the mobs crying "execution" and Frank's security becoming more of an issue, the Georgia governor had him secretly moved to a fortresslike prison complex for his protection. Watson's newspapers soon discovered his location, and with the crowds and the public raging out of control, the ultimate tragedy occurred.

In August 1915 the tension was so great that talk of lynching had penetrated even the prison walls. Then a convict slashed Frank's throat, injuring him severely. Four days later a large mob stormed the prison, hauled off Frank, and lynched him near the girl's home in Marietta.[15] Around the nation people were shocked and bewildered. Yet the *Marietta Journal* pronounced: "We regard the hanging of Leo M. Frank as an act of law-abiding citizens." Watson himself responded to the lynching by boasting, "A vigilante committee redeems Georgia and carries out the sentence of the law . . . Jew libertines take notice."[16]

Although many in the United States were saddened by and abhorred the Frank lynching, during this incident the Ku Klux Klan got their biggest boost in membership since the years of Reconstruction after the Civil War. The trend in membership growth and violent activities for the Klan continued until 1929 when, after the stock market crash, people's energies became more directed toward survival in a depression.

The Influence of Henry Ford   The second example that reveals the magnitude of anti-Semitism in the United States involved the man who came to epitomize the American dream, Henry Ford, Sr. It is unfortunate that as a symbol for the American dream, his dream became a nightmare for the Jewish people. Henry Ford is commonly recognized as the father of American production because of his creation of the assembly line. But many people today do not realize that Ford was the father of the production line for anti-Semitic propaganda as well. His propaganda war against the Jewish people took its primary form in the weekly newspaper he owned, the *Dearborn Independent*. The attitude he harbored against Jews is typical of what Jonathan Sarna calls the conflict between

> the "mythical Jew," that cursed figure of Christian tradition deeply embedded in Western culture, and the "Jew next door," who seemingly gave the lie to every element of the stereotype. Usually, it was the mythical Jew—the unscrupulous moneylender, the eternal wanderer, the satanic Christ-killer—who was flayed by anti-Semites. If they sometimes realized that Jews of their acquaintance did not fit the mold, the mold was often too deeply ingrained to change; it was easier to live with the contradiction. "Them Jews—I don't mean you," is a phrase one upstate New Yorker still remembers having heard from her neighbors.[17]

Like many of America's people in high social order, Ford had strong anti-Semitic sentiments. As a well-respected industrialist, inventor, and folk hero his opinions generally carried considerable weight with the public.

The *Dearborn Independent* issued its first anti-Jewish statement on May 22, 1920. It continued to do so for a total of ninety-one issues. During the time Ford ran the series, sales of the paper dropped, resulting in a loss of nearly five million dollars. But in his opinion it was the best poor investment he had ever made.

Even though American Jews and many non-Jews lost respect for Ford, his influence, both positive and negative, reached deeply into Middle America. Leo M. Franklin, rabbi at a large Detroit synagogue, longtime neighbor and former friend of Ford, remarked to a Detroit newspaper, "Few thinking men have given any credence to the charges offered against Jews. But his publications have besmirched the name of the Jews in the eyes of the great majority, and especially in the small towns of America, where Ford's word was taken as gospel. He has also fed the flames of anti-Semitism throughout the world."[18]

Based on articles written in the *Independent*, Ford published *The Protocols*, statements accusing Jews of subversive actions in business and world affairs. These ideas were further refined in his publication *The International Jew*, which, beginning in the 1920s, became popular in the United States. During the thirties *The International Jew* was even translated into German and helped feed Nazi propaganda, which taught that Jews were making a concerted effort and had a subversive plot to control the world.

By the late 1930s, with his name being increasingly associated with Hitler, Henry Ford wrote a retraction of his earlier publications. One would like to believe he grew and changed over the years, but some evidence suggests otherwise. Gerald L. K. Smith, an acquaintance of Ford and the national director of the Christian Nationalist Crusade in the 1950s, continued to publish *The International Jew*. In his introduction to a copy printed in the fifties, Smith relates that in one of his many interviews with Ford in 1940 "he gave me a sensational and shocking report. He said: 'Mr. Smith, my apology for publishing "The International Jew" was given great publicity, but I did not sign that apology. It was signed by Harry Bennett.' "[19] Whether this story is true will never be known. The letter appears to have Henry Ford's signature. The tragedy is that even if Ford did retract his past offenses toward the Jewish people, he had already done considerable damage. That Smith was able to use Ford to promote neo-Nazi "Christian" nationalism is an example of Ford's destructive influence.

Anti-Semitism persists today and can be found in all elements of society—from the rich to the poor, from the powerful to the not so powerful, and from Washington to Berlin to Moscow to Tokyo. Its roots are deep and have no cultural bounds. Contemporary expressions of anti-Semitism include former president Richard M. Nixon's Watergate tapes, the Reagan administration's visit to the Bitburg cemetery, Kurt Waldheim's (a former Nazi) election as president of Austria, and the violence that requires police to guard synagogues across the United States on Jewish holidays.

An historical overview enhances one's understanding of the immediate circumstances that led to Auschwitz. Psychological explanations of basic problems of human nature, such as the tendency to scapegoat and fear the other, also illuminate the causes of Auschwitz. But Auschwitz goes beyond generalized conditions of humanity. The roots of racial anti-Semitism do not lie merely in the historical conditions that developed in the nineteenth and twentieth centuries. Nor do they exist simply in psychological theories. Rather, one can find the roots of racial anti-Semitism in nineteen and a half centuries of religious persecution of Jews by Christians.

Theological Perspectives

It is difficult for many to recognize that the problem is primarily a religious one. The roots of *anti-Semitism* (a *racial* disease) lie specifically in the warped Christian tradition of *anti-Judaism* (a *theological* disorder).

Destructive Presuppositions

For nearly two thousand years Christians have blamed the Jews for the death of Jesus. But post-Holocaust scholarship in the field of first-century Jewish history demonstrates that this firmly held viewpoint is incorrect.[20] Jesus' death was not the result of a crowd of soured and disillusioned Jews shouting "Crucify him," but of a planned political execution by the Romans and the Roman procurator of the land of Israel, Pontius Pilate. Documents from the first century C.E. suggest that Pilate was a paranoid tyrant. He crucified or beheaded Jewish charismatics who drew attention to themselves because he viewed them, whether they were politically or religiously motivated, as a potential threat to the security of the Empire.[21]

The historical ramifications of Christians labeling Jews as "the Christ-killers" are too easy to dismiss, especially in a secular world. Yet such a position is still common among many Christians in the twentieth century. While most Christians in the Catholic Church and in mainline Protestant churches do not think of themselves as anti-Jewish, the imminent danger of anti-Semitic messages nevertheless remains each time the Gospels are read and expounded without careful scrutiny.

During the reign of the Third Reich most of this century's great Christian theologians and church leaders came out against Hitler and the Nazis' philosophy and actions toward the Jews. But many of these Christians continued to proclaim a rejection and replacement theology of Judaism without making the connection between their theology and anti-Semitism. This failure is evident in the writings of scholars such as Paul Tillich, Karl Barth, and, some argue, Dietrich Bonhoeffer,[22] who died in a Nazi prison camp after an unsuccessful plot to assassinate Hitler.

Alexander Donat's personal memoir, *Holocaust Kingdom,* illustrates the inconsistency between morality and theology. In the context of the Warsaw ghetto, from which hundreds of thousands of Jews were sent to the chambers of death, he focuses on a wife, a husband, and their little boy, who survived both the ghetto and the death camps. Clark Williamson paraphrases the account:

> The parents were fortunate in being able to place their son with a friend who lived outside the ghetto. . . . The parents were shipped off to Auschwitz, separated, and managed by hook and crook to survive the final solution. Neither was aware of the fate of the other or of the child. At the age of five, supplied with a new birth certificate by a Roman Catholic parish, the boy walked out of the ghetto holding the hand of the woman who saved his life. He was spirited away to a Roman Catholic orphanage in the countryside, where he went to church every Sunday, said his prayers twice a day, and learned the Our Father and the Hail Mary. The boy was converted to Christianity by the nun who looked after the children. She taught him that he "would have to give up all Jewish things." He was baptized. He was taught the classic Christian attitudes toward Jews.
>
> When he and his mother were reunited after the war, "he hated everything Jewish." "The Jews," he said, "killed the Lord Jesus."[23]

The nun who converted the young boy was not a bad woman. She was fulfilling what she understood to be her ministry for God; indeed, she became the hands and feet of God in her courageous acts to save children from the ovens of Auschwitz. Nevertheless, the irony of her actions is apparent. As Williamson observes, "The effort to purify the world of Jews begins with the attempt to convert them, to destroy a people and a heritage by spiritual means. . . . That nun may be excused for not having realized something for which, with all our benefit of hindsight, we have no excuse. There is no justification for continuing the theology or behavior that made possible the final solution."[24]

Auschwitz, then, demands an honest and confessional look at Christian tradition, with all its shadows and blood as well as its glories and acts of charity. The veil has been lifted on the church's character by an event so tragic that it precludes turning back to innocence. Therefore, Auschwitz becomes the normative event for doing Christian theology and a new paradigm for practicing the Christian faith. The challenge for faith after Auschwitz is not to fear change—even radical transformation. In the face of the Holocaust one must risk letting go of some traditions and allow the God of Abraham and Paul to lead the way out of the ashes of the past and assure that Auschwitz will never happen again.

The Catholic theologian J. B. Metz sets forth the theological criterion: "not to engage in a theology of any kind that remains untouched by Auschwitz or could have remained untouched by it"; he advises his students to "leave alone any theology which actually could have been the same before or after Auschwitz."[25] Furthermore, Metz writes, "There is at least one authority that we should never reject or despise—the authority of those who suffer. If this applied anywhere, it applies, in our Christian and German history, to Auschwitz. The fate of the Jews must be remembered as a moral reality precisely because it threatens already to become a mere matter of history."[26]

Paving New Roads

This perspective calls for a hermeneutical approach that is rudimentarily different from past approaches. Whether one has started with Scripture and moved in the direction of tradition and experience or vice versa, Scripture has been upheld at all costs. Yet the oven chambers of Auschwitz suggest that some of the traditional foundation doctrines in the

New Testament may be destructive and even present a message contrary
to the central proclamation of Jesus. Whether these doctrines spring
from particular statements in the New Testament or from biased interpretations of Scripture through Christian tradition, the event of Auschwitz confronts every person with questions of identity and beliefs and
calls for radical transformation. One must go where Auschwitz leads.
What does it mean, then, to engage in a theology that has been
touched by Auschwitz? Can one have a Christian theology of, after, or
in the light of Auschwitz? I believe that one can and one must. Unless
the Holocaust engages one theologically, christologically, and typolog-
ically, one is forever in danger of preserving the spark of anti-Judaism
in the church and yielding to the possibility of more flames to destroy
Jewish children and other children of God around the world.

One can solicit a theology of Auschwitz through many means, but
two seem most appropriate—symbol and history. The best approach is
to blend these two, but first one must deal with them separately to grasp
the full meaning of their impact together. One must be cautious, however, in speaking of symbol and history as separate. All speech is symbolic; the very words one uses in the construct of language are symbols
of thoughts, ideas, and events. Thus to speak of historical events one
uses the symbol of language. The following argument about the cross
reflects on a particular symbol as a means of doing Christian theology
after Auschwitz. Then, as part of that discussion, I inquire into an
historical understanding of the cross; that inquiry leads to an analysis
of the scriptural text itself.

The Cross   Perhaps the symbol that best represents a Christian reflection on Auschwitz is the cross. At this point I submit a word of
caution. For Christians, the cross represents the image of trust, liberation, love, and self-giving. For Jews, the image is quite the contrary.

This reality struck home several years ago when I was counseling a
couple who were considering an interfaith marriage. The woman had
grown up in the church. The man had been raised in the synagogue.
She had little question through life that if and when she married the
ceremony would be celebrated in the sanctuary where she heard the
Scripture expounded, partook of the Lord's Supper, and was baptized
as an infant. Since the woman sought to be open to the man's wishes,
and he to hers, they hoped to combine significant parts of the wedding
rituals of both the Jewish and Christian traditions.

But months prior to the wedding, as they walked into the sanctuary for the first time together, the man suddenly jumped back. On the center wall above the chancel area was a large wooden cross. It was clearly the focal point of the room and would be impossible to hide or to dismantle for the wedding. Although the man had recently been inactive in his synagogue, he was very much a kindred soul with his brutally destroyed forebears that day as he glared in distress at the cross. In his eyes one could sense terror, fear, anger. For him, the Christian cross did not represent love and liberation or sacramental hope. Instead, he saw the cross of demonic sacrifice, the cross under which countless numbers of his ancestors had been killed during the Crusades and millions more had been murdered during the Holocaust. In that moment the couple glimpsed the difficulty of an interfaith marriage. They felt the distance between their families, their traditions. For one tradition, the way of the cross leads to light. For another, the way of the cross is a dark, billowing cloud that rises from burnt flesh in machines of death.

Although the cross may be a stumbling block in Christian-Jewish dialogue, it can be a bridge as well. One must take the cross into account; this symbol is central to the Christian encounter with faith. If one looks closely at Paul's understanding of the cross,[27] the cross can even be instrumental in developing a Christian theology after Auschwitz.

The framework from which I reflect on the cross evolves out of what Gustaf Aulen calls the "classic" idea of atonement. This view affirms that in Christ, God fights against and has victory over brokenness and oppression, an evil that leads to bondage and suffering. Through this act, many recognize God's reconciling love toward humanity. In the classical framework, wholeness and liberation require risk; not only the risk of humanity in relation to God but also of God in relation to humanity and the world. The drama of atonement is a work in which God reconciles both the world to Godself and Godself to the world. Thus in the encounter between God and human beings not only do human beings change but God also changes.[28]

One must be careful, however, not to limit God's reconciling love to only one action at one place and time, for this exclusive interpretation of atonement in Christian tradition has helped lay the rails to Auschwitz. The destructive claim of Christian exclusivists asserts a belief that God is limited to only one re-presentation of boundless love—through Jesus Christ.

Even if one attests that God is dynamic and continues to remove the obstacles that prevent humanity from embracing its own God-blessedness when it is understood as only possible through Christ, one limits the love, work, and redemption of God to one normative event and one truth-bearing tradition. This "smaller" God is the same God whom countless Germans misrepresented in their belief that the New Jerusalem had room for only one Aryan race.

The classic interpretation of atonement in principle has room for a bigger, creation-centered God who risks for other peoples and creation through other normative events. Indeed, the dynamic nature of God's love is always risking and reconciling people toward God and God toward people.

At Auschwitz one encounters this God, the God who enters into the human drama of pain and suffering, tears and mourning, joy and laughter, hope and liberation. God is not aloof or dispassionate in the midst of tragedy. Nor does God show compassion on one group and enmity on another. Rather, the God of Abraham and Sarah, Paul and Hildegard is directly in the middle of everything—wounded, yet calling all creation into wholeness.

Therefore, the cross that reminds Christians of the loving, reconciling, and present God who was in Jesus two thousand years ago can also help bridge the gap for Christians to encounter the same God who was present with the Jews at Auschwitz. The millions who were murdered may have not even been aware that in their death God was suffering in love with them for the sake of humanity. Indeed, many of them may have felt as Jesus of Nazareth did when, as Mark's Gospel records, he cried out, "My God, my God, why have you forsaken me?" (15:34). But the God of Jewish and Christian tradition is present in death, pain, and oppression.

It is doubtful that most of the people killed in the Holocaust perceived themselves as martyrs. Just as unlikely is the claim that Jesus understood himself in this way. Jesus and the eleven million people killed in the Holocaust were probably unable to understand or to give meaning to the bureaucratic, systematic, and demonic force that crushed them. Perhaps only in the deepest ontological and existential sense (certainly not in the conventionally rational or theological perception) did some of the victims of torture and humiliation grasp that even in their deaths God was with them—dying, being gassed, and being burned alive. Elie

Wiesel captures the essence of this awareness when he writes about three gallows:

> One day when we came back from work, we saw three gallows rearing up in the assembly place, three black crows. Roll call. SS all around us, machine guns trained: the traditional ceremony. Three victims in chains—and one of them, the little servant, the sad-eyed angel.
>
> The SS seemed more preoccupied, more disturbed than usual. To hang a young boy in front of thousands of spectators was no light matter. The head of the camp read the verdict. All eyes were on the child. He was lividly pale, almost calm, biting his lips. The gallows threw its shadow over him.
>
> This time the Lagerkapo refused to act as executioner. Three SS replaced him.
>
> The three victims mounted together onto the chairs.
>
> The three necks were placed at the same moment within the nooses.
>
> "Long live liberty!" cried the two adults.
>
> But the child was silent.
>
> "Where is God? Where is He?" someone behind me asked.
>
> At a sign from the head of the camp, the three chairs tipped over.
>
> Total silence throughout the camp. On the horizon, the sun was setting.
>
> "Bare your heads!" yelled the head of the camp. His voice was raucous. We were weeping.
>
> "Cover your heads!"
>
> Then the march past began. The two adults were no longer alive. Their tongues hung swollen, blue-tinged. But the third rope was still moving; being so light, the child was still alive. . . .
>
> For more than half an hour he stayed there, struggling between life and death, dying in slow agony under our eyes. And we had to look him full in the face. He was still alive when I passed in front of him. His tongue was still red, his eyes not yet glazed.
>
> Behind me, I heard the same man asking:
>
> "Where is God now?"
>
> And I heard a voice within me answer him:
>
> "Where is He? Here He is—He is hanging here on this gallows. . . ."
>
> That night the soup tasted of corpses.[29]

Christian tradition has allegorically interpreted Isaiah's suffering servant as Jesus Christ, who suffered and died with all of humanity's iniquity upon him. The testimonies of those who died and of those who survived the chambers of death remind one that the suffering servant—this time, the Jewish people and indeed God—continue to die each time God's children are killed. The hymn in Isaiah is not a prophecy or allegory of Jesus; rather, it is an analogy of Second Isaiah's Israel, the early Christians' crucified Lord whom the Romans killed, countless victims of atrocities through the ages, and the death of Israel's six million servants at the hands of the Nazis. As Wiesel poignantly suggests, it was not only Jesus or Israel who was led like a lamb to the slaughter but the God of the universe, who died there on the cross and in the oven chambers. God hurts with God's children and is murdered all the day long when God's children suffer at the hands of another.

The symbol of the cross is indeed helpful and necessary in wrestling with a Christian theology of Auschwitz. Analogy, as a literary genre, requires little reworking of past traditions. Historical inquiry, however, tests the very foundations of faith. Where suffering is present the liberating God calls Christians to grapple with Scripture and the historical interpretation placed upon particular scriptural presuppositions. Thus Christians must reexamine the New Testament, question how the New Testament community interpreted the Hebrew Scriptures, and ask how the church has interpreted and reinterpreted the Christian message for two thousand years. Is it possible in Christianity to embrace a faith claim that is inclusive of other people and all of God's creation? One must recognize that, if examined honestly, some of the foundational assertions of the Christian Scriptures have had destructive results.

An Inclusive Faith   Many theological problems with the New Testament can be creatively addressed in ways that do not shake the foundations. One creative tool is demythologization. If one has difficulties with biblical assertions that are dependent on the prescientific cosmology of the first century, one can still assert the existential claim implied in the text and demythologize the story into a twentieth-century cosmological framework. For example, one may either literally or figuratively affirm the virgin birth in the first chapters of Matthew and Luke; both perspectives can translate the account into today's world as the affirmation of God's presence with Jesus and humanity—Emmanuel, or of humanity's own birthing of God through creative acts of love and compassion.

Another creative approach is to establish an historical context for the document to determine if what is being asserted is relevant only for the time in which it was written or if it has transcultural, timeless validity. For example, Paul's argument in 1 Corinthians regarding the moral issue of eating meat that had been sacrificed to idols is obviously an issue that had specific historical relevance for the church in Corinth, but has little bearing for a modern Christian community rooted in monotheism and a postsacrificial liturgy. But the precept behind Paul's discussion—abstaining from actions that offend others—might be valid today, even though the specific instructions were relevant only to the people whom Paul addressed in the letter.

A third helpful development is the use of inclusive language rather than the exclusively male language of the Bible. The advent of the contemporary feminist movement in the 1960s has resulted in the revision of Bible translations, lectionaries, and worship aids. The process of inclusion is similar to demythologizing in that it requires one to change language that was written in a male-dominated culture into a contemporary language that affirms the equality of male and female.

A fourth approach concerns the issue of liberation. The Third World church and the church rooted in the African American subculture have been particularly instrumental in helping people from a traditional Western theological framework to see new and creative ways of interpreting the Scripture that takes into account liberation. Liberation theology is beginning to address the issue that in Christ "there is neither slave nor free, there is neither male nor female, there is neither abled nor disabled, there is neither straight nor gay," but "neither Jew nor Greek" perplexes those who hold a christocentric theology (as opposed to a theocentric Christian theology) that is theologically oppressive toward other faith communities.

Therefore a theology that evolves out of Auschwitz—a theology particular to the context of one's own faith community yet inclusive of the coexistence and vitality of other faiths—constitutes a unique problem for the church. Unlike the approaches of demythologizing, historical contextualization, using gender-inclusive language, and liberation theology, Auschwitz—like the Crusades—confronts Christianity at its theological base. The rejection and replacement claim that Jesus Christ is the *only* child of God for all of humanity, not just *a* child of God, allowed Christianity to become a religion of intolerance and persecution toward those who do not adhere to its specific claim. Christianity is confronted because this kind of christological framework has no room for the existence of other faith communities.

Although Judaism is a tradition that has at times been intolerant of other groups and even xenophobic, by its very nature it is a faith that does not work out of the rejection and replacement framework regarding other religions. As a result, many Jews today are able to embrace Christianity as a younger sibling more easily than Christians embrace Judaism. But Judaism has never been able to accept Christianity's exclusive claim on God's covenant, which implies that God has revoked the covenant with the people of Israel when they continue to relate to God outside the Christ claim.

Unfortunately, the exclusive claim of Christianity is illustrated numerous times in the New Testament. Although this claim seems quite distinct from what one can discern about the historical Jesus, it appears to have been central to the Jesus kerygma (proclamation) in the early church. Paul also makes a particular claim about Christ, but, as succeeding chapters will demonstrate, he does so without the anti-Judaic fervor and rejectionist foundation through which Augustine, Luther, and countless other Christians have interpreted him.

Many contemporary authors involved in Jewish-Christian dialogue would strongly disagree with this position regarding Paul. They claim that Paul's gospel of Christ was for Gentiles only and regard him as the major bridge for dialogue between Jews and Christians. Although I agree with the latter assertion, the former position seems to be more wishful thinking than a realistic assessment of Paul's teachings. That God called Paul as a Jew to be the apostle to the Gentiles seems accurate. But this statement does not entail the claim that Paul believed that the gospel of Christ is for Gentiles only. Rather, Paul claims that Jews should accept *the gospel* of Christ without asserting that Jews should become Christians (accept *Christ*).

In a study of Christian-Jewish dialogue, Peter von der Osten-Sacken asks: What does one do with the Jews through the ages that have become Christians while maintaining their Jewishness? The early apostles who walked and lived with Jesus were Jewish, as was Paul. Through the Christian ages there is evidence that some Jews, though a minority, held fast to their Jewishness yet affirmed a faith that allowed for the gospel of Christ as well.[30] It is not altogether clear that most of Jewish Christianity today is what Paul meant by Jews accepting the gospel of Christ, but a Christian theology of Judaism that does not at least take into account contemporary Jewish Christians fails to deal with an important aspect of the church's life.

But the chimneys! The claim of Auschwitz haunts one and forces one to reckon with traditional theology. One must follow where Auschwitz leads. One simply cannot ignore that the same Paul who made the particularistic claim of Jesus as Lord also posed the question: "Has God rejected God's people? By no means! I myself am an Israelite, a descendant of Abraham, a member of the tribe of Benjamin. God has not rejected [God's] people whom [God] foreknew" (Rom. 11:2). Is this the same Paul? What can one make of the paradox he presents?

Auschwitz presents Christians with an ultimatum—to reject intolerant theology and to shed the cloak of anti-Judaism worn for two thousand years. After the Holocaust one must recognize that "no longer is it a case of the illegitimacy of Judaism. Unless [Christians] succeed in finding within the New Testament some area which is substantially free of anti-Judaism, the issue becomes the illegitimacy of Christianity."[31] But is it possible for Christianity to cast off its rejection and replacement theology and uphold the foundations on which Christian tradition rests? Yes! Such a theology can be accomplished and it can be demonstrated through Paul.

The ovens of Auschwitz have thrust Christianity into a new era. The potential for more Holocausts always exists as long as people do not embrace one another with the love that comes from the eternal God. Martin Luther King, Jr., eloquently summed up the universality of this mandate when he wrote in 1963 from the Birmingham city jail: "Injustice anywhere is a threat to justice everywhere. We are caught in an inescapable network of mutuality, tied in a single garment of destiny. Whatever affects one directly affects all indirectly. Never again can we afford to live with the narrow, provincial 'outside agitator' idea."[32]

Jews are extending their hands toward Christians not just in love but also in hope—in the great hope that Christians will remember Auschwitz, and that the world will remember not for the sake of sentimentality but to proclaim wholeheartedly: Never again!

A Christian theology of anti-Judaism diminishes the church's theological integrity. As the church stares aimlessly into the fires of destruction, the silent tears of dead Jewish children require Christians to ponder their own existence. It is as if the children ask, "Do not the ovens of Auschwitz engulf Christians in shame before the God of Abraham and God's people?" Thus, it is not a matter of deciding whether the church will move into the fires of Auschwitz. Christians have already entered the oven chambers. There, along with eleven million people, Christian theology went up in smoke. But it was not the end of Christian theology. Perhaps through confession, the church can discover a creative, holistic, and liberative theology that out of integrity testifies to the reality of a living God and a living universe.

2

A Revised
Standard
Version

Just as in the life of an individual the
adolescent breaks away from the parent,
sometimes with much scorn and contempt for
the values and practices of the parent and of the
parent's generation, so too in the history of
religions the new community strikes out verbally
against the parent community. . . . Usually the
closer the family ties had been, the greater is
the viciousness of the denunciations. The verbal
attack is directly against the religious community
that gave birth to and nurtured the new group,
while virtually nothing is said against distant
faith communities not directly involved nor
simultaneously competing for the allegiance of
the same persons.

. . . The Christian tradition—in fact any
religious tradition—should be encouraged to be
critical of itself. Such self-criticism may not be
acceptable during the youth and adolescence of
a religious tradition. . . . Nevertheless, I think
that radical self-criticism is essential to the
health and vitality of the church.
—Norman A. Beck[1]

Life's transitions are traumatic; although not humorous at the time, the
recollection of some of the more awkward occasions often induces laughter. One such episode was my first day of college. That I was unprepared
for both the intellectual and emotional challenge academia thrust upon
me is an understatement. Yet, taking the advice of well-meaning Christians from my hometown, I felt prepared to engage in the battle to
secure my faith from the vipers, the deceivers, the children of Satan—
commonly known to unbelievers as religion professors. Having girded

my loins with blue jeans, having put on the breastplate of righteousness (a T-shirt imprinted with a "One Way" gesture), and having shod my feet with holed (as opposed to holy) shoes, I embarked across campus to class. I took the shield of faith (a silver cross necklace), which I knew would quench all the flaming darts of the Evil One. I had my cowboy hat of salvation, covered with buttons exclaiming "God loves you and so do I," and the sword of the Spirit (my contemporary paraphrased Bible wrapped in a beautiful leather carrying case). With all these, I entered Beginning Greek. After half an hour of stares from upper-class students and a convincing lecture on biblical criticism, I took off my cowboy hat, hid it under the chair, and began to think that the gates of hell had prevailed against me. I was losing my faith—or so it seemed.

This perceived loss of faith proved only to be the first of many confrontations with my religious credulity. The irony is that I was not losing my faith but beginning the process in which everyone must engage in order to have authentic faith. Ken Wilber suggests: "The movement of descent and discovery begins at the moment you consciously become dissatisfied with life. . . . For concealed within this basic unhappiness . . . is the embryo of a growing intelligence, . . . usually buried under the immense weight of social shams. . . . It marks the birth of creative insight.[2]

Today one confronts the atrocities of the Holocaust. The death camps reveal something gone sour, the shadow side of humanity, the way one can twist a religious tradition so as to project on others the sinful disease of anti-Judaism that lay within oneself. The haunting words of Abraham Joshua Heschel make this truth painfully real: "It is with shame and anguish that I recall that it was possible for a Roman Catholic church adjoining the extermination camp in Auschwitz to offer communion to the officers of the camp, to people who day after day drove thousands of people to be killed in the gas chambers."[3] In spite of such testimony, many contemporary Christians have difficulty believing that the roots of anti-Semitism lay partly, and perhaps mostly, in the New Testament and in the Christian tradition. Many make no connection between "putting on the whole armor of God" and the Crusaders' blood-stained armor in the Middle Ages. They draw no parallel between Christians bearing crosses "marching as to war" and the Nazi soldiers with their swastikas— twisted crosses—marching Jews into ovens. Some Christians argue that they have never had anything against the Jewish people, that they do not even know any Jews.

But in the early 1960s, even after the Second Vatican Council had rejected the long-standing assumption that the Jews were to blame for the crucifixion of Jesus, a study of the attitudes of three thousand lay people representing ninety-seven Protestant and twenty-one Catholic parishes indicated a different story.[4]

When asked the question, "Who crucified Jesus?" 80 percent replied that Pontius Pilate desired not to crucify him, with 47 percent claiming that the reason Pilate killed Jesus was because, "a group of powerful Jews wanted him dead." Less than 20 percent attributed Jesus' death to "a group of powerful Romans."[5] "In sum, the traditional images of the historic Jew remain viable features of the contemporary Christian outlook."[6] Sadly, some 40 percent of both Protestants and Catholics felt that "the reason the Jews have so much trouble is because God is punishing them for rejecting Jesus." Among Protestants alone, 33 percent suggested that, "The Jews can never be forgiven for what they did to Jesus until they accept Him as the True Saviour."[7]

With so many Christians espousing moderate to very high anti-Jewish sentiment, one must ask where they learned these views. One could reasonably argue that some of these feelings came directly from personal reading of and reflection on the New Testament and Christian literature. Yet I am convinced that the primary source of misinformation has come from the pulpit, either through uncritical exposition of Scripture or through assumptions, critical and uncritical, about the New Testament that have been influenced by nineteen centuries of anti-Jewish theology in the church.

Furthermore, when the same questionnaire was given to 1,580 clergy, their responses were "so tediously similar [to the laypeople] that they suggest it is precisely in church and Sunday School that the learning takes place."[8] Thirty-two percent of the clergy blamed "the Jews" for the crucifixion of Christ.[9] For those who are called "to preach the Word, read and teach the Scriptures, and engage the people in study and witness,"[10] embracing a new paradigm of inclusiveness will be difficult, but unavoidable if the church's theology is to be credible in the face of oppression.

Can the Christian pulpit rise from the dark entombment of anti-Jewish theology? Can one have an authentic Christian faith after Ausch-witz that links pulpit to pew and pew to society's broken and oppressed people? Perhaps Heschel's words are the answer: "it is with shame." Yet shame is not the same as wallowing in self-pity. Rather, with the shame of Auschwitz, Christianity must confront its distorted anti-Jewish polemic in Scripture and tradition and then move forward into a confessional faith that is characterized by authenticity.

The Gospels

Anti-Jewish theology is visible in the New Testament in many places, especially in the Gospels and Acts, and most clearly in the references to the Pharisees and in the story of Jesus' crucifixion. One must remember that the Gospels and Acts were not written as historical accounts of the life of Jesus and the life of the early church. Each of the evangelists wrote the Gospels "according to" their own experiences of the Jesus proclamation and the specific theological position they intended to convey to their readers.

Most modern scholars agree that the content of the Gospels and Acts reveals more about the period *in* which they were written than the time *about* which they were written. Thus, in dealing with the subject of the Pharisees and of Jesus' crucifixion, one must understand the context in which the Gospels were written and compare this context with extrabiblical writings, noncanonical literature, and archaeological data from the same period to gain a more complete picture of what may have occurred.

The Gospels and Acts were written in Greek in order to be read and circulated in the Greco-Roman world. Their final form was established between the years 65 and 100 C.E., although later variants were sometimes added to and deleted from the texts. Most New Testament scholars think that Mark was the first Gospel of the church's canonical Scripture, written between 60 and 70; that Matthew and Luke-Acts were written between 80 and 95; and that the Gospel of John was written between 90 and 110 C.E.

The most important reason for having a rough estimate of when the Gospels were written is to place them side by side with other historical writings and archaeological data to gain a fuller historical understanding of the period. This critical method of analysis allows one to better determine the historical meaning of the particular passage, even to the point of disagreeing with the scriptural account.

Such an understanding of biblical studies is pertinent to many subjects addressed in the New Testament, but is particularly germane to a post-Holocaust Christian theology. I address two important aspects of this understanding here: (1) the Pharisees and (2) the crucifixion of Jesus. Before moving ahead, I need to note several other historical factors.

First, one must not forget the interaction between the church and the synagogue at the time of the Gospels' writing. The earliest community that congregated around the Jesus proclamation was a sect within Judaism composed mostly of the original apostles, Jewish messianists, and some of Jesus' family. The Jesus sect's base was in Jerusalem, but the sect had probably spread into other Judaean communities. Although some of the sect's leaders (e.g., Barnabas) actively proselytized non-Jews into the fold, the movement's significant thrust toward Gentiles came with Paul of Tarsus and his radical interpretation of a call that suggested that Gentiles are children of Abraham through Christ's death and resurrection without first adhering to the Mosaic law. Through Paul and his missionary zeal the gentile world witnessed many gentile converts to his gospel in places as far from Jerusalem as Asia Minor, Athens, and Rome.

Although Paul's own theology was rooted in Jewish Pharisaism, his upbringing and education in hellenized Tarsus influenced his teaching in ways that differed radically from other Jews in the Jesus movement. Still, he tried to keep a solid bond between his gentile disciples outside Palestine and the small sect of the Way based in Jerusalem. Paul's concern for this bond is seen mostly through his constant appeals to his gentile followers to give money for the brothers and sisters in Jerusalem. Paul may not have wished to face it, but the rift between the Jerusalem church and the rapidly growing gentile churches existed from the moment of Paul's experience on the Damascus road, perhaps even prior to that experience; it is difficult to know just how much influence Paul's missionary predecessors, like Barnabas, had on the Greek world.

Simultaneous with this growing split was the Jews' implicit and explicit rebellion against Rome. According to the Zealots, one was either a slave to God or a slave to Rome. As most Jews gradually realized, they were already slaves to Rome and Caesar; thus rebellion came out of faithfulness to God.

This perception posed a peculiar problem, at least for the gentile Christians. In the eyes of Rome, Christians and Jews were basically synonymous. Yet many of these gentile converts were Roman citizens and resented being grouped with the rebellious Jews. Even so, Jews and Jewish followers of Jesus continued to live out a tentative relatedness with gentile Christians for many decades.

Most scholars place the major break between gentile Christians and, along with all Jews, Jews in the movement of the Way with the destruction of the second temple in 70 C.E. and at the Council of Jamnia fifteen years later. Gentile Christians were quick to establish in their own minds that the destruction was the result of God's judgment on the Jews for rejecting Christ. The irony is that the Jewish faithfulness to serve one God compelled many to rebel against Rome, and that rebellion was the reason Jerusalem was destroyed.

What happened to the Jerusalem church after 70 C.E. is unknown. Like most Jews of Jerusalem, the Jewish Christians were probably killed, enslaved, or dispersed into hiding. Archaeological evidence suggests that some Jewish Christian sects may have survived until as late as the fourth century—even living and perhaps worshiping with other non-Christian Jews.[11] But for all practical purposes, after 70 C.E. gentile Christianity became the dominant Christianity; and for reasons already noted, gentile Christianity wanted nothing to do with Judaism—except to claim inheritance to the Hebrew Scriptures and Israel's God.

Therefore, as Stendahl suggests, "all our writings in the New Testament are directed to congregations containing Gentiles, and . . . there is not a single writing in the New Testament which is not directed to a congregation which is primarily Gentile, including the Gospel of Matthew and the Epistle to the Hebrews."[12] Against this historical backdrop, one can venture deeper into the circumstances surrounding Jesus and his crucifixion. Perhaps this new way of looking at an old story can also clarify the circumstances surrounding the crucifixion of the Jews at Auschwitz.

The Pharisees

Who were the Pharisees? Ellis Rivkin, a pioneer in the study of the Pharisees, believes that contemporary Christianity and contemporary Judaism's self-understanding and dialogue together hinge on a critical and informed knowledge of the Pharisees.[13] The Gospel of Matthew describes Jesus as saying, "For I tell you, unless your righteousness exceeds that of the scribes and Pharisees, you will never enter the kingdom of heaven" (5:20). Throughout the Gospels they are described as "serpents . . . brood of vipers," "hypocrites," "blind guides," and so forth. Unfortunately, this picture of the Pharisees led Joachim Jeremias, one of the most noted twentieth-century Christian authorities on Jesus' parables and New Testament theology, to say, "Where is it that Jesus sees the cancer that is not recognized by the pious men of his day? This becomes clearest in his sayings against the Pharisees, with whom he had most to do."[14]

Jeremias is not alone in this portrayal of the Pharisees. "Pharisee" is often used in Christian pulpits and Sunday schools to describe anyone who is "self-righteous," "coldhearted," or just plain "anti-Christian." This usage has become so common that pharisaism generally connotes hypocrisy, especially in religious or moral matters, a sanctimonious attitude of observing the letter rather than the spirit of a law. Is this an accurate description of the sect upon which Rabbinic Judaism was built?

Blind Guides or On the Seat of Moses?   Although this perspective is most common among Christians today, Matthew gives a glimpse of another perspective. In his Gospel he reports Jesus as saying, "The scribes and the Pharisees sit on Moses' seat; therefore, do whatever they teach you and follow it" (23:2-3). Is this the same author who reported earlier the saying that "unless your righteousness exceeds . . . the Pharisees?" Who were they really? Matthew at least hints that they were an influential group who were highly regarded among Jews at the time of Jesus. Does Matthew 23:2-3 intimate a tradition of the Pharisees that Christians have not known or have ignored?

In keeping with Matthew's brief reference to a different picture of the Pharisees, Rivkin submits that the Pharisees "were so successful in winning over the people to their innovative teachings that in the time of Jesus they are sitting in the chair of Moses, and legitimately so."[15] This expanded understanding of Jesus' statement is dependent on two other primary sources of information besides the Gospels, sources that the church has traditionally ignored. These are the historical narratives of Josephus and the tannaitic literature of the rabbis of Palestine in the late first and second centuries.[16]

These documents and the vast number of secondary sources about them provide a picture of the Pharisees that does not accord with the

Gospels' portrait of "serpents" or "whitewashed tombs." Rather, the Pharisees were conscientious, moral, and well respected among the masses. They were laypeople, not clergy, and were theologically opposed to the strict written interpretation of Torah venerated by the priestly Sadducees. Instead, they preferred an oral interpretation of the written Law. They were learned, but lived with and worshiped with the common people of Judaism.

The Pharisees probably developed as a sect from people who separated from the more sacramental and temple-centered Zaddokites (the predecessors of the Sadducees), who, since the Babylonian Exile, had been the established authority regarding Torah. The Pharisees' hidden revolution began developing even before the Hasmonean revolt of the second century B.C.E., but greatly accelerated with the alliance of the usurping high priest Menelaus and the pagan and hellenizing conqueror Antiochus IV.[17] As one explores the time of Jesus, when the Pharisees were at the height of authority in Judaism, the portrait of the Pharisees that emerges is multidimensional.

Sadly for the church and the children of Auschwitz, this new understanding of the Pharisees that is starting to unfold in Christian circles is the perspective to which Jews have adhered for centuries, particularly through the teachings of the rabbis, the Pharisees' successors. But only since the Holocaust, with Christian theology burned up in smoke along with six million Jews, has the church begun listening to what Jews have been telling Christians all along about the world of Jesus.

Indeed, only as Christianity commences in an unrestricted understanding of its own tradition and begins to recognize the activity of God in history to include territories beyond its own boundaries will it be inspired to see the whole picture of history. Listening with open ears to scholars like Jacob Neusner and Ellis Rivkin transforms the depiction of the Jewish people in the Gospels (as a demonic people doing all in their power to restrict God's creative activity in the world) into a truer representation of the Pharisees. The Pharisees were ironically the Jewish group in Jesus' day that most exemplified the creative action of God in the world.

Jesus and the Pharisees   Most enlightening, and of particular importance for the Christian church after Auschwitz, is the new relationship one begins to see between Jesus and the Pharisees. "As to content, the teachings attributed to Jesus are so remarkably parallel to those of the liberal Pharisees, followers of Hillel (the conservative Pharisees were generally of the school of Shammai) that Neusner declares: 'Some of his [Hillel's] teachings are in spirit and even exact wording close to the teachings of Jesus.' "[18] If Jesus did criticize the Pharisees and the Pharisees criticized him, which seems apparent, "it now appears likely that Jesus attacked only certain groups within the Pharisee movement, not the movement as a whole. . . . In large measure Jesus' battle with 'the Pharisees' needs to be understood as an 'in-house' struggle."[19]

The term "in-house" has particular significance in understanding Jesus and the Pharisees. The Gospel writers also portray groups other than the Pharisees, such as the Herodians, Sadducees, elders, and chief Priests, as sects in conflict with Jesus.[20] These portrayals, like that of Jesus' relationship with the Pharisees, are exaggerated.

Nevertheless, the primary difference between Jesus' relationship with these other sects and his relationship with the Pharisees is that the former was an out of house conflict—not out of the house of Israel, but out of the house of the Pharisees. In other words, Jesus and the Pharisees stood beside each other on most matters, particularly as they related to the other sects of first-century Judaism.

Although Jesus may have held different perspectives from some Pharisees, particularly the more conservative ones, regarding morals, politics, social mores, and theology, few Pharisees agreed on any of these matters. As a teacher, Jesus was similar to some Pharisees in several ways. Although other sects in Judaism held one or two of these characteristics in common with the Pharisees, the comprehensive list reveals a unique persona of first-century Judaism's most popular sect. These include: the methodology used to interpret oral and written law, the frequent references to the prophets, teaching through parables, affirming the beliefs in a resurrection and the impending reign of God, and asking questions and giving answers that twisted the meaning and engaged the other party in conversation.

Moreover, as already mentioned, the open hatred and scheming hostility between Jesus and the Pharisees that the Gospel writers depict probably represents the later hostility between the rabbinic leaders of the synagogue and the mostly Gentile church of the late first century. In his day, Jesus more likely had in-house arguments with the Jewish people.

Leo Baeck, a modern Jewish scholar who survived Theresienstadt during World War II, concludes: "Jesus, in all of his traits, is completely a genuine Jewish character. A man such as he could only grow up on the soil of Judaism. . . . He was a Jew among Jews; out of no other people could a man such as he have been able to have this effect; in no other people could he have found the apostles who believed in him."[21]

Therefore one can affirm a new understanding of Jesus after Auschwitz—that is, new for most Christians—that characterizes the Nazarene not as one who was against the Pharisees or Judaism but as a Jew—he was Rabbi Jesus. A greater awareness of this historical picture enhances Christian-Jewish dialogue, enabling the church to take a firm step forward on the bridge between church and synagogue that exists today. This step is only a beginning.

The Crucifixion

The next step of reinterpretation involves an open look at Jesus' crucifixion. This examination is imperative for all Christians concerned about a Christian theology after Auschwitz for at least two reasons. One is that the cross is the primary symbol of liberation and reconciliation in the Christian church. The second reason, dependent on the first, is that by the sword of the cross—"in the name of Christ"—more people have been killed, humiliated, and dehumanized than under any other banner in the history of humanity. Ironically, until the destructive power of the cross—the killing, humiliation, and dehumanizing in the name of Christ—is put to death, the church will never fully realize the liberative and reconciliatory power of the cross—resurrection and hope.

Franklin Littell, a Christian scholar who has long fought for this awareness to surface in the local church, comments, "I am convinced that—with all the implications involved for theology and church history—the crucifixion and resurrection of the Jewish people are the most important events for Christian history in centuries."[22] In the shadow of the Holocaust, Christians must begin to see the eerie connection between the swastika of Hitler and the church's cross of faith. Only after such recognition can the church convincingly assert the faith claim of resurrection. Without this recognition the church will continue to be the true exemplar of whitewashed entombment.

The Gospels are not uniform in their depictions of Jesus' death, but they do agree on several points: (1) Jesus was brought to trial and crucified on a cross; (2) Pilate, the Roman procurator of Palestine, washed himself from the whole incident and even pleaded (by some accounts) with the crowd to set Jesus free; and (3) the Jewish people were responsible for Jesus' crucifixion.

Most scholars agree with the first generalization, but by examining some of the historical realities during that era of history, one begins to see that the other two are laden with problems.

One of these realities is that it was impossible for the Jewish people, under Torah, to use crucifixion as a form of death. Crucifixion was a Roman form of capital punishment frequently used by Pilate as well as other Roman officials throughout the empire. The Gospel writers seem to be aware of this particular aspect of history. Thus they portray Pilate as being officially responsible for the crucifixion but acting only from pressure to please the crowd. Their portrayal of the Jewish people contrasts dramatically: "Pilate said to [the Jews], 'Here is the man!' When the chief priests and the police saw him, they shouted, 'Crucify him, crucify him!' Pilate said to them, 'Take him yourselves and crucify him; I find no case against him'" (John 19:5b-6). Furthermore, as if Pilate needed reminding of Roman political policy, John writes, "From then on Pilate tried to release him, but the Jews cried out, 'If you release this man, you are no friend of the emperor. Everyone who claims to be a king sets himself against the emperor'" (19:12). The Synoptic Gospels give similar accounts (Mark 15:1-15; Matt. 27:1-26; Luke 23:1-25).

Another inconsistency in the Gospels compared with other historical literature is the portrait of Pontius Pilate. In contrast to the fair, judicial, and somewhat impotent ruler portrayed in the Gospels, Philo wrote in a letter to King Agrippa I that Pilate was "unbending and recklessly hard."[23] Like other Roman procurators in the first century, Pilate had a reputation among the masses (in this case the Jewish people of Judaea) as a tyrannical and paranoid ruler: "He found pleasure in trampling underfoot the Jews' most sacred religious beliefs. In arrogant defiance of their laws, he set up the royal eagles in Jerusalem. The people appeared before him in the arena of Caesarea to petition for a change. He surrounded them with his troops, giving them a choice. They could yield, or they might accept immediate death."[24]

By other accounts than the Gospels, Pilate was an ambitious ruler who desired only to please Caesar and thus to secure his own place in the empire. Geographically distant from Rome, Judaea was to be secured at all costs. Under his rule, charismatics, whether political or religious, were commonly beheaded or crucified. Pilate cared little about the message they proclaimed, but cared a great deal about the crowds and enthusiasm the charismatics generated. Palm waving by spirited crowds worried him.

Political shrewdness was also a characteristic of Pilate. This legacy is revealed in the Gospel's portrait of Pilate as one perceived to have washed his hands from guilt for Jesus' death. As this image of Pilate persisted in the church through the centuries, irony would extend to absurdity in Pilate's canonization (sainthood) in the Coptic Church of Ethiopia and Egypt. As Rivkin states, the truthful portrait of Jesus' crucifixion is that "it was the Roman imperial system that was at fault, not the system of Judaism."[25]

Rivkin does indicate, however, that it would not be inconsistent for Caiaphas the high priest and the Sanhedrin to have been involved in the trial of Jesus. One can explain this involvement in several ways. (1) Caiaphas, as high priest, would have worked closely with the procurator and would have needed the blessing of the procurator to stay in power. (2) Though supposedly representative of the people, the Sanhedrin was made up of individuals who were politically sympathetic to Caiaphas. (3) Even if Caiaphas and the Sanhedrin were unsympathetic to Rome, it would be to their own best interest and the interest of the Judaeans to suppress a charismatic, in fear of Roman retaliation through the mass slaughter of Jews. (4) If Jesus did claim to be the Messiah, his trial by the Sanhedrin would not have led to the sentence of death. The Sanhedrin itself comprised religiously divergent factions. Although Jesus' claim would have sounded extreme to such a group, it would not result in the recommendation of crucifixion.

Thus Jesus' trial and crucifixion was not a religiously motivated process by the Jewish people, but a political process carefully orchestrated by Pontius Pilate and a few of his non-Roman puppets—namely, Caiaphas and the Sanhedrin.[26] "At the time of Christ in Palestine, who did the crucifying? The Romans. Who was crucified? The Jews."[27]

Christian Tradition

The point where Scripture ends and tradition begins is not easily clarified. Scripture is merely canonized tradition. When referring to tradition here, I mean the noncanonized tradition that generally began after the writing of Paul and the Gospels. Thus "tradition" points toward the collective experience of the church in its interpretation or misinterpretation of the Hebrew Scriptures and the Jesus kerygma from the first century C.E. to the present.[28] This section is not a comprehensive examination of Christian tradition; I leave that task to historians and theologians who wish to portray a thorough study of Christian historical theology. Neither does this section list all the known events, people, and documents in Christian tradition that are anti-Jewish in nature. Rather, I highlight some key figures and literature against the Jewish people to reveal a dark side of Christianity—a side that laid the foundation for Hitler's gas chambers and crematoriums in the 1930s and 1940s.[29]

As I stated previously, by the latter half of the first century C.E.— particularly after the destruction of the temple—the cornerstone of anti-Jewish theology was laid in the church. Irving Greenberg recounts how the church must have reasoned:

> But if Jews do not accept Jesus, even after their temple is destroyed, is this not proof that God has in fact rejected them? . . . Would not Gentile Christians conclude that the acceptance of Christianity in the world proves that Jesus came not to continue the old and original covenant, but rather to bring a new covenant to humanity? And since the Jews failed to understand, have they not forfeited the promise? . . . In effect, the response to the destruction created a model of relationship in which the mere existence of the Jews is a problem for Christianity. The obvious temptation—continually given in to—was to solve the problem by getting rid of the Jews.[30]

With the anti-Jewish foundation firmly in place in the early church, Greenberg describes three classic ways Christians, in framing the house of anti-Jewish theology, have dealt with the "Jewish problem." The first way claims that Judaism is a dead religion—the old covenant simply ceased to exist when the new covenant was born. The *New* Testament supersedes the *Old* Testament. A variant of this view is that Jews are children of the devil. The second way attempts to proselytize Jews, to convince them to convert to Christianity. The third way to solve the Jewish problem is to kill the Jews.[31]

In the preface I referred to Raul Hilberg's logical progression of such thinking. Clark Williamson also testifies to this historical sequence in Christian tradition as he affirms Arthur Gilbert's estimate "that fewer than twenty percent of Jews were able to survive *as Jews* in Christian Europe from the fourth century to the twentieth. The other eighty percent were taken care of along the way by forced baptism, expulsion, massacres, pogroms, and sundry mob actions."[32]

One cannot shift the blame for the atrocities of Auschwitz administered by Nazis—themselves anti-Christian in motive—to Christian tradition. Yet Hitler's systematic effort to rid the world of all Jewish people is intelligible only as the apex of a long Christian tradition that has been adverse to the existence of the Jewish people and their religion.[33]

The Church Fathers

Anti-Jewish theology appears in nonbiblical Christian literature as early as the end of the first century. Its primary purpose was apologetic and its themes were supersession and the character of the Jewish people. The polemic among the early church fathers was fairly consistent. It gained great momentum during the patristic period—enough to remain a persistent theme throughout the history of Christian thought. A. Roy Eckardt observes, "Anti-Judaism and the antisemitism that it foments began with the early centuries of the church and culminated in the medieval and Reformation attitudes toward Jews."[34]

Why is this polemic missing from most history books? One contributing factor is that historians of Christian thought have mostly ignored or been ignorant of the subject. Church councils debated anti-Judaism in the format of legislation, not dogma. Most historians of Christian thought have focused on dogmatics and, as a result, have been inattentive to the anti-Jewish disposition of Christian history.[35] Only as the smoke from the chambers of death clears can one take on a post-Holocaust awareness of history.

The Epistle to Barnabas   With this perspective, one may view a work such as the *Epistle to Barnabas*—a tract probably dating from the first century and one of the sacred books read aloud in Christian congregations until the fourth century—as anti-Jewish in content and purpose. The anonymous writer, evidently a gentile Christian from Alexandria, interpreted the Hebrew Scriptures allegorically. The events and people of the Old Testament were relevant only as they pointed toward the Christ-event in the New Testament. As far as Barnabas was concerned, the uniqueness of the history of the Hebrew people had been sacrificed. His main agenda was whether the covenant belongs to us or to them. He not only argued that Jewish worship and fasts have been abolished, but also denied that the Old Covenant had ever been credible.[36]

Justin Martyr   The best-known tract of anti-Jewish literature in the patristic period is Justin Martyr's *Dialogue with Trypho the Jew*, written in the first half of the second century. Addressing his fellow gentile Christians in defense of Emperor Hadrian's destruction of Jerusalem in 135 C.E., he contrived a letter to an imaginary Jew named Trypho. Like Barnabas, he elaborated on the familiar theme that Christians had replaced Jews in God's covenant, but his most important declaration was that the Jewish people suffer today for killing Christ. "Accordingly, these things have happened to you in fairness and justice, for you have slain the Just One."[37]

Marcion   Another person from this period who deserves special attention is Marcion. Although not technically a church father (Christian tradition never officially recognized his teaching), his influence has been lasting. With the idea that the New Covenant has replaced the Old so prevalent in the early church, it was only a matter of time before someone would suggest that the church throw out the Hebrew Scriptures. In the middle of the second century, Marcion did just that. Clark Williamson writes that he even "believed the God known to the Hebrews to be different from and inferior to the God disclosed in and to Jesus; the former created this evil, material world, but the latter is a spiritual being who redeems us from it."[38]

   Although his attempts to sway a majority of church officials failed, his large following is believed to be responsible for a major distinction in the way the church perceives the Scriptures to this day—that of an "Old" Testament and a "New" Testament.[39] John Pawlikowski warns that "among those Christians who have been touched by the dialogue with Jews and the Jewish tradition there exists a growing conviction that a subtle Marcionism still resides in churches."[40]

Anti-Jewish literature was also common among other church fathers such as Irenaeus, Tertullian, Origen, Eusebius of Caesarea, Epiphanius, and Gregory of Nyssa. But the two thinkers whose tracts against the Jewish people most deeply influenced the climate of the Middle Ages were Augustine in the West and Chrysostom in the East.[41]

Augustine   Augustine's comments regarding the Jewish people are numerous and appear in many of his writings. Although he sought to remain faithful to Paul's affection toward the Jewish people, his gentile Christian rootedness in five centuries of anti-Jewish tradition made it difficult for him to understand the Jewish people. Much of what he wrote echoes the remarks of his apostolic predecessors and contemporaries.

Perhaps in seeking to remain loyal to Paul's call in Romans to beware of severing the branch from the tree (11:16b-24), Augustine did not convey a hatred toward the Jewish people, unlike many of his fellow church leaders. Nevertheless, his writings have had a significant negative impact on the Jewish people, because he developed the theory of the Jews as "the witness-people." According to Edward Flannery, by a witness-people, Augustine meant: "they are at once witnesses of evil and of Christian truth . . . ; they subsist 'for the salvation of the nation but not for their own.' They witness by their Scriptures and serve as 'slave-librarian' of the Church; and likewise they give witness by their dispersion and their woes. Like Cain, they carry a sign but are not to be killed (Gen. 4:15)."[42]

To substantiate the theory of the witness-people, or as it is more commonly called "the Wandering Jew," Augustine leans heavily on allegorical interpretation in the Cain and Abel story (Gen. 4:1-16), portraying Cain as the Jews and Abel as Christ. In a tract entitled *Reply to Faustus*, God rejects Cain the gardener's offering but accepts the offering of Abel the (Good) shepherd. Out of jealousy, Cain slays his younger innocent brother. Hence, according to Augustine, Cain and the Jewish people cannot answer God's question, "Where is your brother?" and thus are cast out of paradise forever. Remaining consistent with his allegory to the end, Augustine does say that, like Cain, the Jewish people are not made to suffer. Yet, also like Cain, the Jewish people are "marked" forever (by circumcision) to wander the earth, and their "continued preservation will be proof to believing Christians of the subjection merited by those who . . . put the Lord to death."[43] Therefore, for Augustine, the Jewish people are the witness-people, never entering paradise themselves, but in their shame providing the world with a witness to the crucifixion of Jesus, consequently leading non-Jews to paradise.

John Chrysostom   If Augustine sought to preserve the connection between the branches and the tree, his contemporary from Antioch, John Chrysostom, did everything in his power to burn out the tree, roots and all. The very existence of the Jewish people posed major problems for Chrysostom. Concerned mainly with his own parishioners who were frequenting synagogues and brushing elbows with Jews, the fiery preacher asked rhetorically whether one could accuse the Jews "of their rapine, their cupidity, their deception of the poor, of thieveries, and huckstering? . . . Indeed a whole day would not suffice to tell all."[44] This is precisely what Chrysostom did, but not just for a whole day—for his whole life!

Flannery lists some of Chrysostom's remarks in his castigating sermons: "How can Christians dare 'have the slightest converse' with Jews, 'most miserable of all men (*Homily* 4:1), . . . lustful, rapacious, greedy, perfidious bandits. . . . inveterate murderers, destroyers, men possessed by the devil. . . . They know only one thing, to satisfy their gullets, get drunk, to kill and maim one another . . .' (1:4). . . . Why are Jews degenerate? Because of their 'odious assassination of Christ' (6:4)."[45]

These vehement expressions of Augustine and Chrysostom indicate that the church had entered the theological "Dark Ages" long before the cultural Dark Ages would begin. Yet as Clemens Thoma states, "Beyond those harsh antisemitic statements by the Church Fathers, we must not forget that there is no papal bull officially excommunicating Jewry. . . . On the other hand, we must not forget that the true abyss between Synagogue and Church is much deeper than implied by official and semi-official statements."[46]

The Middle Ages

For the most part, the journey of the Jewish people through the Middle Ages to the present has been a downward path, except for brief interludes of grace.[47] Much of the Christian preaching resulted in pogroms against

Jews. Samuel Sandmel portrays the deadly fanaticism in the twentieth century that developed out of the Middle Ages: "The pogroms in Eastern Europe from which my parents fled began with the ringing of church bells. I remember as an American boy how my mother used to shiver whenever the bells rang in the church near our home."[48]

Haunting Parallels   One of the most vivid expressions of anti-Jewish theology through the Middle Ages was through church law. The Nazis claimed to have never enacted a single measure against the Jews that did not already have precedence in canonical law. "The Nazis 'did not discard the past; they built upon it. They did not begin a development; they completed it.' This fact makes ludicrous any unqualified claim that the Nazis were the enemies of Christendom. In actuality, they were in very large measure the agents for the 'practical' application of an established social logic."[49]

Raul Hilberg gives a detailed and haunting list comparing medieval canonical law with the legislation of the Nazis.[50] Here are a few examples:

▪ The law for the Protection of German Blood and Honor (1935) parallels the Synod of Elvira (306), which prohibits intermarriage and sexual intercourse between Christians and Jews.

▪ Jews are barred from train dining cars in 1939. The Synod of Elvira (306) forbids Jews and Christians eating together.

▪ The law for the reestablishment of the Professional Civil Service (1933) matches the Synod of Clement (535), which disallows Jews to hold public office.

▪ A decree of 1938 allows authorities to bar Jews from the streets on given days (such as Nazi Holidays). The Third Synod of Orleans (538) inhibits Jews from showing themselves in the streets during Passion Week.

▪ The book burnings that occur in Nazi Germany parallel the burning of the Talmud and other books during the Synod of Toledo (681).

• The 1940 *Sozialausgleichsabgabe* enforces a Jewish income tax equal to the party contribution levied on Nazis. The Synod of Gerona (1078) enforces Jews to equal Christian contributions to the church.

• Jews are forced to wear Star of David badges in 1941. The fourth Lateran Council of 1215 mandates the marking of Jewish clothes with a badge.

• Synagogues are destroyed in the entire Reich (1938). In 1222 the Council of Oxford bans the construction of new synagogues.

• Compulsory ghettos for Jews are ordered by Heydrich in 1939, echoing the compulsory ghettos legislated by the Synod of Breslau (1279).

• A 1939 decree mandates the sale of Jewish real estate. The Synod of Ofen (1279) forbids Christians from selling or renting real estate to Jews.

• Nazis pass a law against "Overcrowding of German Schools and Universities" in 1933, matching the Council of Basel (1434), which prevents Jews from obtaining academic degrees.

No Place in the Inn   More than any other people in the Middle Ages, the Jews were made the scapegoat for all that Christendom despised, deplored, and denied about itself. In an age of demons, wizards, and mythic images of hell that could dissuade even a confident Bultmannian from sleeping alone in a musty castle there was no room in the inn for a Jew, the earthly manifestation of the Prince of Darkness. Book burnings, forced baptisms, compulsory ghettos, expulsions, and pogroms were often endorsed not only by fanatic crowds but also by supposedly rational and subdued church leaders and councils.

   In spite of the continuous persecutions, Jewish harassment decreased significantly for brief interludes. One such time was during the Carolingian epoch. "The restrictions of the old Code were all but forgotten, and new legislation sought merely to protect the Church from certain Jewish practices rather than to curb Judaism."[51] Under Pepin (714–68) the Jewish plight lessened visibly. Improvement continued with Charlemagne (742–814) and culminated in some degree of equity while Louis the Pious was king (814–40).[52] Nevertheless, attitudes had reverted to the spirit of Chrysostom by the end of the ninth century. Morris Bishop points out that Jews "had to wear a visible mark, a yellow patch or a star of David, and a horned cap. At Toulouse they were obliged to send a representative every Good Friday to the cathedral to receive a resounding box on the ear. At Beziers the mob had the right to stone Jews' houses during Holy Week until the Jewish congregation, in 1160, annulled the right by a money payment."[53]

Another major turn toward destruction in Christian tradition came in 1095. Pope Urban II launched a campaign to purge the world of the heathen infidels, particularly those who held the Holy Land. Thus, beginning in the summer of 1096, the first of eight Crusades began with an enthusiasm never before witnessed in Christendom. "The crusades began with grotesqueries," and the Jewish people again became the primary scapegoat. "Motley hordes of enthusiasts . . . marched through Germany and the Balkan lands, killing Jews by the thousands on their way, plundering and destroying."[54]

Waving their swords and shields, the Christian mercenaries gave Jews the choice of baptism or death. Flannery states that "in most cases a few Jews were baptized voluntarily, more again were baptized by force, many were killed, and there were numerous suicides."[55] Many of these suicides were Jews who sought to remain loyal to God rather than submit to forced baptism.[56] Such actions are incomprehensible from a church that claims Jesus came that the people might have life, and have it abundantly (John 10:10).

"From January to July of 1096 it is estimated that up to 10,000 [Jews] died, probably one fourth to one third of the Jewish population of Germany and Northern France at that time."[57] This was during the first Crusade alone—before the Crusaders even reached the holy land. The remaining Crusades followed the precedent of the first quest to rid the world of the heathen. Regarding the atrocities of the Crusades, Nicholas Berdyaev leaves Christians in shame with the comment: "Perhaps the saddest thing to admit is that those who rejected the cross have to carry it, while those who welcomed it are engaged in crucifying others."[58]

Many other incidents of the Jewish experience during the Middle Ages deserve mention, but I can touch on only two. One is the concerted effort to expel the Jewish people from Europe. This effort includes the expulsion of all Jews, around sixteen thousand, from England in 1290, from France in 1306 and again in 1394, and from Spain in 1492. The Spanish Jews then fled primarily to Portugal, which expelled them in 1497. Many Jews found haven in the New World, particularly in Brazil under Dutch rule. The first Jews came to New Amsterdam (later New York City) in North America in 1654 when Portugal seized Brazil from the Dutch and expelled all Jews.[59] With no place in the inn for any Jew in Christendom, Augustine's anti-Jewish, yet frighteningly prophetic, labeling of the wandering Jew was still vibrant and virulent.

Another horrifying predicament was forced upon European Jewry during the Great Famine (1315–17) and the Black Death (1347–49). With the famine and the plague taking one out of every three people in Europe, a frantic, starving, and out-of-control Christendom turned toward the one scapegoat that was firmly implanted in their psyches— the Jewish people. With Christians already believing that Jews were murderers and children of Satan, it was logical that by the 1320s Jews had been indicted as witches and sorcerers who had poisoned the wells of Europe. In spite of Pope Clement VI issuing a bull defending the Jews against such accusations, several massacres and mass lynchings occurred in Europe: "Six thousand Jews died in Mainz when the Jewish quarter there was set on fire. Two thousand were burned at Strasbourg. . . . How many thousands of Jewish lives were lost cannot be known. Hundreds of communities were obliterated. The whole Jewish community in Europe was left with permanent damage. Moreover, these charges helped form the image of 'the Jew' that is so useful to modern anti-Semitism."[60]

Economical Scapegoats   One of the ways Christians patronize Jews today is by depicting them as economical scapegoats. This idea was born and evolved in the mind of medieval Christians who perceived Jews as dishonest business entrepreneurs. Christian pulpits began to proclaim this sentiment around the twelfth century, but the underlying mistrust was already part of the foundation. This attention on the Jews as money-lenders had several primary causes: (1) Jews were virtually cut off from controlling even their own money through laws, taxes, and so forth. Guilds and religio-economic associations that were restricted to Christians prevented the employment of Jews in the usual occupations. Thus Jews were confined to a limited number of occupations. (2) The church had a ban on usury that kept Christians from any moneylending practices.

(3) The Crusades opened doors for a world trade not known since Alexander the Great's hellenizing conquests.

Flannery goes a step farther: "the principal reason for the Jew's practice of usury was his own need for money. . . . At every turn, he was faced with special taxes, confiscations, cancellations of credit, expulsions, and threats of death. He had literally to buy not only his rights but his very existence."[61]

Through mistrust and fear, the seeds of Henry Ford's *International Jew* were planted. Even though Christians were eventually allowed to charge interest and had financial successes and failures in reasonable proportion with the Jews, the idea of the Jew as the shrewd businessperson had become a permanent fixture in the Western mind.

For the Jewish people, the Middle Ages were truly the dark ages; even by the sixteenth century, dawn was a long way off. "Of grave significance was the utter deterioration of the Jewish image. . . . The dissociation of the imaginary from the real Jew effected earlier under theological influence was now complete. The terms 'Jewish' and 'diabolical' had become all but synonymous."[62] Under this cloud a troubled Augustinian monk, Martin Luther, changed the course of history after nailing ninety-five theses on the castle church door in 1517 in Wittenberg.

The Reformation

The church's sweeping reforms during the Reformation skipped right over its deeply embedded anti-Jewish polemic and swept any opportunity for rectification under the rug. The Reformation—particularly Luther—did much to intensify the predicament of the Jewish people for centuries to come. I do not mean to diminish the positive challenges Luther posed for the Vatican (many resulting in the ensuing Catholic Reformation); or the new era ushered into the church regarding a more critical biblical scholarship, especially in non-Latin languages; or the Reformation's revitalized emphasis on humanity's dependence on God's grace. Yet because Luther has been so influential in both Protestantism and post-Reformation Catholicism, his negative and destructive thoughts—in this case, toward the Jewish people—have also carried tragic consequences.

Martin Luther   Martin Luther (1483–1546) started his reforming days with good intentions for the Jewish people. In 1523 his pamphlet entitled *Jesus Christ Was Born a Jew* urged Christians to treat Jews in a caring manner. He felt that if Jews were introduced to the true gospel (a Reformed and non-Catholic gospel, as he understood it), their conversion to Christianity would follow soon after: "They (the papists) have dealt with the Jews, as if they were dogs rather than human beings . . . we in our turn ought to treat the Jews in a brotherly manner in order that we might convert some of them . . . we are but gentiles, while the Jews are of the lineage of Christ. We are aliens and in-laws; they are blood relatives, cousins and brothers of our Lord."[63] This pamphlet was reprinted nine times in twelve months.[64]

Not everything went according to plan for Luther. His reformed message did not bring about the conversions expected. Indeed, sometimes the open dialogue that he encouraged between Protestants and Jews resulted in the conversion of Christians to Judaism. Thus, nineteen years after writing the first pamphlet, a disillusioned and angry old man published *Against the Jews and Their Lies*. It is haunting and grotesque to read his words through eyes filled with smoke from Auschwitz. In summary, Luther said:

> What then shall we Christians do with this damned, rejected race of Jews? Since they live among us and we know about their lying and blasphemy and cursing, we cannot tolerate them if we do not wish to share in their lies, curse, and blasphemy. . . .
>
> First, their synagogues . . . should be set on fire. . . .
>
> Secondly, their homes should likewise be broken down and destroyed. . . .
>
> Thirdly, they should be deprived of their prayer books and Talmuds. . . .
>
> Fourthly, their rabbis must be forbidden under threat of death to teach any more.
>
> Fifthly, passport and traveling privileges should be absolutely forbidden to the Jews. . . .
>
> Sixthly, they ought to be stopped from usury. All their cash and valuables of silver and gold ought to be taken from them.
>
> Seventhly, let the young and strong Jews and Jewesses . . . earn their bread by the sweat of their noses as is enjoined upon Adam's children. . . .
>
> To sum up, dear princes and nobles who have Jews in your domains, if this advice of mine does not suit you, then find a better

one so that you may all be free of this insufferable devilish burden—
the Jews.[65]

"His writings resulted in the expulsion of Jews from Saxony in 1543.
Luther's last sermon, preached a few days before his death, importu-
nately appealed that all Jews be driven from Germany."[66] For the next
two hundred years, so-called Christian nations worked to enforce a
movement that Jews would later call "the age of the ghetto."[67]

It is difficult to understand what happened to Luther in those nineteen
years between tracts; perhaps what lay deeply embedded, through centuries of Christian tradition, won out. To be Christian was to be anti-
Jewish. The humanist Erasmus of Rotterdam wrote perceptively and
candidly, "If it is the part of a good Christian to detest the Jews, then
we are all good Christians."[68]

John Calvin   Among the many other reformers, the best known was
John Calvin (1509-64). Unlike Luther, Calvin was more harsh toward
Jews in his earlier years of influence, but more humane in his later
years. He was content to keep Jews out of Geneva, particularly early
on; he can be commended for his opposition to the Marcionism that
continued to plague the church. He believed strongly that the Hebrew
Bible is equal to the New Testament as the inspired Scripture of God.
His insistence that Christians adhere to the Jewish law and his earnest
respect for the Hebrew Scriptures during the Reformation brought a
fleeting glimpse of hope regarding Christians' attitudes toward the Jewish
people,[69] but the prevalent picture of anti-Judaism remained undaunted.

The Modern Period

One may best describe the period following the Reformation as the era
marked by Christian rationalism and the Jewish struggle for emancipation. Emancipation first came to the Jews in the American colonies.
Although Roger Williams gave birth to religious freedom at the founding
of Rhode Island in 1688, it was not juridically guaranteed for all the
states until 1789 with the attachment of the Bill of Rights to the Con-
stitution. Real freedom is an ideal, however, and has not even today
been fully realized for Jews and other minorities in America. France
was next to declare religious freedom while other European countries
took steps for partial Jewish emancipation along the way.

Rational Anti-Semitism   One of the most significant developments of the modern period was the stimulation of the rational mind. Although the Renaissance was marked by intellectual growth, the Enlightenment thrust Christianity into an era where fiction was replaced by fact, the intangible by the tangible, and the mythical by the scientific. Here rational anti-Semitism came into full fruition.[70] In spite of the struggle to give reasonable explanations for the existence of Jewry without the use of faith and mythical images from the past, the deep-seated hatred toward Jews penetrated the walls of rationalism into the hearts of many thinkers of this period.

This kind of destructive thought was particularly common in the writings of men like Voltaire (the nom de plume of François-Marie Arouet), Karl Marx, Denis Diderot, F. C. Bauer, and Jean Jacques Rousseau. Ironically, one of the first great modern anti-Judaists of the rational school was himself a Jew, Baruch Spinoza.

Even more important for the history of Christian thought was the anti-Jewish sentiment of the German philosophers and biblical theologians. Thinkers like Johann Fichte, Georg Hegel, Friedrich Schleiermacher, and Adolf von Harnack most evidence this sentiment.[71] Perhaps these earlier philosophers laid the foundation for twentieth-century Christian rationalists, such as W. H. Montgomery, who wrote a book entitled *Jesus Was Not Jew* (1935). By using rational sounding, yet uncritical methodology, Montgomery attempted to prove that the Jesus he loved and the Jews he hated had no relationship whatsoever—except the cross, where the Jews killed Jesus.[72] Montgomery is representative of the extremely prejudiced segment of American society, where more tolerance prevailed. Even though most scholars would have rejected Montgomery's arguments, other well-respected theologians and politicians advocated anti-Judaism in subtle, less extreme venues.

Paradoxical Neoorthodoxy   Modern Christian thought in the twentieth century has depended heavily on the writings of these religious thinkers of the eighteenth and nineteenth centuries. But the most influential Christian theologians prior to and at the same time as the Holocaust were those who espoused neoorthodoxy. Neoorthodoxy is another one of the great ironies in church history and anti-Judaism. While its theologians—H. Richard and Reinhold Niebuhr, Paul Tillich, Karl Barth, and Dietrich Bonhoeffer—adamantly opposed the atrocities of Hitler, they also embraced a theology whose core was anti-Jewish, albeit un-intentionally.[73] By its very nature, neoorthodoxy sought to revive an adherence to particular theological doctrines of the Reformation. Although opposed to the rational liberalism of the nineteenth century, it sought to use a critical method of biblical interpretation and advocate a rational faith.[74]

Of the neoorthodox theologians just mentioned, Bonhoeffer is the most perplexing. He strongly opposed Hitler, the death camps, and the physical destruction of European Jewry. After an unsuccessful effort to assassinate Hitler, Bonhoeffer himself died in a death camp. As a result, Holocaust survivors call him "a righteous Gentile" and many Christians remember him as a martyr for the faith. But Bonhoeffer's thinking also reflected the tremendous influence of Christianity's rejection and replacement theology of Judaism. Before the Holocaust, Bonhoeffer stated that "the church of Christ has never lost sight of the thought that the 'chosen people,' who nailed the redeemer of the world to the cross, must bear the curse for its action through a long period of suffering."[75] No doubt the great martyr would never have uttered these words had he known what lay ahead for European Jewry.

Obviously, Bonhoeffer did not advocate Hitler's final solution of death for the Jewish people. Rather, he fought for their survival as persons. Despite his strong moral convictions, Bonhoeffer's vision was not for Jews to live as practicing Jews. Instead, he advocated that they have the opportunity to convert to Christianity. Clark Williamson observes, "Hitler and Bonhoeffer were united in seeking a world without Jews. One would extinguish them physically; the other would convert them—eliminate them religiously. The choice was between spiritual and physical genocide, genocide being the cutting off (*caedere*) of a people (*genos*) by whatever means. It was the old medieval option of baptism or death, except that with Hitler, there was no choice."[76]

Still, contemporary criticism of one like Bonhoeffer should be confessional, that hindsight always has greater clarity than foresight. How many people today would have been willing to stand up against the evil empire of Nazism to the point of death? I imagine that if Bonhoeffer had the luxury of reflecting back on, rather than dying in, the Holocaust, he would be one of the champions today in criticizing the anti-Jewish theology that buttresses anti-Semitism. He did not have the benefit of the post-Auschwitz dialogue that has only recently called into question classical assumptions.

Another prominent neoorthodox theologian who resisted Hitler and was outwardly against the destruction of the Jewish people was Karl Barth (1886–1968). Nevertheless, his sentiments about the Jews were mixed; he too was full of theological complexities. Even before World War II was over he began to recognize some inconsistencies in his own theology regarding the Jewish people. Barth was convinced, however, that the Jewish faith was "outmoded and superseded" by Christianity. Echoing Augustine's idea of the Jews as "the witness-people," Barth wrote in 1942: "The Jews of the ghetto give this demonstration involuntarily, joylessly and ingloriously, but they do give it. They have nothing to attest to the world but the shadow of the cross of Christ that falls upon them. But they, too, do actually and necessarily attest Jesus Christ Himself."[77]

Barth never completely affirmed the idea that Judaism stands on its own apart from Christianity and that the Jewish people's witness to God is independent of the existence of Christianity. Yet, his theology began moving in the direction of embracing Jews as Jews after Auschwitz. Always struggling and wrestling, Barth was growing toward the position of a post-Holocaust Christian theology. In his *Dogmatics in Outline* Barth expresses the elements of confession and shame not evidenced in his earlier statement. Perhaps his struggle had much influence on the passionate post-Holocaust theology espoused by his son, Markus Barth.[78] Karl Barth's grappling is exemplified in these words written after the Holocaust:

> And don't you see, the remarkable theological importance, the extraordinary spiritual and sacred significance of the National Socialism that now lies behind us is that right from its roots it was anti-Semitic, that in this movement it was realised with a simply demonic clarity, that *the* enemy is the *Jew.* . . .
> We must strictly consider that Jesus Christ . . . was *of necessity a Jew.* . . . The problem of Israel is, since the problem of Christ is inseparable from it, the problem of existence as such. The man who is ashamed of Israel is ashamed of Jesus Christ and therefore of his own existence.
> . . . The attack on Judah means the attack on the rock of the work and revelation of God, beside which work and which revelation there is no other.[79]

Robert McAfee Brown asks a question that Christians struggling with Auschwitz must confront: "By what right does someone like the present author—non-Jew and noninhabitant of the death camps—participate in the dialogue at all? . . . *We live in a different universe.* Ours is a universe in which Auschwitz has never entered; theirs [Jewish survivors] is a universe from which it is never absent."[80] Any non-Jew, like myself, must wrestle with and ponder constantly this question. Nevertheless, "the unavoidable question, How can we dare to speak?, has an unavoidable answer, *Simply because we cannot dare not to speak.*"[81]

I have not written this chapter to point the finger outwardly. Rather, as a Christian—as one intricately linked to all Christians of the past, present, and future—the finger points inwardly as one who claims to be Christian. Confessional analysis of past failures is always an in-house appraisal. If, indeed, Christians affirm their faith by proclaiming, "I believe . . . in the communion of the saints," they must honestly confess that they commune with Augustine and Luther, in both their goodness and their attacks against Judaism and the Jewish people.

Even so, how can Christians dare speak about the Holocaust of the Jews? As a non-Jew who was not even born during the Holocaust, I cannot begin to grasp the horror that survivors of Auschwitz carry in their memories every day and night of their lives. In this sense, I cannot speak. But the Christian story is my story. Out of confession, I must tell my people's part in the story—that we went into the Holocaust sure of ourselves, wearing the full armor of God, and left amidst the ashes, stripped of our armor and the theology it represented. The link between the cinders of Auschwitz and Christian Scripture and tradition is undeniable. Therefore, although unable to speak, I cannot—the church cannot—dare not to speak!

In this chapter I have demonstrated the confessional movement toward Jewish brothers and sisters through the attempt to draw a portrait that has more dark shades than light. But another picture provides the most imminent hope for understanding between Christians and Jews: a portrait of the apostle Paul. The new portrait of Paul in the subsequent chapters affirms a real hope for the world. It comes not through the pen of Augustine or from the pulpit of Martin Luther, but through the cinders of Auschwitz. The risk for Christendom is that it might have to change some of the basics. The mandate is that if Christians do not change, the silence, the ineptness in dealing with painful truth, encourages future final solutions. If the church is to thrive with integrity, it must commit to be a voice of discontent amid all atrocities everywhere. It must also proclaim truth, even at the risk of dismantling familiar tenets of dysfunctional theologies within its tradition.

3

In a
Mirror
Dimly

When I was a child, I spoke like a child, I thought like a child, I reasoned like a child; when I became an adult, I put an end to childish ways. For now we see in a mirror, dimly, but then we will see face to face. Now I know only in part; then I will know fully, even as I have been fully known. And now faith, hope, and love abide, these three; and the greatest of these is love.

—1 Corinthians 13:11-13

Children for me evoke war, thunder and hate, shouts, screams, dogs howling, children in the street hunted, beaten, humiliated. I see them walking and running like the old men and women who surround them, as though to protest, as though to protect them without protecting them. There is no protection for Jewish children. . . . You watch them marching, marching, and you know they will never come back; and yet you go on seeing them, but they no longer see you.

—Elie Wiesel[1]

I write to understand as much as to be understood. Will I succeed one day? Wherever one starts from one reaches darkness. . . . A million children massacred: I shall never understand.

—Elie Wiesel[2]

One of the most beautiful gifts of life is to reexperience the inquisitiveness, the world of fantasy, and the limitless expectations within oneself when one witnesses a child's extraordinary ability to encounter the world with freshness and vivacity. A child's world is always new—in the discovery of a mother robin feeding her young; in the excitement of carving a pumpkin for the first time at Halloween; in the innate ability of a three-year-old to transform a dining room table, some chairs, and an old blanket into a wonderful castle.

It is unimaginable that at least a million Jewish children were brutally murdered in modern machines of destruction between 1933 and 1945—that when, in 1944, the gas chamber near the crematorium at Auschwitz was out of order, children were thrown onto a pile and burned alive. A. Roy Eckardt comments: "There is in this world an evil that is more horrible than every other evil. This is the evil of children witnessing the murder of other children, while knowing that they also are to be murdered in the same way, being absolutely aware that they face the identical fate."[3]

Paul compares life before Christ's return to that of a child's life before adulthood—innocent, hopeful. He likens it to looking into a mirror dimly, still unable to make out the full reflection. But even more significant is that Paul's waiting is evinced with an assurance, a confidence, that could sustain the Christian community through various hardships. Their time in the "not yet" was cradled in the "already" of faith, hope, and love, the greatest of these being love.

Had Paul been a child in Warsaw instead of Tarsus, had he lived in the 1940s instead of the early part of the first century C.E., his analogy would have been markedly different. Innocence for Jewish children in the 1930s and 1940s was stripped away in an untimely fashion by the darkened corners of secret hiding places, by the stench and suffocation of boxcars, and finally, if they were not yet completely robbed of their childish ways, the bonfires of Auschwitz and Treblinka completed the systematic task. Rather than equating his waiting with that of a person peering into a mirror dimly, the reflection of Paul's face in a mirror at Auschwitz would have been vividly darkened by his tightened skin, his sunken cheeks, and his glazed eyes. Instead of life being a testimony to faith, hope, and love, Paul's triad might have been starvation, hopelessness, and death. In this context, I enter into an analysis of the apostle Paul.

In Search of Paul

The Classical Perspective

Of all the great individuals since the proclamation of Jesus began, perhaps no one has been more misinterpreted, misquoted, and misrepresented than Paul. As the first known writer of Christendom and one whom the early church deemed significant enough to label his letters (and those attributed to him) as Scripture, Paul has always been and will continue to be a crucial figure for Christians to engage.

Augustine   One of the first Christians to wrestle significantly with Paul was Augustine. "It was he who first applied Paul's doctrine of justification to the problem of the introspective conscience, to the question: 'On what basis does a person find salvation?' And with Augustine, Western Christianity with its stress on introspective achievements started."[4]

The idea of Paul as the father of the introspective conscience never caught on in the Eastern churches during the Middle Ages.[5] By contrast, since the time of Augustine the Western church has been preoccupied with the inner self, contributing to a markedly individualistic worldview and an overwhelming enchantment with theological and psychological navel gazing.

Martin Luther   Thus it is no surprise that Luther, an Augustinian priest, turned to Paul with the eyes of Augustine to find salvation and expiation from the inner turmoil and guilt that troubled him. Finding particular solace in Paul's words from Romans 7, Luther deduced that Paul's struggle with the law was identical to his own obsession with works-righteousness and the practice of paying indulgences enforced by the papacy.

Equating guilt with law, and forgiveness with grace through Christ, Luther and his protege, Melanchthon, developed a sophisticated theology contrasting law and gospel that became a theological obsession among Protestants for centuries to come. Luther associated the negative "law" with Jews, the "Old" Testament, and the people of Israel. He assumed that "gospel" represented the more positive salvation by God's grace through faith in Christ, a faith that the Jewish people have forfeited out of their adherence to Torah and because they reject Christ. Stendahl writes that in the Reformation, "the Law, the Torah, with its specific requirements of circumcision and food restrictions becomes a general principle of 'legalism' in religious matters. Where Paul was concerned about the possibility for Gentiles to be included in the messianic community, his statements are now read as answers to the quest for assurance about man's salvation out of a common human predicament."[6]

Reading Paul through writers such as Augustine and Luther contributes greatly to many misunderstandings about Paul. Paul's situation could not have differed more from Luther's. For Luther, life was unhappy and guilt-ridden. In every effort to uphold the life-style of a righteous servant, he was plagued with an inner anguish of never measuring up. For him, the theological and existential question of life was, "How am I to find a gracious God?"[7]

In contrast to Luther, Paul was fulfilled as a Jew, free from the anguish of guilt, both before and after his Damascus road experience. Does it sound like a person preoccupied with an Augustinian Fall-Redemption-centered theology who, in reflecting on the time before his experience on the road to Damascus, writes, "as to righteousness under the law [I was] blameless" (Phil. 3:6)? Paul's Letters give no indication that he felt unable to fulfill Torah. Romans 7 is often cited to illustrate Paul's anguish with the law, but as I will demonstrate in chapter 5, such an interpretation is incorrect. Paul goes from "glory to glory" rather than, like Luther, from despair to glory. The only regret Paul mentions is that he had persecuted the church.[8]

Augustine's and Luther's impact on how Christianity has understood Paul is immeasurable. The idea that justification by faith is the main emphasis for Paul became the central way of reading Paul and of doing Christian theology.

Contemporary Biblical Theologians   One can see such an understanding of Paul in writers—even Jewish writers—who have profoundly influenced theology today, such as F. C. Baur, Hans Lietzmann, and Julius Wellhausen.[9] Regrettably, renowned and respected scholars still maintain that Paul adhered to a Fall-Redemption-centered theology. One of the more notable contemporary figures with this viewpoint is Ernst Käsemann: "It has rightly been repeatedly noticed that the apostle's message of justification is a fighting doctrine, directed against Judaism."[10]

Krister Stendahl calls attention to Käsemann's antiquated thinking by asserting that the function of justification by faith in Paul's writings, especially in Romans, is "not primarily polemic, but apologetic as he defends [against 'boasting' Jews] the right of Gentile converts to be full members of the people of God." Furthermore, Stendahl responds to a critique by Käsemann:

> Käsemann sees my line of thinking as a serious threat to Protestantism—which for him means a threat to an authentic understanding of both Paul and Jesus. I share with him a deep concern for the

theological consequences of exegetical work, but I am not sure that "the gospel" can be so easily summarized under the rubric of "the justification of the ungodly" (Rom. 4:5, cf. 5:6; Käsemann, p. 75, 78 *et passim*)—or, for that matter, in any other single theme, Pauline or not. Similarly, I am not convinced that the insights of the Reformation depend on perpetuating such an interpretation of Paul as Käsemann champions.[11]

It is most unfortunate that Käsemann and many other Pauline interpreters fail to comprehend the direct correlation between the fiery pulpit of Luther and the oven chambers at Auschwitz.[12] Their concern may be that one not change the Scripture to accommodate what·one would like it to say—a legitimate concern indeed. But these scholars miss the mark in their inability to see that the tragedy of the Holocaust leads past the Christian tradition packed with anti-Judaism to the original intent of Paul in the New Testament—a creation-centered theology that included liberation for all Gentiles as well as Jews.

Searching out Alternatives

Not everyone has retained a pre-Holocaust perspective in this post-Holocaust world. A new awareness among many Christians has gradually emerged that points out the anti-Jewish statements in the New Testament. As Christian scholars have become aware of the negative images of Judaism in the Gospels, they have also discovered apparently anti-Jewish polemic in the letters of Paul. Unfortunately, in trying to be faithful to a critical and post-Holocaust look at Paul, some scholars have perceived a negative image, that Paul was "the true 'founder of Christianity.'"

This anti-Jewish Paul is espoused in writings of notable contributors to Jewish-Christian dialogue such as Edward Flannery's *Anguish of the Jews* and Rosemary Ruether's *Faith and Fratricide*.

It is understandable that many Jewish scholars also view Paul in this way. Although sympathetic to the historical figure of Jesus, both Christian and Jewish scholars label Paul as the great apostate rather than apostle, meaning that Paul is the founding father of anti-Jewish theology. Early in the post-Auschwitz era even Jewish scholars who sought to be sympathetic to Paul—scholars like Joseph Klausner, Hans Joachim Schoeps, and Samuel Sandmel—adhered to this view.[13]

But what about the fact that Paul was a Jew? How could he be so anti-Jewish? Out of this question, the persistent work of scholars like Krister Stendahl, E. P. Sanders, Lloyd Gaston, Matthew Fox, Clark M. Williamson, and John G. Gager is lifting the veil on Paul. Their careful historical analysis is revealing that the anti-Jewish Paul hailed by people such as Augustine and Luther is so ingrained in Judeo-Christian minds that many have missed Paul the Jew. It is not Paul who is anti-Jewish, but Augustine, Luther, and other historical figures on which many rely to interpret Paul.

What then have these scholars discovered anew about the great apostle? They have discovered that the Western church has indeed been correct that Paul was in turmoil, but his struggle was not resolved *after* his Christ experience. Rather, on that road to Damascus, the real anguish began.

Contrary to Luther, Paul's anguish was not, How am I to find a gracious God? but, How do I understand a salvation history that keeps God's promises to Israel intact, while insisting on the faith claim of Christ crucified and resurrected?[14] To this anguish, this turmoil, I now turn.

Rediscovering Paul

Emil Brunner wrote that Paul was a man "in whose heart and life took place the whole argument about the difference between Judaism and the Christian Community."[15] When one evaluates Paul's writings and wrestles with the agenda that concerns him, it is evident that his primary issue is the relationship between Jews and Gentiles.[16]

Paul and the Law

One of the great myths held by the more classical interpreters of Paul is that he believed "Christ, as the end of the Law, abrogates the Law as a way of salvation, leaving Jews outside the saved community."[17] This twisted perspective of Paul and his gospel has brought about much unnecessary struggle for Jews in Western society. Such an interpretation, which reflects Luther's evaluation of Paul, is also articulated in the writings of others sensitized to Luther's polemic against Judaism. Two such examples are the renowned Roman Catholic theologian, Rosemary Ruether, and the intertestamental expert, Samuel Sandmel.

Torah Abrogation View   Ruether depicts Paul's theology as saying, "The Jew, who has the Law, then becomes the 'lawbreaker' par excellence." Thus for Paul "Christians, not Jews, are the true offspring of Abraham and heirs of the promise."[18] In similar fashion, Sandmel wrote, "[Paul] repudiated [the laws in the Pentateuch] as obsolete and annulled. Indeed, he proceeded beyond annulment to an attitude that can be described as one of contempt."[19]

This anachronistic view portrays a Paul who believes that the higher religion of Christianity superseded Judaism. He is understood as an antinomian ex-Jew who adheres to a replacement theology of gospel rather than Torah, of salvation by grace through faith rather than salvation by works-righteousness. This traditional understanding has allowed Christian theologians, preachers, and laity, either advertently or inadvertently, to use Paul to contrast Christianity with Judaism, Jesus with Pharisaism, grace with Torah, faith with works, and God with Satan. Why did Luther seek to exclude the New Testament's Letter of James from canonical Scripture? Perhaps it was too Jewish in relation to what he understood to be Christian.

But this view is not myth, one might reason, for all one needs to do is read in Paul's own letters of his lashing out against Jews and the law.[20] Does one just ignore Paul's obvious indictments against the law in Galatians and Romans? What about Romans 10:4—"For Christ is the end [*telos*] of the law, that everyone who has faith may be justified." Can one misinterpret the apostle's position regarding the law in Romans 7? "While we were living in the flesh, our sinful passions, aroused by the law, were at work in our members to bear fruit for death. But now we are discharged from the law, dead to that which held us captive, so that we are slaves not under the old written code but in the new life of the Spirit" (vv. 5-6).

The classical or traditional view of Paul's relationship to the law is a misrepresentation; it implies a link between the law and "the fruit of death" that has catastrophical implications. Barry Cytron similarly reflects that the traditional view is "not only unsatisfactory, but dangerous. That reading Paul as if he abrogated the Law, and therefore abrogated Judaism, denied the covenant with Israel [and] had an enormously corrosive impact on the ways Jews were treated."[21]

But what can one make of such passages? Is it only wishful thinking to read Paul any other way? In rereading the apostle is one not in danger of what Cytron calls forcing "a new anachronistic view of Paul?" If so, "we are just as guilty [of misreading Paul] as Luther."[22]

Yet the silent cry of dead children in Auschwitz reminds one that exclusivism continues to exist; in rereading Paul one must risk another misreading of Paul. If the Christian church is to continue to understand Paul's writings as canonical Scripture, it must recognize that for too long only some words of Paul have been heard and others silenced. Are Christians afraid to listen to silent voices? Can Christians dare not hear the silenced words of Paul echoing into the silent cries of God's children at Auschwitz? These words of Paul are hard to reconcile to the anti-Jewish Paul:

> I ask, then, has God rejected [God's] people? By no means! I myself am an Israelite, a descendant of Abraham, a member of the tribe of Benjamin. God has not rejected [God's] people whom [God] foreknew. (Rom. 11:1-2)
> So I ask, have they stumbled so as to fall? By no means! (Rom. 11:11)
> So that you may not claim to be wiser than you are, brothers and sisters, I want you to understand this mystery: a hardening has come upon part of Israel, until the full number of the Gentiles has come in. And so all Israel will be saved. (Rom. 11:25-26)
> As regards the gospel they are hostile[23] for your sake; but as regards election they are beloved for the sake of their ancestors; for the gifts and the calling of God are irrevocable. (Rom. 11:28-29)
> O the depth of the riches and wisdom and knowledge of God! How unsearchable are [God's] judgments and how inscrutable [God's] ways! (Rom. 11:33)

Christians have largely ignored these verses for many centuries. Any form of salvific condemnation toward the people of Israel is simply out of the question for Paul. His metaphor of the olive tree in Romans 11 suggests that some gentile Christians already adhered to a rejection and replacement theology toward Judaism. Paul warns: "But if some of the branches were broken off, and you, a wild olive shoot, were grafted in their place to share the rich root of the olive tree, do not boast over the branches. If you do boast, remember it is not you that support the root, but the root that supports you. . . . So do not become proud, but stand in awe" (vv. 17-18, 20).

Since the Second Vatican Council, many scholars have sought to resolve the conflict between Paul's seeming antinomian position and his

firmly embedded belief that "all Israel will be saved." Although they
disagree on details, these scholars are united by their common conviction
that God has not rejected the Jewish people. These scholars exemplify
a confessional self-awareness of what it means to call oneself Christian
in the face of dead Jewish children. Their passionate commitment toward
the assurance that such an atrocity will never happen again buttresses
the words of their writings and lectures. Several credible alternatives
to the Torah abrogation view have developed since 1960 that are noteworthy and offer possibilities in rereading Paul.

Dual Covenants View   The first alternative describes Paul as supporting
a theology that upholds Torah for Jews and Christ for Gentiles. Jews
and Gentiles have distinctively different covenants. Major advocates
who have brought credibility to this understanding are Krister Stendahl,
Paul van Buren, and Clark Williamson. Through careful analysis of Paul's
writings, particularly Galatians and Romans, these scholars break radically from the classical understanding of Paul as one who abrogates the
law and Judaism. The primary recipients of Paul's gospel are Gentiles.
Therefore his adamant remarks not to live according to the law are
directed at Gentiles, not Jews. Jews experience the righteousness of
God on the ground of their faith, which is Torah. This righteousness
was made known before the law through the faith of Abraham (Rom.
4:3). Abraham is the forebear not only of the Jews but of the Gentiles
as well. "For this reason it depends on faith, in order that the promise
may rest on grace and be guaranteed to all his descendants, not only to
the adherents of the law but also to those who share the faith of Abraham
[the Gentiles], for he is father of all of us" (Rom. 4:16).

Paul asks his recipients, "Or is God the God of Jews only? Is [God]
not the God of Gentiles also? Yes, of Gentiles also, since God is one;
and [God] will justify the circumcised on the ground of their faith and
the uncircumcised through that same faith? (Rom. 3:29-30).

In this understanding of Paul, faithful Jews are those who ground
their faith in Torah. Torah allows them to experience God's righteousness,
a right relationship exemplified in Abraham. Faithful Gentiles are those
former strangers to the God of Abraham who now commune in covenantal
relationship with God and Israel through the faithfulness of Jesus Christ.
"Through the church's preaching of Christ, we who once were without
God in the world . . . have been brought near to God and Israel."[24]

Paul's gospel is one in which Gentiles are grafted into covenant relationship with God and with the Jewish people. In this relationship Christians and Jews participate together in the righteousness of God. Law is upheld; Christ is upheld. Separate people have separate paths, but out of God's faithfulness both Jews and Gentiles are brought together in one promise. "The original writings of Paul in all their uniqueness are indispensable to the Christian community as they picture his call to be our champion, a Jew who by vicarious penetration gives to us Gentiles the justification for our claims to be God's children in Jesus Christ."[25]

Stendahl and others supporting this position have cut through long years of tradition to reread Paul as one who did not negate Torah; but they have not dealt with one particular aspect of the apostle's theology—his demand in Romans 11 that Jews embrace his gospel. In failing to give adequate attention to this issue, the dual covenant position bypasses Paul's strong belief that Jews should accept the gospel of Christ. It also leaves little room for those who claim to be Jewish Christians today (although Jewish Christianity may not be what Paul meant by Jewish acceptance of the gospel of Christ).

Linked to this problem is the question of what to do with Peter, James, John, and the others in Jerusalem. What of Paul, a Jew, as well? Even if the followers of the Way in Jerusalem and others of Jewish ancestry understood Jesus more in terms of the Jewish Messiah than the Greek Christ, one must still account for them. Peter von der Osten-Sacken brings this point home when he notes that Paul's "apostolic service *to the Gentiles* is the way in which Israel is to be made 'jealous.' . . . Paul certainly then expects Israel's future yes to Jesus Christ. But . . . he is silent about the how and when of this yes."[26] I am convinced that Paul is not silent about how or when, as I will make clear in chapters 4 and 5. The view that Torah is for Jews and Christ is for Gentiles—dual covenants—is simply inadequate unless it deals with Paul's insistence on the Jewish acceptance of his gospel.

Third Entity View A second major post-Holocaust position that seeks to reconcile Torah and Christ is that of the third entity, an idea developed particularly by E. P. Sanders. He directly addresses the problem of dual covenants:

> The crucial point is that Paul applied the entrance requirement "faith in Jesus Christ" to Jews as well as to Gentiles. Even Peter

> and Paul, who had lived as righteous Jews, had to do *something else* in order to be members of the people of God; they had to have faith in Christ (Gal. 2:15f.). . . . Gentiles who enter the people of God do not, after all, in Paul's view, join Israel according to the flesh. It is not the case that Israel is established and that Gentiles are admitted to it on its own terms. The terms change. But moreover the new terms apply also to the chosen people: righteousness is by faith in Jesus Christ and not by works of law whether one is Jewish or Gentile; one is a true descendant of Abraham who belongs to Christ (Gal. 3:29), not otherwise.[27]

At first glance this perspective seems no different from the traditional understanding of Paul and the law—Torah abrogation. Yet Sanders's view differs in at least one major respect—Christ does not cancel the law.

Sanders's assertion that Christ does not cancel the law appears somewhat perplexing, particularly with Sanders maintaining that for Paul righteousness is not by works of law. A deeper probe into this understanding describes a Paul who believes not that Christ cancels the law but that Christ transcends the law. Torah is considered good and relevant to living for Jews, but Paul's "attack on righteousness by the law is against making acceptance of the law a condition of membership in the body of those who will be saved."[28]

Sanders states that Paul maintained the same requirements for Gentiles. They too are sinners and are in need of God's liberative grace. Although in former days Gentiles were unaware of the law through Moses (Romans 1), they are subject to the law that was made known through nature (Romans 2). Neither path is adequate for righteousness. Therefore both Jews and Gentiles are on the same footing—"all have equal opportunity to be righteoused [sic] by faith in Christ."[29]

Similarly to Sanders, Gager states that "according to this interpretation, Jews no longer have a separate identity apart from Christ."[30] The third entity view of Sanders is different from the abrogationist interpretation, having a more complimentary picture of Torah, but it also results in another form of the rejection and replacement theory (which Sanders, to his own dismay, recognizes).[31] Sanders believes that one can understand other statements, such as Romans 11:25-26 ("and so all Israel will be saved") only in the light of a Pauline theology that does not leave room for Judaism apart from Christ.

With great anguish Sanders concludes "that Paul's view does not provide an adequate basis for a Jewish-Christian dialogue."[32] In an earlier article Sanders had commented: "[Paul] thought that the only way to be saved was through Christ Jesus. If it were to be proposed that Christians today should think the same thing, and accordingly that the Jews who have not converted should be considered cut off from God, and if such a proposal came before a body in which I had a vote, I would vote against it."[33] More recently, he remarked, "I still would. I am now inclined to think that perhaps Paul would too."[34]

Sanders has struggled to be faithful to the true Paul. In his effort to reread the apostle with a post-Holocaust sensitivity, he has been able to move past Luther's anachronistic view of Torah abrogation. Although Sanders tends to agree with Stendahl's perspective that says simply: Christ is for the Gentiles and Torah is for the Jews, he is also straightforward in stating that Stendahl's view is not Paul's. His helpful perspective has sought to avoid wishful thinking and to allow for ambiguity. Still, Sanders anguishes in having discovered a Paul that is inadequate for Christian-Jewish relations in a world charred by Auschwitz. Is Sanders's perspective the last word on Paul and the Jewish people? If so, one must conclude that being Christian, at least in regard to how Paul understood "Christ crucified," is no longer a credible faith today. But another perspective on Paul deserves examination.

The perspective needed regarding Paul is one that remains faithful to Paul's text and does not fall into a rejection and replacement theology of Judaism. Like Stendahl's view, it allows Torah to stand on its own for Jews, and for Gentiles to hail Christ. Like Sanders's view, it takes stock of Jews who adhere to the gospel of Christ. Yet it is an interpretation that also opens the door for Paul to be the bridge between Christians and Jews after Auschwitz. Such a perspective is what I call the Inclusive Promise.

Inclusive Promise View   My inclusive promise hypothesis of Paul and Torah hinges on the subtle but consistent distinction in Paul between faith in Christ and faithfulness of the gospel of Christ. It requires Christians to take a quantum leap into uncharted territory—the theology of a Jewish Paul that had a particularistic cosmic claim regarding the Christ-event yet included Jews without calling them to conversion. When surveyed accurately, Paul's gospel upholds the law for Jews and makes it unnecessary for gentile Christians. Christ is for Gentiles what Torah is for Jews. Nevertheless, Paul indeed believes that God wills for Jews to accept the gospel of Christ. Paul is convinced that this gospel is God's will for both Jews and Gentiles, but it means something different for each. This is the "how" that Peter von der Osten-Sacken claims is unknown about Paul's gospel. If not explicitly clear, the inclusive covenant view makes Paul's "how" implicitly understandable.

Venturing into this uncharted territory poses major problems from the outset. Although Paul does not write with an anti-Jewish bent, the early church included the Pauline Letters into canonical Scripture because "they were universally read as confirming both the rejection of the old Israel and the abrogation of the ritual commandments. . . . The process that led to the canonization of the Pauline letters has also determined an anti-Jewish reading of them in all of subsequent Christianity."[36] But the church cannot abandon Paul's Letters. They present an incredible irony: Paul's Letters, and his alone, are the only New Testament sources that move directly toward a theology including the Jewish people and still upholding the integrity of proclaiming Jesus as the Christ. Had Irenaeus and other patristic leaders recognized Paul's favorable position toward the Jewish people, Paul's Letters would probably not have been canonized. "Paul was not really accepted by the church until Irenaeus, and only then as a domesticated Paul, a Paul remade into a catholic Paul."[36] Had the early church interpreted Paul's Letters as including the Jewish people, they quite possibly would have remained as obscure to most Christians as gnostic texts such as the *Gospel of Thomas*.

In chapters 4 and 5 I show in detail how Paul unequivocally believed in an inclusive promise for Jews as Jews and Gentiles as Gentiles. He developed the idea of an inclusive promise without compromising his belief that God wills for both Jews and Gentiles to accept the gospel of Christ. Given the exclusivity of tradition, inclusiveness occurs only when one stretches beyond the boundaries of tradition and seeks to recover the liberative currents from tradition's fringes. Although it is never possible, or even desirable, completely to shed traditions, one must attempt a recovery of Paul's original intentions. The best recovery is to probe the immediate context of his letters.

The Centrality of Galatians and Romans

Galatians and Romans are the two Pauline letters that deal primarily with Torah and the Jewish people. Most scholars believe that Romans is the last letter Paul wrote that was included in the New Testament, and that Galatians reflects the same theological precepts as Romans. One should remember that Paul is not a systematic theologian. His letters reveal that his theology is much more developed in his last letters than in his earlier works. These writings are correspondence, not theological credos. Erwin Goodenough observes correctly that "method or plan is the first problem in trying to reconstruct the 'essential Paul.' None of Paul's letters conveys exactly the impression of any other, especially in details, and some seem quite different in kind."[37] As such, they are directed to specific people in particular circumstances.

Paul remains amazingly consistent. Goodenough asks:

> In view of these apparent fluctuations, is it legitimate to attempt to extract from a single letter what we take to be the essential message of Paul? I believe it is, since in this letter, Romans, he is provoked by no outside vagaries or problems; he is expounding the message of Christ, the theme of which is salvation. He does this quietly and as systematically as I think his mind ever could work. He becomes deeply emotional in places, but the gospel was a very deeply emotional message and he a deeply emotional person. Nevertheless, his intent in this letter is clear; he is simply telling to the Romans the gospel of Christ as he understands it.[38]

At the core of all Paul's letters is his "overwhelming preoccupation . . . with the religious status of Gentiles in relation to the Torah,"[39] the primary focus in both Romans and Galatians.

Gaston notes that in meeting with the Jerusalem pillars, Paul clearly understands himself as the apostle to the Gentiles (Gal. 2:7-9). Therefore his gospel is written primarily, if not completely, for Gentiles. Gager concurs: "Paul agreed to aim his Torah-free Gospel exclusively at Gentiles. . . . It is equally apparent that Paul's gospel was not merely directed at Gentiles but was principally *about* Gentiles: 'Scripture foresaw that God would justify the Gentiles. . . .' (Gal. 3:8)."[40]

This view conflicts directly with the classical view that Paul's congregations were a mix of Jewish and gentile Christians. The main argument for the classical position is that Paul would make sense only to an audience with a Jewish education. John A. T. Robinson represents such a position: Romans "presupposes a Jewish, Old Testament and rabbinic background and would be unintelligible to those who knew nothing of it."[41] Against such a hypothesis, Sanders states simply: "It seems that Paul's 'basic meaning' is usually clear enough" and is not dependent on having a background in the Hebrew Scriptures.[42] Sanders agrees with Johannes Munck in thinking that "the contents of the letters need not reflect the presence of Jews, whether natives or proselytes, in Paul's churches. Paul's quotation of Scripture does not require that his readers themselves be adept at arguing from Scripture. They only had to realize *that* he was quoting an authoritative text, not to be able to appreciate how cleverly he argued, much less to be able to formulate counter arguments."[43]

I now turn to a more detailed discussion of Paul's understanding of the gospel as reflected in Galatians and Romans.

4

Galatians: Before Moses Was Abraham

For Philo, as for Paul and for the rabbis, a fundamental problem regarding Abraham is the relationship between Abraham, the ancestor, and the descendant, Moses, and his Law. If Moses' Law was the divine law, how could Abraham . . . have flourished without it?
—Samuel Sandmel[1]

In Philo (and in Paul), the patriarchs are regarded as the norm, and the Mosaic Laws need to be brought into conformity with the patriarchs.
—Samuel Sandmel[2]

Before Moses was Abraham, at least as far as Paul was concerned. Paul was convinced that the law was a gift from God and provided the grounding of Jewish faith. Like most of his contemporary Pharisees, Paul was familiar with the Law and the Prophets. Along with Jewish people the world over throughout the ages, he would have frequently recited the story of liberation for his people, the Exodus-Sinai event. Unlike most Jews in his day, however, Paul looked behind Moses and God's covenant given through Moses to focus on the patriarchs, particularly Abraham.

Although the law was a blessing, a binding covenant never to be revoked, Paul believed that the law was also a curse. Marcion and most Christians since Marcion have understood this curse to apply to all, including Jews. But this idea is not what Paul had in mind. Instead, he increasingly became convinced that a Gentile convert to Judaism would always remain at a disadvantage in relating to the Law compared to Jews who had grown up with the Law and Jewish tradition. Therefore, no matter how sincere his or her loyalty to the Law, the Gentile convert to Judaism would only remain frustrated and "cursed" by his or her inability to keep the Law.

According to Paul, the law is a curse only in the sense that from the beginning it was intended only for Jews. Although the God of Israel loved Gentiles, Paul believed that God loved them in their ignorance. The only way Gentiles could have an enlightened zeal for the Lord God was to convert to Judaism, with all its laws and customs. Paul had been a strong proponent of this perspective, even to the point of persecuting the church when it deviated from his understanding of orthodoxy. But all of this changed one day as he traveled on the road to Damascus.

Paul was transformed on that road, but not from Judaism to Christianity. Rather, he became convinced that Jews had an unfair advantage over Gentiles. Even if Gentiles converted to Judaism, were circumcised, and adopted the law as their standard for living, Jews would have an advantage just from growing up Jewish.

At this point Abraham comes into the picture in Paul's unfolding drama of salvation history. Abraham existed before the law, yet flourished as a faithful servant of God. How was this possible without the law?

Like some of his Jewish contemporaries, Paul was deeply troubled over this seeming inconsistency in theology. Philo of Alexandria is a good example of one of Paul's contemporaries who struggled with similar questions. Philo became prominent in the generation before Paul, but their lives overlapped. It is impossible to know whether Paul ever read Philo, but the similarities in thought suggest that they were driven by some common questions. Samuel Sandmel observes:

> For both there existed somewhat similar problems in the Law of Moses. . . . The problem for both is that the Laws are presented only in Exodus, raising the question of the relation of the patriarchs who flourished before Moses to the laws inaugurated in his time. Briefly stated, Philo and Paul have it in common that the patriarchs in Genesis are regarded as the true norm of proper religion, and the laws in Exodus and following books needed in some way to be related to that true norm.[3]

Philo resolved this conflict by developing a sophisticated philosophy based on the divine *Logos*, which was active before written laws. For Philo, "Abraham observed the law of nature, and Abraham himself was a law; the Law of Moses is the copy of the law of nature, and the Law of Moses derives its specifications from those specific things which Abraham (and other patriarchs) did."[4]

Paul responded to this question quite differently. Although he was like Philo in many respects, Paul departed from Philo by drawing upon the more rabbinic emphasis on salvation history; but instead of focusing on the Jews, Paul used Abraham to present God's promise to the Gentiles.

According to Paul, God made the binding promise with Abraham and Sarah that they would bear children, becoming the parents not only of the Hebrew people but of the nations (Gentiles) also. Abraham trusted God. He demonstrated faith in the faithfulness of God. For Paul this promise was primary and preempted the covenant God made at Sinai. In Paul's thinking, the Abrahamic promise was inclusive of all people, Jews and Gentiles alike. The Mosaic covenant was for Jews only. The Law provided an order for Jewish society to live out God's inclusive promise given through Abraham and Sarah.

Traditional interpreters of Galatians and Paul's writings in general have held that Paul abrogated Torah at this point: Paul believed that the law was inadequate and impossible to fulfill. But Paul never proposed such a belief. Instead, he upheld the law. All covenants are binding. Paul argued that Gentiles have been embraced as God's beloved since the time of Abraham without becoming Jewish. This embrace is fully realized in a new event—"Christ crucified." Now Gentiles are not only beloved but can fully participate in the covenantal life with God while remaining outside the law. The law had become a block for Gentiles, because from the start it was not intended for them. Jews continue to share in God's promise through Abraham grounded by faithful living within the law. Paul demonstrates this perspective in his allegory of Hagar and Sarah.

Hagar and Sarah

Galatians 4:22-31 contains one of the most confusing allegories in biblical literature. The allegory contemplates the story of Abraham, his two sons, and their mothers (Gen. 21:9-12), and relates the story to Paul's present situation of the Gentiles' place in salvation history. Hagar and her son, Ishmael, represent birth "according to the flesh." Sarah and her son, Isaac, represent birth "through promise" (4:23) and "according to the Spirit" (4:29). Ishmael's birth and Hagar are related through Sinai and slavery. Isaac's birth and Sarah are understood as an extraordinary event—the fulfillment of God's promise to Abraham.

Unfortunately, traditional Pauline scholars associate Hagar with Jews who continue to rely on the law and on works-righteousness. In contrast, they portray Sarah as the faithful servant of God who helped bring God's promise of "laughter" (*Isaac* means "laughter") into being. According to these interpreters, God's promise is fulfilled by all who have faith in Christ.

But this argument has a major flaw. If Paul wrote Galatians to Gentiles exclusively, then his argument is directed toward Gentiles, not disobedient Jews. Isaac symbolizes hope for both Jews and Gentiles. Gentiles infatuated with Jewish ways and those encouraging this action (gentile troublemakers) are trying to put their trust in Hagar. Because the law was originally intended for the Jewish people, it is a block for Gentiles, and Gentiles who focus on Moses and the law miss the significance of the Abrahamic promise for their lives. All people, Jews and Gentiles, are in the tradition of Abraham-Sarah-Isaac. Charles Cousar comments: "Their life comes from the new age, where God who once fulfilled a promise to Abraham and Sarah about the continuance of their family has fulfilled another promise to Abraham—'In thee shall all the nations be blessed' (3:8; Gen. 12:3)."[5]

The Troublemakers

Most scholars agree that Paul's pastoral concern in Galatians was that his recipients not allow themselves to be influenced by the Judaizers. The "Judaizers" is only a relatively recent name for these unknown troublemakers in Galatians. The use of this term is unfortunate. Not only does the term "Judaizers" have derogatory connotations, but it also implies that the troublemakers might be Jews.

Paul speaks of the troublemakers as "them," not "you," which seems to indicate that they were an outside group proclaiming a different gospel from Paul. Gager comments: "The bearers of this new gospel had urged the Gentile Christians to Judaize, that is, not to abandon Christianity for Judaism but to incorporate certain elements of Jewish ritual observance, including circumcision (5:6), into their beliefs and practices."[6]

Classical interpreters of Paul believe that the troublemakers were Jews trying to sway Christians in Galatia away from the gospel. This view has been discredited by the awareness that practicing Jews would have been concerned with Gentiles' full conversion to Judaism rather than the mere adoption of some Jewish practices. Charles Cousar agrees with the scholarly consensus today that the troublemakers were not Jews but "Jewish Christians . . . with no specific support from the Jewish authorities in Jerusalem." He reasons that they were "probably Christians of Jewish origin who lived in the Dispersion."[7] Yet this claim also has difficulties.

The only Jewish bearers of Christ's gospel that Paul mentions in Galatians is the group in Antioch connected with the leaders in Jerusalem (2:11-12). Many scholars assume that the troublemakers mentioned in Galatians refer to the same or a similar group of Jewish Christians. But Paul cannot be speaking of these Jews here. He indicates in his letter that he does not know the identity of the troublemakers (5:10). In addition, Paul writes that the troublemaking persuasion is not from God (5:8). It is unlikely that he would make this claim against Christians of Jewish origin, regardless of how much he disagreed with them.

The argument that the troublemakers are a different group of Jewish Christians from the party in Antioch also breaks down because Paul gives no indication that the letter "to the churches of Galatia" (1:2) is directed to any people other than gentile Christians (4:8-11). Had Paul known of Jewish Christians in the churches in Galatia, he would have addressed them as well as gentile Christians in the letter.

Clark Williamson suggests another possibility—"that the troublemakers were Gentiles infatuated with Jewish ways, people who are playing at being Jewish. . . . Would Paul need to remind a Jew that 'I testify again to every man who receives circumcision that he is bound to keep the whole law' (Gal. 5:3)? . . . These verses imply that the troublemakers were neither Jews nor Jewish Christians."[8] Thus Gager insists, "Judaizing, not Judaism, is the issue. And in all likelihood those who were advocating the virtues of Judaizing were Gentiles rather than Jews."[9] The troublemakers were clearly not practicing Jews. Nor is it likely that they were Christians of Jewish origin. Hence the evidence suggests that the troublemakers were probably Gentiles playing at being Jewish without coverting to Judaism.

In reading Galatians one recognizes that the classical Torah abrogation hypothesis does not hold up. For Paul, the law is unnecessary only for Gentiles. If anyone is abrogating Torah it is some Gentiles in the Galatian church who are nullifying Paul's gospel to take on one that incorporates elements of the Jewish faith.

Galatians also provides ample evidence to discredit the dual covenants perspective, which seeks to prove that the law is exclusively for the Jewish people and that Christ is exclusively for the Gentiles, but which fails to account for Paul's belief that Jews accept the gospel. For in chapter 1, Paul already writes about Peter (Cephas) and James ("the Lord's brother"), followers of Jesus who were Jewish, not Gentile.

Although Galatians does not provide enough data clearly to distinguish the inclusive promise view from the third entity perspective, it does lay the groundwork for understanding Torah in Romans. Romans distinctively portrays the inclusive promise as Paul's view.

The new suggestion that Galatians does not abrogate the law and that the troublemakers are Gentiles breaks radically from the traditional understanding of the letter. It is therefore necessary to analyze some of the key issues that might raise the question of the legitimacy of this hypothesis. One issue is the way Paul seems to discredit the legitimacy of Torah in the latter half of chapter 2 through chapter 3 after he establishes its legitimacy in chapter 1 and the first half of chapter 2. A second issue is the meaning of "under the law" and "works of the law." A third is the use of "curse" in reference to the Torah. The last issue is the meaning of "the Israel of God" in chapter 6. Each issue illustrates a Paul who embraces the law for the Jewish people, even though at first glance Galatians appears to say quite the opposite.

Gentiles' No to Torah

After establishing the credibility of his gospel by referring to the pillars' blessing and their dissociation with the "false believers" (1:6—2:14), Paul presents his own position to the Galatians (2:15—3:5) in a way that resembles the discreditation of the law. This point is somewhat confusing, particularly after Paul just affirmed the legitimacy of Peter's gospel to the circumcised (2:7). Thus the key question is, Is Paul discrediting Torah for *all* people, including the Jews? To the contrary!

Peter and others in Jerusalem believed that Christ did not nullify the law for Jews. They not only continued to practice Torah but initially had some difficulty in understanding how Paul could preach to Gentiles about a relationship with God apart from the law. Before Paul's visit ended, "the right hand of fellowship" (2:9) was extended to Paul and Barnabas from those of repute—an action that represented compromise for both parties. Essentially, Paul said to Peter, "You preach the gospel among Jews and practice the law"; and Peter said to Paul, "You preach the gospel among Gentiles without the law." Therefore Paul's arguments against "works of the law" are geared toward his gentile recipients. In Paul's reasoning, "Torah signified only one thing for Gentiles, namely, condemnation."[10] This view is echoed in Romans: "Circumcision indeed is of value if you obey the law; but if you break the law, your circumcision becomes uncircumcision" (2:25).

Yet if Paul truly believed this way, what can one make of his use of personal pronouns ("we" and "I") when he talks about the law? Because Paul was a Jew, might this use suggest that he believed that Christ superseded the law for all people, both Gentiles and Jews? This suggestion is unlikely, especially in the light of Paul's portrait of faithful Jews apart from Christ in Romans.

Lloyd Gaston argues that Paul's use of personal pronouns does not suggest that he believed that all Jews should give up the law for Christ's sake. Rather, Paul means just what he says—"I." For the sake of the gospel—that in Christ Gentiles have been brought near to the God of Abraham—Paul has "died to the law" in order to identify totally with Gentiles (Gal. 2:19a). John Gager summarizes his argument:

> Thus v. 19a states: (a) that Paul has "died to the law," that is, that he no longer submits to the covenant of Israel or its commandments; (b) that this came about "through the law," meaning either "law" in the sense of the new law of Christ or perhaps more likely, that his apostasy is in accord with the divine will that Paul should preach Christ among the Gentiles (Gal. 1:16); and (c) "so that I might live to God," which, following on the second sense of "through the law," simply expresses Paul's belief in the divine character and origin of his mission. Finally, in v. 19b-20, Paul completes the appeal to his apostasy by emphasizing his total dependency on Christ. Gaston uses Paul's own language to summarize its bearing on the case of the Judaizers: "I beseech you, become as I am, for I also become as you are!" [Gal. 4:12].[11]

Paul's argument in 1 Corinthians serves as a point of reference in understanding his use of personal pronouns in Galatians.

> To the Jews, I became as a Jew, in order to win Jews; to those under the law I became as one under the law (though I myself am not under the law) so that I might win those under the law. To those outside the law I became as one outside the law (though I am not

free from God's law, but am under Christ's law) so that I might win
those outside the law. To the weak, I became weak, that I might
win the weak. I have become all things to all people, that I might
by all means save some. I do it all for the sake of the gospel, so
that I may share in its blessings. (9:20-23)

Paul testifies that "whatever gains I had, these I have come to regard
as loss because of Christ" (Phil. 3:7). His call to bring the good news to
Gentiles becomes the mandate of his life. Paul is willing and even
compelled to do whatever is necessary, including becoming an apostate
to Torah, in order that he might live out his call to preach among the
Gentiles.[12] Although he certainly did not see himself as an apostate to
Judaism, he understood his chameleonlike behavior as the way to maintain the integrity of his call to the Gentiles. Indeed, Paul would be the
first to admit that such a perspective in no way invalidates the practicing
of Torah among other Jewish witnesses of the gospel such as Peter.

Again, Paul's argument in Galatians was not against Jews practicing
the law but against the troublemakers. The intensification of his "I" in
2:18-20 says to the Judaizers: "If I, a Jew, know that Gentiles are no
longer justified by works of the law, how can you Gentiles possibly
undertake observance of it?"[13] By arguing that he has "already . . .
abandoned observance of the law as part of his apostleship to the Gentiles," Paul tried to show his Gentile recipients how ridiculous it would
be "if he were now to permit or encourage Gentiles to observe the
law."[14] Paul did not discredit the legitimacy of the law for Jews; rather,
he credited the law's illegitimacy for Gentiles.

"Works of the Law" and "Under the Law"

A second issue raised by classical interpreters of Galatians is what to
make of Paul's use of "works of the law" (2:16; 3:5) and "works under
the law" (3:23; 5:18). Scholars have assumed that both phrases describe
the Jews in relation to the covenant.[15] The traditional rendering has Paul
writing "that a person is justified not by the works of the law but through
faith in Jesus Christ . . . because no one will be justified by the works
of the law" (2:16). Further, "Now before faith came, we were imprisoned
and guarded under the law until faith would be revealed" (3:23). Thus
the traditional conclusion is that Jews who adhere to Torah are imprisoned, guarded, lacking in faith, and are not justified by God. Hence,

according to this argument, Jews who do not accept Jesus as the Christ live by the letter and not by the spirit of the law.

To reach such a conclusion one must presume that Paul is speaking of Jews as well as Gentiles. To make Paul's words abrogate Torah one would also have to change genitives to datives and accusatives (as in the translation just cited). But if Paul remained consistent through Galatians, directing it toward the gentile troublemakers, the verses above might read: "a Gentile is not made righteous by means of works of the law but through faithfulness of Jesus Christ . . . by means of works of the law shall no Gentile be made righteous" (2:16). Affirming such a reading, John Gager states "that *anthropos* in v. 16 must refer to Gentiles is clear enough from the context, for Paul's sole concern here is the Gentile Judaizers."[16]

The view that Christians have come to call "legalism" was not even an issue among Jews in Paul's day. Lloyd Gaston argues that legalism— "the doing of certain works in order to win God's favor and be counted righteous—arose as a gentile and not a Jewish problem at all."[17] Buttressing this point, Markus Barth states that the phrase "works of the law" appears in early Christian writings "only in contexts where the imposition of some legal elements upon the Gentiles is discussed."[18] One can only conclude, then, that "the term 'works of the law,' not found in any Jewish texts, refers to the Gentile habit of adopting certain Jewish practices as a means of self-justification."[19]

Pauline commentators have given less attention to the phrase "under the law," but they generally assume that it refers to the Jewish people. This assumption appears to apply in Romans 3:19, but in other contexts (particularly 1 Cor. 9:20-23 and throughout Galatians) one can see that it cannot refer to the Jewish people. In 1 Corinthians, Paul mentions "those under the law" between the terms "Jews" and "those outside the law"; therefore they seem to represent another group. Gager sums it up:

> Thus they can be neither Jews nor those completely unrelated to Judaism. It is unlikely that they are proselytes, since Jews and Gentiles alike agreed that proselytes were no longer Gentiles. . . . That [Paul] was never "outside the law" is obvious; that he feels no need to distinguish himself from Jews is equally obvious. What other group is there to which he did not belong? There is but one real possibility, namely, that "those under the law" refers to those

many and widely-attested Gentiles who undertook to observe se-
lected elements of the Mosaic commandments but stopped short
of full conversion.[20]

Those who adhere to "works of the law" and those "under the law"
are the same group—the gentile troublemakers.

The "Curse" of Torah

A third issue in Galatians concerns the use of "curse" and "law" together.
Those who hold the Torah abrogation theory assume that Paul regards
Jews, "who rely on works of the law," as the ones who "are under a
curse" (Gal. 3:10). An SS officer might similarly reason: "The charred
bodies of dead Jewish children—How can we call them 'innocent'? After
all, are they not the misled babes 'cursed' to be burned alive, these
Jews who 'rely on works of the law' for salvation?" If one reads Paul out
of context, this twisted interpretation is comprehensible: "For all who
rely on works of the law are under a curse; for it is written, 'Cursed is
everyone who does not observe and obey all things written in the book
of the law.' Now it is evident that no one is justified before God by the
law. . . . Christ redeemed us from the curse of the law" (3:10-11, 13).

The problem with prooftexting this passage is that it does not take
into account the immediately preceding words: "And the scripture, foreseeing that God would make righteous the Gentiles by means of faithfulness, preached the gospel beforehand to Abraham, saying, 'In you
shall all the nations be blessed.' So then, those who are persons of
faithfulness are blessed with Abraham who had faith" (3:8-9, au. trans.).

This translation significantly changes the understanding of who is
cursed. It is not the Jewish people but the troublemakers—Gentile
Christians infatuated with some Jewish laws. Therefore, I read Paul as
saying: "For all [Gentiles] who rely on works of the law are under a
curse; for it is written, 'Cursed is every one who does not observe and
obey all things written in the book of the law.' Now it is evident that
no [Gentile] person is made righteous before God by the law. . . . Christ
reconciled us [Gentiles][21] from the curse of the law" (3:10-11, 13).

Paul concludes this segment with these appropriate words: "In Christ
Jesus the blessing has come upon the Gentiles, that we might receive
the promise of the Spirit through faithfulness" (3:14, au. trans.).

The full impact of this argument comes in 4:4-5: "When the time had fully come, God sent forth [God's child], born of woman, born under the law, to reconcile those who were under the law, so that we might receive adoption as [children]."[22] Here "under the law" means something slightly different than it did before. It previously referred to the troublemakers. Now the topic is the "curse." Does this verse mean that Jesus, as a Jew, was cursed? No! This interpretation would be inconsistent with Paul's thesis that Jews who follow the works of the law are not cursed. In this case, Paul is not referring to Jesus the Jew, but to Jesus the child of God. Paul understands Jesus in the same framework as himself—as one who became outside the law in order to win some (i.e., Gentiles)—outside the law (1 Cor. 9:21). This interpretation is the only way to make sense of Galatians 3:13-14a: "Christ [reconciled] us from the curse of the law by becoming a curse for us—for it is written, 'Cursed is everyone who hangs on a tree'—in order that in Christ Jesus the blessing of Abraham might come to the Gentiles." Thus, according to Gager, "Jesus assumes the Torah only for the purpose of redeeming those who stand under its curse. . . . Jesus' sole function, so it would seem, is to bring to fulfillment the promise of Abraham regarding the Gentiles."[23]

"The Israel of God"

Another major problem in understanding Galatians is the meaning of the phrase "the Israel of God" in 6:16. One's theological biases weigh especially heavily in the interpretation of this verse. Again, it is important to look closely at the context of the entire letter, and specifically at 6:12-16. My parenthetical comments help illumine Paul's assumptions underlying the text.

> It is those who want to make a good showing in the flesh [Gentile troublemakers] that try to compel you to be circumcised—only that they may not be persecuted for the cross of Christ. Even the circumcised (Gentile troublemakers and those persuaded by them) do not themselves obey the law, but they want you to be circumcised so that they may boast about your flesh. May I never boast of anything except the cross of our Lord Jesus Christ, by which the world has been crucified to me, and I to the world. For neither circumcision nor uncircumcision [for Gentiles who have been called to proclaim the Inclusive Promise among Gentiles] is anything; but

a new creation [the Inclusive Promise] is everything! As for those who will follow this rule [Gentiles]—peace be upon them, and mercy, and[24] upon the Israel of God (Jews).

The New Common Lectionary places this passage in year C, among the Sundays after Pentecost. The lectionary lists the epistle reading as Galatians 6:7-18. The change in subjects between verses 10 and 11, however, indicates a break here. Verses 7-10 are linked with the preceding verse and focus on generosity. Paul uses the familiar metaphor that one reaps what one sows. Verses 11-18 serve as a summary of the letter by returning to the subject of the relationship between the Gentile in Galatia and Torah. This is one of the principal issues of understanding Paul after Auschwitz; thus I focus on verses 11-18.

The mood of these verses is primarily polemical. Classical interpretation has maintained that the polemic is directed against the Jewish people, and that Paul advocates the abrogation of Torah.[25] Some scholars have more recently asserted that Paul's polemic in Galatians is not against the Jewish people but against the troublemakers. Because these troublemakers advocate circumcision, scholars have assumed that they must be Jewish Christians who are trying to persuade gentile Christians to take on some aspects of Judaism.[26] Indeed, this passage seems to assert such a position. But some evidence suggests that these troublemakers are Gentiles infatuated with outward signs of Torah. In addition to the reasons already stated, Galatians 6:11-18 alone demonstrates in three ways that the troublemakers are Gentiles.

First, Paul does not believe that Christ abrogates Torah. Faithful observance of Torah is possible for Jews apart from Christ. By maintaining their Jewishness, Jewish Christians (i.e., Jews who hailed Jesus as their Messiah or Jews who believed that through Christ Gentiles have been made righteous by God) believe that one remains faithful to all of Torah, not just outward observances such as circumcision (vv. 12-13).

Second, verses 12 and 13 are written in parallel form. The polemical action in each verse is against the same group that Paul has attacked all along—the troublemakers. They are those "who want to make a good showing in the flesh" (v. 12) and "the circumcised" (v. 13). Paul gets angry because the troublemakers "compel *you*" (v. 12) and want *you* to be circumcised" to validate what *they* have done (i.e., "that *they* may boast about your flesh," v. 13). Indeed, Jewish Christians would not be those Paul accuses of making a good showing in the flesh—receiving circumcision—in order to avoid persecution for the cross of Christ (v. 12). If they are Jewish Christians, they would have received circumcision on the eighth day after their birth like all Jewish males, not in order to avoid persecution.

Third, the direction of God's action in 6:11-18, as in the whole letter, is toward the inclusion of Gentiles as Gentiles. Paul is not against Jews as Jews. Therefore Paul's frustration in verses 11-18 is not with either group per se. Rather, Paul expresses his anger with Gentiles who put on an outward showing—circumcision—but do not become Jewish. The gentile Christian troublemakers are those who play at being Jewish and compel other Gentiles to do likewise.

I have established through verses 12-13 that the troublemakers in this passage are Gentiles. It is important to discuss here why Paul believes that these Gentiles desire circumcision and why the trouble-makers want to win over other Gentiles to circumcision. According to Paul, their troublemaking emerges from the fear of being persecuted for the cross of Christ.

Through Christ these Gentiles' perception of their status has changed, even though Paul believed their actual status changed in God's promise at the time of Abraham. Their new-found faith in the God of Abraham and Sarah through Christ put them in direct conflict with Roman law. Roman law required all citizens, and even noncitizens, of the empire to worship Caesar as lord and savior. In peaceful times this law was not strictly enforced, particularly as it pertained to Jews. Jews were often allowed to worship the God of Abraham and Sarah without worshiping Caesar as long as they rendered to Caesar what belonged to Caesar. But Rome was not lax in times of tension. Galatia was an area on the fringes of Roman dominion, under constant attacks by the barbarians from the north. Roman authorities naturally felt more nervous about anything they perceived as disloyalty. Living in Galatia, therefore, was much more tense for Christians and Jews than living in the heart of the empire.

Most Romans were polytheistic, and worshiping Caesar as lord and savior involved only adding another god to the existing pantheon. Gentile Christians and Jews stood alone in their worship of one God. They also adhered to the same authoritative writings—the Law and the Prophets. (No New Testament writings yet existed and the Hebrew Scripture Canon containing the Law, the Prophets, and the Writings was not closed until the Jewish Council of Jamnia in 90 C.E.). Although not

Jewish themselves, the early gentile Christians in Galatia felt a particular kinship to the people of Israel and wanted the Jewish community to accept them as beloved and legitimized children. Perhaps this is what Paul means when he wrote of their compelling desire to be circumcised, "and only in order that they may not be persecuted (or annoyed) for the cross of Christ" (v. 12).

Cousar notes correctly that "the Greek verb for 'persecute' here may imply no more than 'annoy.' "[27] Furthermore, Paul does not say the undisclosed group (the Jewish community) is annoyed at these Gentiles for believing in Christ crucified, only that the Gentiles want to make a good showing in the flesh so that they may not be an annoyance for the cross of Christ. Indeed, these Gentiles wanted acceptance—if not by the Romans, then by the Jews. Thus their desire for circumcision did not stem from wanting to be Jewish (hence they did not keep the law). Instead, circumcision was a way for these monotheistic Gentiles to belong, even if only in the flesh, to the already established Jewish community in Galatia.

Paul shifts his focus in verse 14 to "the cross of Christ," to which he alluded in verse 12. While verses 12 and 13 clearly parallel, verse 14 contrasts with verses 12 and 13. The contrast is between what the gentile troublemakers glory (boast) in—seeing other Gentiles circumcised along with themselves (v. 13)—and what Paul glories (boasts) in—"the cross of our Lord Jesus Christ" (v. 14). "Christ crucified" is that event by which Gentiles discover authentic existence in the gift and demand of God's boundless love, which occurred through the Abrahamic promise. Helping Gentiles discover this ancient promise is the central focus of Paul's gospel and of his individual call as apostle to the Gentiles.

When Paul writes that by the Christ-event "the world has been crucified to me, and I to the world" (v. 14b), he is lifting himself up as an example for the gentile Christians in Galatia. In order that he might win some (help them discover God's promise) outside the law, Paul himself became as one outside the law—like a Gentile. His call to preach the righteousness of God among the Gentiles became the center of his life after his Damascus road experience. By the cross of Christ, the world (meaning everything in the cosmos except the preaching among Gentiles) "has been crucified to me, and I to the world." Paul seems to ask "Why are you Gentiles trying to become like Jews? The meaning of 'Christ crucified' is that you Gentiles have been embraced apart from circumcision. Nothing else in the world is more important."

Verse 15, then, serves as Paul's "therefore" to the Gentiles in Galatia. The traditional reading has noted this verse as an example of the abrogation of Judaism and Torah. But Paul has something else in mind. He believed that he has been crucified to circumcision (circumcision no longer counts for anything) for the sake of the Gentiles. (As part of his unique call to preach among the Gentiles, Paul did not expect other Jews to give up Torah, except, as in the case of the followers of Jesus in Jerusalem, in the presence of Gentiles.) Likewise, through the cross of Christ, Gentiles have been crucified to uncircumcision (uncircumcision no longer counts for anything). What is important is inner transformation, new birth, a new creation, not the outward appearance.

> Outward religious performance is nothing; inward religious transformation is everything (verse 15). Religious rituals, such as circumcision, have no value in and of themselves (1 Cor. 7:19; Gal. 5:6; Rom. 2:25-26). They are nothing. The performance of a religious act, qua religious act, is a meaningless performance, hollow and devoid of significance. What counts is whether it attests an inner change that results in a new creation (cf. 2 Cor. 5:17; Rom. 6:4; 12:2; also Rev. 21:5).[28]

Perhaps the most important verse in the section is verse 16. Interpreters have spent more energy trying to fit it into a prescribed theology than any other verse in Galatians. The problem is Paul's use of "the Israel of God." One can get a clear picture of different theological presuppositions by reading verse 16 in various translations.

> Peace and mercy be upon all who walk by this rule, upon the Israel of God. (RSV)

> As for those who will follow this rule—peace be upon them, and mercy, and upon the Israel of God. (NRSV)

> Peace and mercy to all who follow this rule, who form the Israel of God. (Jerusalem Bible)

> As for those who follow this rule in their lives, may peace and mercy be with them—with them and with all of God's people. (Today's English Version [Good News Bible])

> And as many as walk according to this rule, peace be upon them, and mercy, and upon the Israel of God. (Authorized Version [King James Version])

Whoever they are who take this principle for their guide, peace
and mercy be upon them, and upon the whole Israel of God! (New
English Bible)

In Greek this benediction is *eirēnē ep' autous kai eleos, kai epi ton
Israēl tou theou*, literally "Peace upon them and mercy, and upon the
Israel of God." It is similar to the Jewish benedictions, particularly the
nineteenth, the *Birkat ha-Shalom* ("Blessing of Peace") of the Shemoneh
Esreh (Babylonian recension).[29] "Bestow peace, happiness and blessing,
grace and loving-kindness and mercy upon us and upon all Israel, your
people."[30] This benediction is at least as old as Paul. Hans Dieter Betz
states that "there can be little doubt that the Apostle is dependent upon
one of the forms of the benediction, if not the Shemoneh Esreh itself."[31]

The controversy that surrounds verse 16 does not have to do with its
historical roots, however, but with its meaning in Galatians. Classical
interpreters have allowed their presuppositions to dictate the meaning
here. If Paul is abrogating Torah, if Christianity supersedes Judaism,
then the verse can mean only one thing: "Israel of God" refers to the
church.

Carl Holladay supports the traditional understanding of Paul: " 'New
Creation,' or inner transformation, provides the real clue to our identity
before God. Those who see and truly understand this constitute the real
'Israel of God' (verse 16), and theirs are the eschatological blessings of
peace and mercy."[32]

Similarly, Betz claims that "Israel of God" is an expression that

> does make sense as a critical distinction between a "true" and a
> "false" Israel. There is no doubt that Paul makes such a distinction,
> even if he uses other terminology. . . . Although admittedly there
> is no proof, the suggestion can be made that Paul took over this
> expression from his Jewish-Christian opponents, in whose theology
> "Israel of God" would identify them as the true Judaism *vis-à-vis*
> official Judaism. Just as Paul transfers Jewish prerogatives to the
> Gentile-Christian Galatians elsewhere in the letter, he would pick
> up another concept here and apply it, rather provocatively no doubt,
> to the readers of the epistle, that is, to those who will remain loyal
> Paulinists. However, one must also include in the blessing that part
> of Jewish Christianity which had approved and still approves, per-
> haps, of the agreements of the Jerusalem Council related to the
> Pauline mission. . . . Clearly excluded and under the curse are the
> "false brothers" back then (cf. 2:4-5) and now (cf. 1:6-9).[33]

With such a theology of rejection and replacement of Israel, the only way one could interpret verse 16 is for the Greek *kai* to mean "even" (an infrequent use) rather than "also" (a more frequent use) or "and" (the most frequent use).

Cousar understands "Israel of God" slightly differently from classical interpreters. Instead of claiming that "Israel of God" cannot refer to the Jewish people, he contends that the phrase cannot refer to Israel alone: In light of Paul's efforts to redefine God's people as those who belong to Christ, the most plausible understanding of verse 16 is that of

> the church now joined with the people of the old covenant to be "the Israel of God." . . . This is reflected in RSV (and JB, NIV), where "all who walk by this rule" and "the Israel of God" are understood as two descriptions of the same group, not two groups. Paul is affirming that "the Israel of God" now includes those who have been crucified with Christ and live in his new creation, even un-circumcised Gentiles.[34]

Classical interpreters of Paul and some with slight revisions such as Cousar seem to ignore that Paul never refers to the church as the "Israel of God." E. D. Burton observed this point as early as 1920 when he wrote that Paul never used Israel "except of the Jewish nation or a part thereof."[35] Furthermore, by comparing the nineteenth blessing of the Shemoneh Esreh with verse 16, Peter Richardson concludes that in one version "peace" also precedes "mercy," hence in Gager's words, verse 16 "must be punctuated and translated so that the blessing falls on two separate groups: those who follow Paul's standard *and* the Israel to whom God will show mercy, namely, 'all of Israel.'"[36]

Traditional scholars have correctly asserted that Galatians 6:11-18 is a summary not only of Galatians but of Paul's theology as a whole. Through Galatians and Romans Paul maintains that all Israel is beloved. Now, through Christ, Gentiles may discover and embrace that God loves them as well. Nonetheless, even though Gentiles are beloved, Paul calls only Jews "the Israel of God." Therefore, one must go beyond what Burton wrote about the possibility that this phrase could refer to only part of Israel. Peace and mercy are upon all the gentile Christians who live according to what Paul has said, *and* peace and mercy are upon the Israel of God (which means *all* the Israel of God). "The blessing thus stands in the concluding words penned by [Paul's] own hand, as a summary of the Pauline gospel as a whole."[37]

The liberating action of God in Galatians 6:11-18 and Galatians as a whole is directed toward the gentile Christians. Paul's tone moves from anger and frustration to peace and mercy. The Galatian text is Paul's story about God's inclusion of the Gentiles, but it maintains that peace and mercy are upon God's Israel (the Jewish people).

Although Paul is clearly frustrated by and quick to judge Gentile troublemakers who insist on trying to be like Jews without converting to Judaism, the underlying theme of Galatians is one of grace: an inclusive kind of peace and mercy embraces Gentiles, the kind that comes only from the God of Abraham and Sarah, the kind that before Christ only Jews discovered. The transformation of Paul's gentile recipients does detract from others' experience of faith (namely, the Jews), but is new and fresh for the Gentiles. God initiates this change, which occurs apart from any personal effort of the Gentiles.

5

Romans: The Inclusive Promise of God

For Paul, "Christ crucified and risen" means "it is in him that God's power is effective for the defeat of powers of 'this age,' in him that the righteousness of God is revealed, in and through him that God's reconciling love is bestowed. He is the summation of what God gives and the fullness of what man may receive. He is, in this double sense, *the event of grace.*"

—Victor Paul Furnish[1]

Jesus' death and resurrection—the Christ-event—is for Paul the greatest event of all time. Through Christ God has acted and continues to act to dissolve all distinctions between Jew and Gentile, free and slave, and male and female (Gal. 3:28; Rom. 10:12). Paul reasons that Jews will no longer have an advantage over Gentiles as inheritors of God's grace. Through God's promise to Abraham and Sarah all are called, including those outside the law, to inherit the promise of God's love.

> For the promise that he would inherit the world did not come to Abraham or to his descendants through the law but through the righteousness of faith. . . . For this reason it depends on faith, in order that the promise may rest on grace and be guaranteed to all his descendants, not only to the adherents of the law but also to those who share the faith of Abraham (for he is father of all of us. . . .) (Rom. 4:13, 16)
> And if you belong to Christ, then you are Abraham's offspring, heirs according to the promise. (Gal. 3:29)

Paul bridges the story of Abraham and Sarah to the story of Christ. The Christ-event is the fulfillment of the Abrahamic promise. The promise is not new to Gentiles, but they are now made fully aware of it, apart from the law, through the death and resurrection of Christ. God has called into existence that which formerly did not exist—the Gentiles. Even though Gentiles have been fully embraced as God's beloved since the time of Abraham, Paul believed authentic existence can not occur for them without their awareness of God's promise. The Christ event is their discovery of love made possible through Paul's witness. Paul concludes, "As it is written, 'I have made you the father of many nations'— in the presence of the God in whom he believed, who gives life to the dead and calls into existence the things that do not exist" (Rom. 4:17). I now turn specifically to Romans. What did Paul communicate through this letter? How does it differ from other epistles, especially Galatians?

Romans and Torah

Paul's Letter to the Romans is the other primary piece of Pauline material besides Galatians that deals with the law and the Jewish people. Before moving into specifics, I need to discuss the context of Romans. Much less is known about the circumstances surrounding this letter than those of Galatians. Romans is unique in the Pauline corpus of the New Testament because it is Paul's only letter to a church community that he had not established or nurtured.

The twentieth-century Christian church has been engaged in a great Romans debate, actively challenging the evaluation espoused by Melanchthon, Bultmann, and Nygren that Romans is a "compendium of the Christian religion."[2] Since the Holocaust, Christian scholars have become increasingly aware that the central issue of Romans is the relationship between Jews and Gentiles.[3] Like those addressed in Galatians, the letter's recipients are mostly, if not entirely, Gentiles: "I want you to know, brothers and sisters, that I have often intended to come to you (but thus far have been prevented), in order that I may reap some harvest among you as I have among the rest of the Gentiles" (1:13); "Now I am speaking to you Gentiles" (11:13).

It is not known whether the topics Paul addressed are responses to specific problems in Rome. One does sense distinctly that he was trying to unite the already divided Christian community in Rome. Yet his impassioned tone indicates that he was addressing a deeply personal matter that goes beyond the realm of his normal pastoral letters. In Romans Paul seemed to be seeking to bridge a gap within his own soul—

a soul that both affirms God's covenantal promise to Israel and avows a faith that has brought Gentiles into that promise. The pain of each group's disdain and exclusiveness of the other must have been gut wrenching for Paul.

The great passion with which Paul wrote has left some gaps in understanding its context. Thus "in the final analysis the letter of Romans must stand by itself and serve as its own guide for any interpretation."[4]

Romans does offer some hints to its interpretation. These are represented in the specific language and themes used throughout the letter. Here Galatians becomes pivotal. As Gager asserts, "the significant overlap of terms, themes, illustrations, and arguments in Romans and Galatians should serve as a warning against considering the two letters as completely unrelated. . . . The specific circumstances of Paul's earlier difficulties in Galatia and elsewhere are still very much in his thoughts."[5]

One of the major differences between Galatians and Romans is that the latter is not preoccupied with troublemakers. Unlike Galatians, the issue in Romans is exclusiveness, first on the part of Jews (chaps. 2–4) and later, as a warning, on the part of Gentiles (11:17-36). But the premises behind Paul's argument in Galatians ring loud and clear in Romans also: The law is not necessary for Gentiles and is not nullified for Jews.

Paul gives much attention to Torah in Romans. Unfortunately, the traditional reading of Romans has misunderstood Paul's view of Torah. As one rereads Romans with post-Auschwitz sensitivity, some vital issues come into focus. The overarching thesis is God's inclusion of the Gentiles. Paul spoke of this theme primarily through his discussion of boasting.

First I discuss Paul's thesis of gentile inclusion. Then I focus on boasting. Next I explore the Abraham story as the key to the gospel. Then I deal with the problem passages (chap. 7; 10:4), traditionally used to illustrate Paul's supposed abrogation of Torah. Finally, I examine Paul's message in chapters 9–11. Each of these foci has been used to substantiate the abrogation of Torah. Here I shed new light on these subjects, out of which a fresh image emerges for Jewish-Christian dialogue today.

Inclusion of the Gentiles

Most of Paul's classical interpreters have held that the central theme in Romans is justification by faith. But recent grappling with the text points to a more overarching theme—God's inclusion of the Gentiles in salvation history. To understand this theme one needs to address two key Pauline concepts: righteousness and gospel.

The Righteousness of God   The terms "righteousness" and "justification" are variations on the same Greek root *dikaio-*. The emphasis has historically been on the word "justification," but recent scholarship points to the term "righteousness" as being much more in line with Paul's intentions. Even though their translation into English can imply two different ideas, from a literal standpoint they represent the same Greek term. Hence one could say that one who is "justified" is· "made righteous."

The principal understanding of "righteousness" in Romans is found in Paul's expression "the righteousness of God." Sam K. Williams points out that since the "key to Romans" is *dikaiosynē theou*, "the argument of [Romans] . . . is thoroughly theocentric." In the past most theologians' emphasis on righteousness has been linked primarily to the human choice of faith or to Christ's act of faithfulness on behalf of humans. These are part of Paul's thinking, but the primary thrust of action in Romans is neither the response of humanity nor the act of Christ. Rather, it is God's action—the righteousness of God—that is primary. God keeps God's promise to Abraham not only by making right the descendants who adhere to the law (the Jewish people), but also the descendants who are apart from the law (the Gentiles) (Rom. 4:9, 16). Williams concurs with Franz Leenhardt, who affirms the link between God's righteousness and God's inclusive promise in Romans: "'the whole process of God's self-revelation and saving work is linked with the promise once made to Abraham.' Indeed, the foundation stone of Paul's whole argument is that God keeps his promises 'to the father of us all'" (4:16).[6]

The Gospel of God   It is also imperative to grasp Paul's concept of "gospel." His frequent use of the term indicates its importance. The literal meaning of "gospel" (*euangelion*) in the New Testament is "good news." Christians have traditionally referred to the four books of Matthew, Mark, Luke, and John as "the Gospels." The use of the term "gospel" in Matthew, Mark, and Luke always refers to the good news of God's impending reign. John does not use the term.

Christian tradition has used "gospel" variously. Luther contrasted "law" and "gospel." Others use it synonymously with being Christian, as in "believing in the gospel." In Western culture, even outside the church, "the gospel truth" or "this is gospel" (meaning truth) are common expressions. Thus "gospel" carries many meanings both biblically and culturally. In grappling with Paul's meaning of gospel, one must temporarily set aside these other meanings.

The concept of gospel is central in Paul's theology. He refers to "the gospel of God," "the gospel of Christ," and "my gospel." The classical understanding of what Paul means by gospel is "Christ crucified and risen," or the Christ-event. This understanding is correct, but the classical interpretation has often skewed what Paul means by "Christ crucified and risen." Therefore the relationship between "gospel" and the Christ-event deserves careful scrutiny before proceeding further.

I develop what Paul means by gospel through four related points. The first point is that Paul's gospel is always God-centered. The second is that Paul's gospel is primarily the good news of God's inclusion of the Gentiles. His call and whole existence focus on the good news of God to the Gentiles. The third point is that Paul hints to his gentile recipients that the gospel, at its base, is inclusive of Jews as Jews in addition to Gentiles as Gentiles. Fourth, Paul yearns for the Jewish people to embrace his gospel to the Gentiles, but this embracing does not mean that Jews are to become Christians.

First and primary to understanding Paul's view of gospel is that this good news is theocentric, not christocentric. Paul is not a systematic theologian. His theology matures through his letters, but he remains consistent in his recognition that God is the Actor of reconciliation and liberation. Christ does not make the Gentiles righteous. Rather, their righteousness is *promised* by God through Abraham and *realized* by God through Christ.

Furthermore, Paul never uses "God" and "Christ" as synonyms. One can see by the context that "gospel of Christ" always means God's gospel is manifest through Christ. Likewise, when Paul says "my gospel," he is not implying that he is the actor of reconciling and liberative love. Instead, the implication is that Paul is the proclaimer of the good news of God's love to the Gentiles.

The second point is that, as it comes to those today who are the heirs of the Gentiles, Paul's gospel is "Christ crucified and risen." "And the scripture [Torah], foreseeing that God would justify the Gentiles by faith, declared the gospel beforehand to Abraham, saying, 'All Gentiles shall be blessed in you' " (Gal. 3:8). Paul understood the inclusion of the Gentiles as good news because with the Inclusive Promise Gentiles did not have to convert to Judaism to experience God's love. Through the Christ-event the nations have discovered that they are descendants of Abraham along with Israel. J. Christiaan Beker notes that "for Paul, the gospel means the extension of the promise beyond Israel to the Gentiles, not the displacement of Israel by the Gentile church (Barnabas)."[7]

Proclaiming to Gentiles the good news that God has included them in love is the very essence of Paul's vocation or call.[8] Reflecting back on his Damascus road experience, he explains to his brothers and sisters in Galatia that God "had set me apart before I was born, and called me through [God's] grace, was pleased to reveal [God's child] to me, so that I might proclaim Christ among the Gentiles" (Gal. 1:15-16).

Paul again focuses on the aim of Christ crucified and resurrected as the event that reveals the closeness of God to the nations. This gospel is reflected upon and is indeed the main focus of his Letter to the Romans. In words similar to Galatians 1:15-16, Paul says to the Romans, "For I tell you that Christ has become a servant of the circumcised on behalf of the truth of God, in order that he might confirm the promises given to the patriarchs, and in order that the Gentiles might glorify God for [God's] mercy" (Rom. 15:8-9).

When Paul writes about the gospel while discussing Jews and Gentiles, he always focuses on the Gentiles' inclusion, an inclusion that occurred in God's promise through Abraham. When Paul speaks of "gospel" without referring explicitly to Gentiles his constituency is gentile Christians only. Paul makes it clear: The purpose of Christ's coming is to discover God's inclusion of the Gentiles. Christ—meaning Christ crucified and resurrected—is the gospel of God for Gentiles.

The third point in Paul's development of gospel is that, at its very root, the gospel is inclusive of Jews as Jews. How could Jewish inclusion be the case if Paul means by gospel, "Christ crucified and resurrected"? Would not such a gospel indicate that Paul intends for Jews to become Christians? No, indeed. It is time to unpack tradition again. The classical position has been that Paul believes both Jews and Gentiles should come to Christ. The church has assumed this position for nearly two thousand years. Yet every time he writes about his call, Paul clearly points to a ministry among Gentiles. The focus of the Christ-event is on the inclusion of the nations. The church has missed Paul's assumption that the good news already belongs to the Jewish people. The good news is discovered by Gentiles apart from the law through Christ. Paul's good news was never intended to be bad news for the Jewish people. But because the church failed to see Paul's basic assumption, the good news for Gentiles has become bad news for Jews.

In Romans 1:16 Paul states that the issue at hand is God's faithfulness, to the Jew first and also to the Gentile. The standard interpretation of this verse has been that both Jews and Gentiles must have faith in Christ. Such an interpretation ignores Paul's assumption that Jews already know the good news of God's love. Paul never says or implies that in the Christ-event God has rejected the Jewish people and replaced them with Christians. Indeed, he unequivocally refutes such a claim, fearing perhaps that Gentiles might interpret him erroneously.

Paul makes it clear that God's faithfulness is the essential ingredient for being made righteous. Abraham represents God's faithfulness toward Abraham and Abraham's faith is the model of such faithfulness and faith for both Jews and Gentiles. But Paul lifts up Abraham for another reason. The Abraham story of faith is a story in Torah. Yet the story witnesses (thus Torah witnesses) to descendants of Abraham outside Israel (the Gentiles) who share in God's righteousness with God's Israel. Most Jews in Paul's day associated Moses with the law. By using the Pentateuch and pointing to Abraham, who lived prior to the law, Paul reasons that he is giving ground in Torah itself for the Gentiles' inclusion which has been discovered and finally realized by non-Jews through Christ.

Faith like that of Abraham is required for Jews and Gentiles. But Paul asserts that God's faithfulness makes Jews and Gentiles righteous quite differently. Jews experience the righteousness of God by God's faithfulness grounded in Torah, and Gentiles experience God's righteousness by God's faithfulness through Christ (3:30). Paul never says that Christ is the only way to experience God's love. Rather, the Christ-event is how God manifests love to Gentiles, and Torah is the way God manifests love to Jews. According to Schubert Ogden, the Christian message "is not that the Christ is manifest only in Jesus and nowhere else, but that the word addressed to [people] *everywhere*, in all the events of their lives, is none other than the word spoken in Jesus and in the preaching and sacraments of the church."[9]

Paul does make one reference to the good news that explicitly points to God embracing Jews as Jews and Gentiles as Gentiles. Although the traditional interpretation of this passage has been rejectionist of Jews as Jews, the passage gives no indication of christology. "For I am not ashamed of the gospel; it is the power of God for salvation to everyone who has faith, to the Jew first and also to the Greek. For in it the righteousness of God is revealed through faithfulness for faith; as it is written, 'the one who through faithfulness is righteous will live' " (Rom. 1:16-17, au. trans.).

The gospel, the good news, is that God's righteousness—the power of God for salvation—is for both the faithful Jew and the faithful Gentile. The traditional reading of this passage focuses immediately on Christ. If one studies the language, recognizes whose action is primary, and takes into account the preceding argument, it is clear that Paul focuses on Abraham. He is not trying to establish that Jews are included. He does not have to. That is his starting, not ending, point. Instead, Paul says that God is impartial, and now, through Christ, God's inclusion of Gentiles promised through Abraham is fully realized. The good news is God's inclusive good news. The gospel did not come into existence with Christ. It was already in existence at the time of Abraham.

The fourth point in Paul's understanding of gospel is that Paul yearns for the Jewish people to embrace the gospel to the Gentiles, but he does not intend for Jews to become Christians. Paul's vision that Jews will embrace the gospel of Christ is the place where E. P. Sanders and others view Paul as exclusive toward Jews. Paul does hope that eventually all Jews will embrace the gospel. But here lies the key: Paul insists that Jews embrace the gospel of Christ, not that they embrace Christ.

If gospel is understood in the narrow sense, as Christ crucified and resurrected, Paul's assertion seems confusing. But if by gospel Paul means the good news that God has included Gentiles apart from becoming Jewish (discovered and fully revealed in the Christ 'event), then he is calling Jews to embrace the fact that God has included Gentiles apart from the law. Jews already know that God embraces them on the grounds of God's faithfulness in Torah. They are the beloved of God. For Paul the gospel means that the door has opened wider than the way most of his fellow Jews viewed it, not that the door has closed on the side of the Jews. Through God's inclusive promise, according to Paul, Gentiles do not have to become Jews in order to experience God's grace.

Through Christ Gentiles discover that God loves them as Gentiles. To say that God closes the door on the Jews while opening the door to Gentiles vitiates what Paul claims. Paul envisioned the eschaton as the time when the inclusive promise would be fully manifested. It is not the time when the branches will reject the root. Do the branches know they cannot survive without the root? Indeed, based on Paul's argument, if Hitler had been successful Christianity would have ceased to exist along with Judaism. The important distinction between accepting Christ and embracing the gospel of Christ will become clearer as I examine Romans in more detail.

Boasting in the Law

Paul begins Romans with his usual greeting and almost immediately leaps into an argumentative expose about boasting. The first object of God's wrath is the Gentiles. By the end of chapter 1 Paul has established that the Gentiles, who "exchanged the glory of the immortal God for images resembling mortal human beings, or birds or four-footed animals or reptiles" (v. 23), are saturated with sin and do not escape the wrath of God to come (vv. 18-32).

Crediting God with showing no partiality (2:9-11), Paul establishes that he too is impartial when he turns his argument to the other group of concern. The second object of God's wrath is the Jewish people. "All who have sinned apart from the law [the Gentiles] will also perish apart from the law, and all who have sinned under the law [the Jews] will be judged by the law. For it is not the hearers of the law who are righteous in God's sight, but the doers of the law who will be made righteous" (2:12-13). Paul is not being vicious. He merely points out that God's wrath and God's righteousness are universal and impartial, whether one be Jew or Gentile.

Does Paul have an underlying agenda? Why is it so important to establish God's nonpartisan status? Classical interpreters have used this section to show God's disdain for the Jews' practice of the law. Is this Paul's intention? It cannot be; nothing here suggests the Torah's abrogation. The underlying concern of Paul's discussion has to be that some group, or perhaps some people within a group, believe that God is partial to them. Thus in this instance the boastful ones are *some* Jews. Paul Achtemeier comments that "Paul here singles out the Jews precisely because their status as chosen people could have tempted one to assume they were exempt from the wrath of God about which Paul has been speaking."[10]

Paul's frustration is neither with the law nor with the Jewish people. Rather, his frustration is that, according to his perceptions, some Jews "boast in the law" (2:23). John Gager asserts that Paul's "sole point of contention is Israel's claim to exclusive access to God's righteousness and thus to the privileges that flow from it."[11] Boasting as a theme in Paul's theology is not a light matter. Boasting is not simply a passing emphasis in the big picture of salvation history. Paul understands Israel's boasting to threaten the legitimacy of his apostleship and gospel. For if Paul's gospel is that Christ is "the fulfillment of God's promises concerning the Gentiles, the one major point of controversy would be Israel's claim to enjoy an exclusive relation to God. This boast would collide directly with Paul's gospel that the Gentiles *as* Gentiles have received sonship not through Israel but through Christ."[12]

One cannot overemphasize the importance of Paul's concern with boasting. Boasting is central to understanding his discussion of Torah and sin as well as to grappling with a comprehensive post-Auschwitz picture of Paul. Because the verses dealing specifically with boasting (2:12—4:25) are compounded with pre-Holocaust images, one must examine them carefully.

For Paul, boasting is the outward expression of exclusionism. In the context of Romans, exclusionism is manifest on the part of some Jews who do not embrace the gospel of Christ. Faithful Jews in the first century, as well as now, believed that God's love extends beyond the people of Israel. Paul is aware that his reference to Abraham as the parent of many nations is common knowledge among Jews. Thus if Paul insists that some Jews are being exclusive, he is probably not referring to Jews who believe that God is not manifest among the Gentiles. What, then, does he mean by "boasting" or "exclusionism"?

One possibility is that some Jews are boasting that the way God's righteousness is manifest to them—by faith grounded in Torah—is better or more complete than the way God's righteousness is realized for Gentiles—by faith outside the law (through Christ). The boasting may have manifested itself in denying that Jesus is the Christ (or Messiah) for Gentiles. But this explanation is unlikely, because in the discussion of Abraham Paul never focuses on the Christ-event specifically (4:23-25 are usually considered a transition into the christological section beginning with 5:1).[13] He never insists that Jews take Jesus as their Messiah, only that they embrace the gospel of Christ—that through Christ, Gentiles enjoy the full experience of God's love.

Even if the boasting about which Paul writes in Romans refers to Jews who believe that God's righteousness through Torah is superior to the righteousness through Christ, such a position among Jews would not detract from their own embrace by God. Also, these boasting ones would still believe that God's love extends beyond the covenant of Torah.

A second possible explanation of "boasting" is that Paul means, quite literally, that some Jews do not believe that God's love is manifest among the Gentiles apart from conversion to Judaism. But most Jews in Paul's day, and today, believe that God hears the prayers of non-Jews, including Christians. By "boasting," Paul may refer simply to a few Jews ("some") who do not believe that God's love extends beyond the Jewish people. In Paul's thinking, and in the thinking of most Jews then and now, such a perspective is bad Jewish faith, and is unrepresentative of Judaism as a whole.

The Jewish concept of an inclusive God is often difficult for Christians to grasp. The exclusionism of Christianity argues that the Christian faith is true, hence non-Christian faith is false, or at least misses the mark. God replaces the "old" covenant with a "new" covenant. Although exclusionism exists within Judaism, it is quite different from Christian exclusionism. In contrast to Christian boasting, Jewish exclusionism says that particular criteria (e.g., Jewish faith, Jewish parents) define what it means to be Jewish. Those who do not meet these criteria are not Jewish.

In the twentieth century, progressive Jews feel that such exclusive claims by more fundamentalist Jews are unacceptable in a pluralistic society. Perhaps the Essenes, Pharisees, Zealots, and Sadducees held similar positions of exclusionism in the first century. Exclusionism exists in Judaism, as it does in every religion, but exclusive Jews do not say that God hears only their prayers. Rather, exclusionism manifests itself in the form of preserving tradition, what many Hasidic and Orthodox Jews call "true Judaism." Even if some Orthodox Jews do not recognize Conservative, Reconstructionist, or Reform Jews as Jews, they still acknowledge that God loves and hears the prayers of other people different from themselves, including fellow Jews and Christians. Stated simply,

Jews, even those who are exclusive, believe that God loves non-Jews. Thus, boasting grounded in this kind of exclusionism cannot be what Paul is referring to in Romans.

Christian exclusionism is unlike Jewish exclusionism; the former insists that God does not hear the prayers of Jews, nor does God hear the prayers of those with different Christian beliefs. If those who "boast" refers to Jews who believe that Torah is the only way God's righteousness is presented to humanity, most Jews would agree with Paul that such a position is not good Judaism.

Another issue in Romans concerns the identity of those about whom and to whom Paul speaks. This issue is particularly important today when Christians tend to place Paul into current categories (e.g., Christians and Jews, faith and works-righteousness, grace and works). These categories are foreign to Paul. Thus, I contend that in Romans Paul speaks primarily, if not exclusively, to Gentiles intermittently about Jews and Gentiles.

Some scholars disagree with this position by insisting that when Paul refers to "Jews" he means Jewish Christians. This view is unlikely, however, because the Jews to whom Paul alludes are boasting about their exclusive favor with God through Torah and do not accept the gospel of Christ, which in Paul's understanding is that Gentiles are "made righteous by the faithfulness of Christ apart from works of law" (3:28).

When Paul speaks of those "enemies" (11:28) of his gospel of inclusiveness toward Gentiles, he is not referring to Jewish Christians. He is speaking of Jews who cannot accept that in the Christ-event Gentiles have been granted "the power of God for salvation" (1:16). Paul's only requirement of Jews is that they accept that Gentiles are blessed with full access to the promise of God's boundless love through Christ. His requirement is not that Jews become Christians. Thus Jews are to accept the good news but in a different way from Gentiles.

Paul's "boasting Jews" in Romans, then, cannot be Jewish Christians. According to Paul, Jews faithful to the gospel (I prefer this expression over "Jewish Christians") accept that an inclusive promise for Gentiles through Christ has been fully manifested apart from Torah. Exclusive Jews are those who boast. These are the ones about whom Paul speaks. Thus "Jews" in Romans refers to those who are "unfaithful" (3:3) and "hostile" (11:28) to the gospel of God's promise to the Gentiles through Abraham (chap. 4). Even so, "as regards election" Jews who do not adhere to Paul's gospel "are beloved for the sake of their ancestors" (11:28). "Will their faithlessness nullify the faithfulness of God? By no means!" (3:3). "For the gifts and the calling of God are irrevocable" (11:29).

To convey his point about boasting, Paul elaborates that God shows no partiality about sin or election. In God's eyes it does not matter whether people are Gentiles (those "without the law") or Jews (those "under the law"). All who sin are diminished (2:12). It is not enough to know right from wrong (to be "hearers"); one must be a "doer" of right in order to be made righteous (or justified) by God (2:13). No one has an excuse. Jews experience the righteousness of God through the law, and Gentiles have heard it "instinctively" (written on their hearts) and are a "law to themselves" (conscience) (2:14-15 and 1:19-29), but now fully experience God's righteousness apart from the law through Christ.

Paul writes Romans with his flame ignited. He is not at a loss for words as his main agenda surfaces: the exclusiveness of some Jews toward Gentiles (2:17-24). "But if you call yourself a Jew and rely upon the law and boast of your relation to God. . . . You that boast in the law, do you dishonor God by breaking the law?" (2:17, 23).

Paul here does not say that Jews abrogate Torah or reject the Jewish people, contrary to the traditional understanding. Rather, Paul undermines boasting and shows "that doing the law is superior to hearing it; Jews who hear the law but fail to do it forfeit any advantage."[14] Gentiles sin because "they know God's decree" (1:32) in their hearts, and yet "exchanged the truth about God for a lie and worshiped and served the creature rather than the Creator" (1:25). Some Jews sin because they "rely upon the law and boast of [their] relation to God" (2:17), and yet those who "boast in the law . . . dishonor God by breaking the law" (2:23). Divine equity is confirmed for Israel and the nations. "If [Paul] was committed to a view that Gentiles now stood on an equal footing in relation to God [through Christ], then Israel's boast would become the primary danger."[15]

Before I go on to the next verses, two notations about 2:17-24 are helpful. First, Paul never singles out all Israel in this boasting. He says, "But if you call yourself a Jew and rely upon the law and boast of your relation to God . . ." (2:17). This statement does not indicate that Paul believed that all Jews, or even most Jews, have a problem with boasting.

Just a few verses later, Paul says, "the Jews are entrusted with the oracles of God. What if *some* were unfaithful?" (3:2b-3a, italics mine).

Second, Paul gives a glimpse of his understanding of the law. This passage is foremost a polemic against those who boast, but Paul, in pointing out how some Jews are unfaithful to the law, indicates his high regard for the law and what "doing" works of the law means. Jews who fail to ground the law in faith, who are only "hearers," miss the law's promise to the nations, who are also descendants of Abraham and Sarah. Thus they blaspheme "the name of God . . . among the Gentiles" (Rom. 2:24).

Such a perspective clarifies the meaning of Paul's next words: "Circumcision indeed is of value if you obey [do] the law; but if you break the law, your circumcision becomes uncircumcision" (2:25). This is the first hint that "faithfulness" is what Paul means by doing the law. Circumcision is a sign of faithfulness. Verses 26-27, then, do not indicate that the "[Gentile] man" is an honorary Jew (as it has traditionally been interpreted), but that a Gentile can adhere to what circumcision symbolizes—faithfulness—without being circumcised.

Speaking again about Jews, Paul says in 2:28-29 that true adherence to the law is not merely knowing the law and being physically circumcised. Rather, true adherence to Torah means doing the law out of faithfulness—an inward motivation that reveals the full purpose of God's righteousness. Boasting is not necessary, then, since faithful Jews do not need human praise. Faithful Jews need to please only God. "For a person is not a Jew who is one outwardly, nor is true circumcision something external and physical. Rather, a person is a Jew who is one inwardly, and real circumcision is a matter of the heart—it is spiritual and not literal. Such a person receives praise not from others but from God" (2:28-29).

After this strong attack on Israel's "unfaithful" and exclusive boasters, Paul seems to think that his gentile recipients are beginning to see that they are on equal footing with Jews in regard to sin. He then makes a powerful, positive statement about his fellow Jews: "Then what advantage has the Jew? Or what is the value of circumcision? Much, in every way. For in the first place the Jews are entrusted with the oracles of God. What if some were unfaithful? Will their faithlessness nullify the faithfulness of God? By no means! Although everyone is a liar, let God be proven true" (3:1-4).

Here Paul introduces a theme that recurs in Romans, particularly in chapters 9–11: even though some Jews are unfaithful (boasting that God's promise is fully enjoyed by them exclusively while ignoring that God's promise to Abraham includes Gentiles), God remains faithful to the Jewish people. Indeed, as Paul later says, "For the gifts and the calling of God are irrevocable" (11:29).

Now Paul's pastoral pendulum swings to the Gentiles. But instead of speaking of "the Gentiles" and "you Jews," Paul switches pronouns to say "we Jews." He is not talking of a pre-conversion experience, as traditional understandings claim. Nor is Paul saying that the law is nullified and that Jews who have not been faithful to Torah are condemned. The purpose of his harsh polemic (3:5-18) is again to demonstrate God's impartiality—that all people, including himself, are sinners: "What then? Are we any better off? No, not at all; for we have already charged that all, both Jews and Greeks, are under the power of sin" (3:9). Jews are neither advantaged nor disadvantaged. This message is directed toward exclusionists, not toward people who have been excluded themselves.

The next set of verses (3:19-31) is probably the most difficult to grasp in this section, but these verses are crucial to understanding Paul's position toward Torah. In verse 19 Paul reminds the Gentiles of what he has said all along—that "[Jews] who are under the law" are well aware what the law says, that it lets them know that everyone in the world is held accountable to God, both as sinners *and* as heirs to God's promises. Thus, "[Jews]" should quiet their boasting mouths.

Verse 20 is difficult mainly because of interpretations in the traditions of Augustine and Luther. The NRSV reflects these traditional biases: "For 'no human being will be justified in [God's] sight' by deeds prescribed by the law, for through the law comes knowledge of sin." This rendering sounds as if Paul is saying that since human beings know about sin from the law (the law makes humans feel guilty), one must give up law for gospel, guilt for grace. If one continues to try to save oneself through works-righteousness in the law, one never experiences God's righteous-making grace and God's freedom from the guilt of the law.

One major problem contemporaries have with this version of verse 20 is based on presumed understandings dependent on Augustine's Fall-Redemption-centered theology, Luther's struggle with guilt, and Wesley's tormented heart that was strangely warmed, but little to do with

Paul himself. The NRSV places the paragraph break after verse 20, but such a break reveals an underlying presupposition that verses 20 and 19 go together and that both refer to the Jewish people. A closer examination of Paul's argument, however, indicates that the natural break is after verse 19. Verse 19 is part of the section of verses 9-19, which focuses on the Jewish boasting. Having established that Jews should be aware through the law that the whole of creation—including Gentiles, not just Jews—is accountable to God (v. 19), Paul turns to the Gentiles (v. 20). Verse 20, then, is linked to verses 21-26, which refer to the Gentiles only.

Thus Paul establishes in verse 20 what he has said in Galatians and in the preceding verses of Romans—that Gentiles are not made righteous through remaining faithful to the Mosaic covenant. The law serves to convict Jews of sin, but also to fulfill their faithfulness through doing, not just hearing, the law. As Paul argues in Galatians, the law is a curse for Gentiles: it convicts them of sin without giving them the opportunity to experience God's righteousness. Their righteousness comes from God apart from the law in the faithfulness of God made fully accessible through Jesus Christ. Hence I read Romans 3:20-21 as saying, "For no [Gentile] will be made righteous in God's sight by deeds prescribed by the law, for through the law comes [only] knowledge of sin. But now. . . ."

This is the culmination point of chapters 2 and 3. John Gager asserts correctly that "the traditional view . . . holds that in verses 21-26 Paul replaces Torah with Christ as the manifestation of God's righteousness and that 'faith in Jesus' becomes the sole basis for justification. Against this reading let us ask whether it is possible to read this passage as speaking not to the exclusion of Judaism but rather to the inclusion of Gentiles."[16]

This is one place where it is crucial to realize of whom Paul speaks. Paul is speaking only about the Gentiles. Several keys enable one to shed traditional biases in order to see Paul's original intent in these passages.

One key recalls that Paul's polemic is not against the law or Jews but against the boasting of some Jews. This section, which incorporates verse 20, is lodged between verses 9-19 and verse 27, all of which focus on boasting. Whatever Paul says in verses 20-26, then, illustrates the reason Jews have no reason to boast. Verses 20-26 are clearly about God's inclusion of the Gentiles "apart from the law" through Jesus Christ. Paul even mentions the Gentiles' "former sins" in verse 25—a direct reference to chapter 1. [17] Thus while reading this passage one should be aware that the term "Gentiles" is implied with such terms as "all" (3:22, 23), "they" (3:24), and "he" (3:26).

A second key is to remember that the boasting of some Jews threatens not a lighthearted conviction of Paul but the very gospel he proclaims (15:8-9). Paul asserts the exclusion of boasting on the part of some unfaithful Jews because God has extended righteousness apart from the law also to include Gentiles.

A third key focuses on the use of the Greek word *pistis*, which means "faith" or "faithfulness." Christian translators have taken much liberty in deciding which translation to use, and even more liberty in changing grammatical cases. The traditional understanding of Paul as an abrogationist of Torah has greatly skewed the ability of translators to decide on the more appropriate word or case in many instances. For example, in verse 22 the NRSV translates "through faith in Jesus Christ." The Greek here is the genitive case, not the dative case. The genitive case usually expresses possession; the dative is usually the case of the indirect object. Most changes in the translation of *pistis* have been from a possessive form to an indirect object. The genitive may have many senses other than possession, but translators generally assume that Paul did not intend the possessive usage because it does not fit with the logical presumptions usually made about Paul. Such an interpretation is forced and unwarranted. Sam K. Williams argues a strong case for maintaining a possessive interpretation by observing that "Paul's point is so important that he surely would have taken care to avoid unnecessary ambiguity; had he meant 'faith *in* Christ' he would have used a preposition to say that clearly.[18] Furthermore, *pistis* or its other genitive variants "is followed by the genitive of person or personal pronoun twenty-four times in the Pauline corpus. Twenty times this instruction refers to the faith of Christians, once to the fidelity of God (Rom. 3:3), twice to the faith of Abraham (Rom. 4:12, 16), and once to anyone who believes upon God (Rom. 4:5). In all these cases the phrase refers to the faith of the person, not to the faith in him.[19] Thus the best translation of 3:22 is, "through [the] faith [or faithfulness] of Jesus Christ."

Applying the precepts just described, one may translate: "But now the righteousness of God has been manifested apart from law, although the law and the prophets bear witness to it, the righteousness of God

through the faithfulness of Jesus Christ for all [Gentiles] who have faith"
(3:21-22, au. trans.).

Having made this radical statement about the Gentiles' inclusion,
Paul turns again to boasting in verse 27. Beginning a series of rhetorical
questions, Paul asks, "Then what becomes of our boasting? It is excluded.
On what principle? On the principle of works? No, but on the principle
of faithfulness" (3:27, au. trans.). In other words, he says, "So, fellow
Jews, God's inclusion of the Gentiles excludes our boasting. On the basis
of works under the law? No, God does this quite apart from the law.
Well then, on what principle does God do this? On the principle of
God's faithfulness through the promise to Abraham, which Gentiles
access fully now through Jesus Christ."

Continuing, Paul says, "For we hold that a [Gentile] is made righteous
by God's faithfulness apart from works of law" (3:28, au. trans.). Then,
just to drive the point home again, he asks sarcastically, "Or is God the
God of the Jews only? Is [God] not the God of Gentiles also? Yes, of
Gentiles also" (3:29).

The climax of Paul's argument in chapters 1–4 follows in 3:30. Here
Paul states pointedly what he has been arguing from the beginning: (1)
God is impartial ("since God is one"), (2) God promises to call both Jews
and Gentiles beloved and legitimate children ("God will make righteous
the circumcised . . . and the uncircumcised," au. trans.), (3) People are
made righteous out of God's faithfulness to the promise made through
Abraham, but on different terms for the two groups ("God will make
righteous the circumcised on the ground of faithfulness and the uncircumcised through faithfulness"; au. trans.).

What a difference in interpretation from assumptions based on Torah
abrogation. Does tradition's anti-Jewish influence still prevent modern
readers from seeing what Paul said? One needs to examine closely Paul's
language to grasp the importance of this verse. The Greek indicates that
God's righteousness occurs to the circumcised (Jews) *ek pisteōs* and to
the uncircumcised (Gentiles) *dia . . . pisteōs*. Both *ek* and *dia* are genitive
prepositions, but Paul clearly intends different meanings. The NRSV's
"circumcised *on the ground of*" and "uncircumcised *through*" distinguish
them well, although the phrases do not make the meaning of this distinction clear. Nevertheless, it is evident that Paul deliberately differentiates between Jews and Gentiles regarding what God does to make
God's righteousness fully experienced by each group.

This verse makes sense only if one recognizes that Paul is distinguishing between the circumcised and the uncircumcised, as he has done in the entire argument up to this point and as he does in the context of God's promise through Abraham in chapter 4. Is it possible that "made righteous the circumcised on the ground of faithfulness" (3:30, au. trans.) means that God will make Jews righteous by God's faithfulness grounded in Torah? Is this not what Paul meant in 2:13 that "doers," not "hearers," of Torah are made righteous? Is it then possible that "made righteous the uncircumcised through faithfulness" means that God has made Gentiles righteous through the faithfulness of Jesus Christ? This interpretation must be taken seriously as a credible explanation.

Paul apparently feared that some of his gentile recipients might misunderstand this whole gospel. It is doubtful that he could have imagined that his gospel would be misunderstood to the point of a world where shirtsleeves bore the insignia of a twisted cross. He warns, "Do we then overthrow the law by this faith? By no means! On the contrary, we uphold the law" (3:31).

The Gospel Key: Abraham's Story

For this reason it depends on faith, in order that the promise may rest on grace and be guaranteed to all [Abraham's] descendants, not only to the adherents of the law but also to those who share the faith of Abraham, for he is the father of all of us, as it is written, "I have made you the father of many nations"—in the presence of the God in whom he believed, who gives life to the dead and calls into existence the things that do not exist. Hoping against hope, he believed that he would become "the father of many nations," according to what was said, "So numerous shall your descendants be." He did not weaken in faith when he considered his own body, which was already as good as dead (for he was about a hundred years old), or when he considered the barrenness of Sarah's womb. No distrust made him waver concerning the promise of God, but he grew strong in his faith as he gave glory to God, being fully convinced that God was able to do what he had promised. Therefore his faith "was reckoned to him as righteousness." Now the words, "it was reckoned to him," were written not for his sake alone, but for ours also. It will be reckoned to us who believe in [God] who raised Jesus our Lord from the dead, who was handed over to death for our trespasses and was raised for our justification. (Rom. 4:16-25)

The New Common Lectionary places this passage in year B, the second Sunday of Lent. The lectionary passages from the Hebrew Scripture do not always correspond easily with a New Testament passage, but Paul's focus on Abraham in the epistle lesson has provided an opening to use corresponding passages about Abraham from both Genesis 17:1-10, 15-19; and Psalm 105:1-11. The common thread of these passages is God's promise with and through Abraham. Paul places much importance on the figure of Abraham for understanding God's action through Christ. In order to grasp Paul's meaning, one must be familiar with the Genesis account. Here I do not study Abraham in depth, but I examine the particular aspects of the Abraham narrative that pertain to Paul's argument.

That Paul elevates Abraham as the exemplar of faith for gentile Christians is perplexing for modern Christians with a christocentric theology. After all, Abraham was not a Christian, but neither was he bound to Torah. He preceded the Law. Therefore, Paul's main interest in Abraham is that he existed before the law and Moses yet exemplified the kind of faith required by Jews grounded in the law. In addition, Paul believes that the promise of God through Abraham held the key for understanding the Christ-event in the first century. His argument makes sense only if one recognizes that he is developing what one might call a Jewish liberation theology of the gentile people. Based partially on the law itself (a story out of the Pentateuch), the theology Paul develops allows for Gentiles to enjoy the experience of God's boundless love apart from the law.

Paul Achtemeier notes that Paul's use of Abraham as a key figure in theology "is following a line of thought familiar to his Jewish contemporaries. . . . Abraham was regularly cited as a person who was regarded as righteous before God. . . . Unlike the view held by his contemporaries, which stressed that Abraham's faithfulness in trial and his keeping the covenant led God to count him as righteous, Paul wants to assert that God regarded Abraham as righteous (Gen. 15:6) before Abraham had been either tested (Gen. 22) or circumcised (Gen. 17:10; see Gal. 3:17-18)."[20]

Carl Holladay expounds further on this point: "for Paul, it was crucial that in the storyline of Genesis Abraham was said to have been justified by God prior to his receiving the covenant of circumcision, and he pushed this distinction to its logical limits."[21] The "logical limit" in classical interpretations of Paul is that Torah is abrogated. In reflecting on Paul's discussion of Abraham, Ernst Käsemann advocates such an understanding: "Paul is thus arguing against the background of the Jewish tradition and problems, and he is using the methods these provide with the same conciseness as the rabbis do. Nevertheless, he does this polemically and with a very different intention. The promise has nothing in common with the law positively. Rather it is antithetical to it."[22]

Taking 4:13-15 out of context would suggest that the classical view of Paul articulated by Käsemann and others is correct. "The promise of Abraham and his descendants, that they should inherit the world, did not come through the law but through the righteousness of faith. If it is the adherents of the law who are to be the heirs, faith is null and the promise is void. For the law brings wrath, but where there is no law there is no transgression."

But one must contend with the total context. The perspective that Paul advocates the abrogation of Torah does not hold up against statements like verses 9 and 16: "Is this blessing pronounced only upon the circumcised, or also upon the uncircumcised? [See also 3:29.] We say that faith was reckoned to Abraham as righteousness. . . . For this reason it depends on faith, in order that the promise may rest on grace and be guaranteed to all his descendants, not only to the adherents of the law but also to those who share the faith of Abraham, for he is the father of all of us."

Paul is clearly not suggesting that the law is annulled. Contrary to traditional interpretation, Paul is not polemical, at least in regard to rejection of the Jewish people or abrogation of the law. He assumes that the adherents of the law—the Jewish people—will continue to ground their faith in Torah. They already depend on the faith of Abraham. But a promise made long ago to Abraham has now been fulfilled: other descendants share with the adherents of the law the faith of Abraham—the Gentiles.

How can one make sense of Paul's account of Abraham, particularly in Romans 4? Three related interpretive notes clarify the direction of his argument. First, Paul says that the law itself is not primary; Abraham had faith before the law. In addition, Paul implies the same about Christ. Standing strictly on Paul's arguments, if one concludes that Torah is abrogated, one must also assume that God might annul the Christ-event as a decisive re-presentation of boundless love. But Paul is not making such a proposal. Faith is neither Torah-centered nor Christ-centered—it is God-centered. Here Paul argues for faith in God and the faithfulness of God. By faith in God's faithfulness, both Torah and Christ are full means of experiencing the gift and demand of God's boundless love for different groups of people.

Why does Paul refer to Abraham to explicate a God-centered theology? "Abraham is of great significance. . . . He is the bearer of God's promised blessing to all peoples (4:11-12)."[23] Paul reasons that if God's righteousness is dependent on the law, Gentiles as Gentiles would never share in the promise of righteousness (v. 13). Therefore Paul points toward Abraham, a figure who preceded Moses. (See the following chart.) The whole argument of the Gentiles' inclusion apart from the law rests in Paul's emphasis on the covenant of promise on behalf of Israel *and* "the nations" (Abraham), instead of the covenant of Torah (Moses), which is for Jews only.

At first glance verses 14 and 15 appear to contradict this point, but a closer look reveals that they strengthen Paul's argument. The traditional understanding of these verses proposes that the adherents of the law are not the heirs of the promise. But such a position ignores what becomes clear in verse 16—that the promise is guaranteed to all Abraham's descendants, including the adherents of the law.

God's Plan

GOD'S INTENDED PLAN OF SALVATION
God's Faithfulness
in
ABRAHAMIC PROMISE

(Abraham is father of Israel)	(Abraham is father of many nations)
JEWS	GENTILES
↓	↓
ENLIGHTENMENT and righteousness *grounded in* LAW (Mosaic covenant) ↓	UNENLIGHTENMENT but beloved by God ↓

Jews experience | Gentiles experience
authentic existence | authentic existence
and | yet
call to witness to nations ⟶ | embraced in God's love
| *outside the Law*

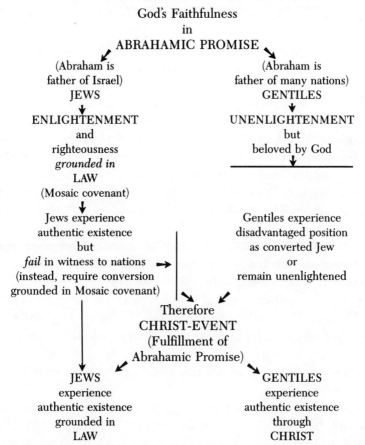

GOD'S AMENDED PLAN OF SALVATION
God's Faithfulness
in
ABRAHAMIC PROMISE

(Abraham is | (Abraham is
father of Israel) | father of many nations)
JEWS | GENTILES
↓ | ↓
ENLIGHTENMENT | UNENLIGHTENMENT
and | but
righteousness | beloved by God
grounded in | ↓
LAW |
(Mosaic covenant) |
↓ |
Jews experience | Gentiles experience
authentic existence | disadvantaged position
but | as converted Jew
fail in witness to nations ⟶ | or
(instead, require conversion | remain unenlightened
grounded in Mosaic covenant) |

Therefore
CHRIST-EVENT
(Fulfillment of
Abrahamic Promise)

JEWS | GENTILES
experience | experience
authentic existence | authentic existence
grounded in | through
LAW | CHRIST

The best way to make sense of Paul's argument here is to recognize that he presents a hypothetical situation in verses 14 and 15 that parallels directly his rhetorical dialogue in 3:29: "Or is God the God of the Jews only? Is [God] not the God of Gentiles also? Yes, of Gentiles also." The argument in Romans 3 continues in chapter 4. As a Jew, Paul practices his own principle of grounding faith in Torah (3:30) by grounding his own argument in the Torah story of Abraham.

Thus 4:14 and 15 serve as a sarcastic scenario of the idea that God is the God of the Jews only. Showing that such a scenario leads only to unenlightened acceptance of God for Gentiles, Paul uses 4:16-22 as the scriptural grounding for his affirmation that God is the God of the Gentiles also. Paul thus opens the theological door for non-Jews also to experience and enjoy authentic existence made possible through God's faithfulness.

To sum up my first point: Paul regards the faith *of* Abraham, faith *like* (example of), and God's faithfulness through Abraham as primary to what follows for both Jews and Gentiles—Torah and Christ respectively. Faith for Jews is grounded in Torah, and faith for Gentiles is "through" Christ crucified (3:30). Paul does not say that the law is unimportant for Jews or that Christ is unimportant for Gentiles. Rather, he gives Jews and Gentiles a course in pre-law and in pre-Christ. This course is entitled "faith." Paul knows that Jews are already familiar with the course, and most would have incorporated some of Paul's ideas into the way they lived Torah. But the faith course is new for Gentiles, who are probably the main, if not the only, recipients of Paul's Letter to the Romans. In Paul's thinking, one cannot be "schooled" in the law or in Christ without faith preceded by God's faithfulness. The promise rests on faith—faith in God and in the faithfulness of God.

A second important aspect of interpreting chapter 4 evolves out of the first point. I have already mentioned that Romans 4 is Paul's scriptural grounding (in Torah) for his argument in chapters 1–3. The theme of "boasting" on the part of some Jews connects the first three chapters; thus one can reasonably assume that "boasting" is an important theme in chapter 4.

Contrary to traditional interpretation, 4:1-2 do not discount law. Paul says only that works of the law are not enough by themselves. The faithful Jew must ground works of the law in the faith of Abraham (v. 3). Thus Paul writes, "Now to one who works [the Jew], wages are not reckoned as a gift but as something due" (v. 4). In other words, Jews now have no room for boasting. In addition, the arms of God are open to embrace those who do not adhere to the law: "But to one who without works [the Gentile] trusts [God] who makes righteous the ungodly

[Greek *asebēs*, meaning literally 'without God'—the Gentiles], such faith is reckoned as righteousness" (v. 5).

The third interpretive note is that Paul argues not to chastise Jews but to clear a path for Gentiles to experience and enjoy the righteousness of God through faith. Paul accomplishes this aim by referring directly to Abraham's promise in Torah (Gen. 17:5; 15:5): "as it is written, 'I have made you the father of many nations'—in the presence of God in whom he believed, who gives life to the dead and calls into existence the things that do not exist. Hoping against hope, he believed that he would become the 'father of many nations'; according to what was said 'So numerous shall your descendants be' " (4:17-18).

The key word in Paul's use of Scripture is *ethnē* (nations). Paul's use of "nations" here "incontestably . . . means the Gentiles."[24] As I have asserted from the outset, Paul does not say that Gentiles are the only descendants of Abraham. Nor does he assert, contrary to traditional interpreters of Paul, that Jews can be true descendants of Abraham only if they abandon works-righteousness and take on faith in Christ. Paul contends that whether one adheres to Torah (Jews) or shares the faith of Abraham outside of the Law (Gentiles) with the adherents of Torah (Jews), one must ground one's existence in the promise of Abrahamic faith in order to be called a faithful descendant of Abraham.

Particularly interesting in Romans 4 is Paul's comparison of Abraham and Sarah, the Gentiles, and the cross and resurrection of Christ (vv. 17-19). The parallels are among the barrenness (of Abraham and Sarah), the formerly nonexistent faith of the uncircumcised (the Gentiles), and the dead (Christ). He contrasts these parallels with the birth of Isaac, the inclusion of the Gentiles, and the resurrection of Christ. Unlike the Hagar-Sarah allegory in Galatians 4:21-31, here Paul does not use allegory, which would imply that he identifies these figures with each other. Rather, he uses analogy, to show the direction of God in history: God always, in both the past and the future, "gives life to the dead and calls into existence the things that do not exist" (Rom. 4:17).

Endnotes to the Law

Romans 7—Paul as the Metaphorical Gentile   No discussion of Paul and Torah is complete without addressing Romans 7. This Pauline text more than any other has come to represent the Western mind at work, or rather, in turmoil. When one thinks of Luther's great freedom from guilt one thinks of this passage. Even those not familiar with Luther would tend to interpret this text in a similar fashion. Whether secular or religious, persons in modern culture who struggle with the Western problems of conscience interpret Paul introspectively. "It is equally true about the average student of 'all the great books' in a College course, or the agnostic Westerner in general."[25] It is not undesirable to be introspective, but to interpret Paul in this way is to express Paul's writings in post-Pauline, hence, non-Pauline thinking.

Some scholars have recently given much attention to the question of whether chapter 7 reflects Paul's pre-Damascus road or post-Damascus road experience. Contrary to earlier scholars, most now agree that this chapter expresses a post-Damascus road turmoil. But scholars still tend to generalize this chapter, applying it to all persons, and to miss the fact "that Paul is involved in an argument about the law."[26] This tendency has, "at its worst, . . . succeeded in turning Paul's argument into the very opposite of his original intentions."[27]

One can assume that Romans 7 is not about a pre-Damascus road experience for two reasons. One is that Paul simply does not discount the law. The argument that this chapter concerns a pre-Damascus road experience depends on the classical presupposition that Paul previously adhered to the law but now has abrogated it. According to this view, the only purpose of his argument here is to remind his readers of sin and of the need for freedom from the law's restrictions. But Paul says clearly that the law is good, and that sin operates independently of the law. Paul explains his point by his common stratagem of following rhetorical questions with his own interpretation: "What then should we say? That the law is sin? By no means!" (7:7). "The law is holy, and the commandment is holy and just and good" (7:12). "Did what is good, then, bring death to me? By no means!" (7:13). "We know that the law is spiritual" (7:14). "I agree that the law is good" (7:16).[28]

The second reason this chapter cannot refer to his life before the Damascus road experience is that in his other references to that time he is free of guilt and blameless as to the law.[29]

The most significant problem in interpreting chapter 7 is the tendency to generalize Paul's discussion to refer to all human beings. Many assume that Paul is speaking about both Jews and Gentiles. I have already demonstrated that Paul does not discount the Jewish people or the law. Could chapter 7—indeed, chapters 5–8—have only Gentiles in mind? Lloyd Gaston has suggested a number of factors that point in this direction. One is the statement in 6:15 that "we are not under the law but under grace." As I have previously illustrated, Paul uses this phrase when speaking about how Gentiles, apart from the law, are distinguished from Jews. Gaston suggests that an additional factor is the relationship between Gentiles and curse, which Paul addresses in Galatians 3:10. Romans 4:15 also alludes to the curse for Gentiles in the law: "For the law brings forth wrath [to Gentiles], but where there is no law there is no transgression [for Gentiles]."[30]

Hence Paul's consistent claim is that for the Gentiles the law leads only to frustration, sin, and death. Thus in 7:15-23 the struggle between knowing what is good and doing what is unwanted is a struggle of the Gentiles, not the Jews. Gager agrees that the dilemma in chapters 5–8 "is uniquely that of the Gentiles. Unlike Jews, they had always been without recourse. Now Jesus Christ has done for them what Torah could not do. Now, there is no condemnation, for Christ has set 'me' free from the body of sin and death."[31]

As in Galatians, Paul's use of personal pronouns in Romans 7 again reveals his personal identification with his gentile recipients. The imagery here illustrates his ability to grasp their situation even more dramatically than in Galatians. Through rhetorical drama in Romans 7 Paul uses himself as the metaphor of the hypothetical Gentile. In reflecting on how incorrectly scholars have interpreted this chapter through the ages, Krister Stendahl leaves modern Christians with a penetrating question: "We should venture to suggest that the West for centuries has wrongly surmised that the biblical writers were grappling with problems which no doubt are ours, but which never entered their consciousness."[32]

Romans 10:4—Christ as the Aim of the Law   Another unresolved issue regarding the law is Paul's statement in Romans 10:4, "For Christ is the [*telos*] of the law, that there may be righteousness for everyone who believes." The term *telos* has traditionally been translated as "end," "termination," "goal," or "fulfillment." Charles Cranfield suggests that it is difficult to maintain that "termination" is the correct translation, particularly in the light of Paul's other statements in Romans 3:31; 7:12, 14; 8:4; and 13:8-10, which speak of fulfillment of Torah, Torah being good, holy, just, and spiritual. The early church fathers, Aquinas, and Luther supported the meaning "fulfillment" or "goal," but they often meant "termination."[33]

Käsemann presents another perspective. He insists that "as a Jewish-Christian [Paul] does not yet undertake" the position of the reformers, for whom the law was "extended to legalism." Still, Käsemann views Paul as leaning toward abrogation when he contends that "the apostle lays the foundation for this generalizing in his interpretation of *nomos*."[34]

The position most grounded in the context of what Paul writes in Romans 10:4 is that of G. E. Howard. Howard maintains that when one observes carefully, the immediate and remote contexts are "dominated by the theme of the inclusion of the Gentiles."[35] Gager asserts that several keys enable one to recognize this theme. One is that, contrary to its classical reading, 10:3 refers not to individual Jews trying to institute their own righteousness before God, but to Jews who are unwilling to submit to the claim of God's righteousness promised to Abraham that includes Gentiles who do not convert to Judaism. In short, " 'being ignorant of the righteousness that comes from God' has to do with the exclusivity involved in 'boasting in the law.' "[36]

A second key is that Christ is the *telos*—the aim or goal—of the law in two ways: "first, because from the very beginning God's righteousness and the Torah pointed to the ultimate redemption of the Gentiles (chapters 3–4) and second, because faith was the proper response to the covenant, from the beginning for Jews and in the present for Gentiles (chapters 3–4)."[37]

A third key is recognizing Paul's use of biblical proofs in 10:5-13, 18-20, to establish the legitimacy of the Gentiles' inclusion. As a Jewish thinker, Paul believed that all claims should be substantiated by Scripture from the Law and the Prophets.

A fourth key is in 10:9, where Paul admonishes the Gentiles in terms of their faith to "confess with your lips that Jesus is Lord." This passage is often generalized to mean all people, but Paul couches his claim in the context of Gentiles, not Jews.

Finally, it is important in reading 10:4 to see the way Paul wraps up this entire section—by affirming God's impartiality (10:12).[38] When taken out of context, 10:4 appears to be christocentric, but should be viewed as a point of summary for Paul that God's love is impartial and includes all people.

In summary, I have scrutinized various theories about Paul's position toward the law. Contrary to the classical understanding, Paul upholds Torah; he does not abrogate it (Rom. 3:31). In Paul's mind, *hearing* the law is not enough for Jews. To fully enjoy God's righteousness they must also ground the law in faith by *doing* that which they know is right (2:13). Part of what it means to experience the righteousness of God is for Jews to recognize that this righteousness is also granted apart from the law for non-Jews: Gentiles fully enjoy God's righteousness apart from works of the law through the faithfulness of Christ (3:21, 28). Paul's frustration is not over the Jewish people's inability to accept Jesus as their Messiah, but over some Jews who boast in Torah and their relation to God (2:17, 23; 3:27). By approaching the law through faith they would see that the gospel—God's promise to Abraham—is for Gentiles as well as Jews (4:16).

This gospel of inclusiveness for Gentiles through Christ has indeed been the aim of Torah all along (10:4). What if some Jews are unfaithful to the Gentiles' inclusion? Does their faithlessness nullify the faithfulness of God? By no means (3:3-4b)! Although some are exclusive, God remains faithful to the inclusive promise.

Paul and Israel

Having demonstrated in detail that Paul does not abrogate Torah, I now focus on Romans 9–11, where Paul's argument about the Jewish people climaxes. Indeed, these chapters are the best resource for discussing Paul's position toward the Jewish people, even though his argument of inclusiveness stands on its own in chapters 1–4. Paul's perspective does not change in chapters 9–11 from what he has already said in Galatians and Romans 1–4. In chapters 9–11 he relates his arguments about Jews and Gentiles to God's total plan of salvation history. Chapters 9–11 are, as Stendahl asserts, "the climax of Romans."[39]

Many scholars think that Romans was written as different homilies that Paul merged together. Most authorities on Paul agree that all of Paul's letters were written to be read aloud in their respective communities. Chapters 1–4 and 9–11, which focus on the theme of Gentile inclusion, represent the first homily; chapters 5–8, which are more christological in nature, represent the second homily. Chapters 12–16 are surrounded by several theories but are generally considered to be

summary commentary on the preceding eleven chapters. The relationship of homily one and homily two is important for understanding the
point Paul tries to establish. The content and the structure of the two
homilies differ totally from each other. Chapters 5–8 tend to be repetitive
and circular; chapters 1–4 and 9–11 develop and integrate one basic
theme in linear fashion. The theme of the first homily is the relationship
between Jews and Gentiles; a number of quotations from Hebrew Scripture characterize this homily. The second homily never mentions Israel
or quotes Scripture. It is very liturgical and includes a number of refrains
(5:10-11; 5:21; 6:11; 6:23; 7:6; 7:24-25; 8:11; 8:29-30; and 8:39), which
always come at the end of a section. These refrains carry the same basic
message—victory of the life of Christ over death. Each refrain also
repeats the terms "death," "life," and "the Lord Jesus Christ" throughout.
Paul uses these terms sixty-nine times in chapters 5–8 and only seven
times in chapters 1–4; 9–11. He uses "Christ" twenty-four times in
chapters 5–8 and only ten times in chapters 1–4; 9–11. Perhaps most
interesting is that "faith(fulness)" occurs only three times in chapters 5–
8 and forty-five times in chapters 1–4; 9–11. Both homilies appear to
be authentically Pauline.

This terminological evidence is another illustration of how chapters
1–4 and 9–11 try to establish, through *Israel's* history, the inclusion of
the Gentiles, and of how chapters 5–8 instruct *Gentiles* in the meaning
of the faithfulness of Christ apart from the law. The close tie between
chapters 1–4 and 9–11 is one indicator that, according to Paul, understanding Abraham is very important for understanding the place of Israel
in history.[40] Other letters of Paul that are more christological than Galatians and Romans 1–4; 9–11 (such as Philippians and Thessalonians)
are similar in genre to Romans 5–8. As in the second homily of Romans,
in these other letters the Jewish question does not come up because
the focus is on God's action through Christ on behalf of the Gentiles.

Just as Paul affirms to the Romans that the inclusion of the Gentiles
through Christ does not abrogate the law (3:31), he also proclaims unequivocally that "God has not rejected [God's] people whom [God]
foreknew" (11:2). Nevertheless, classical Christian theologians who preceded the Holocaust have used chapters 9–11 to prove that God has
rejected the Jewish people and to validate their own rejection of Judaism
and of the Jewish people. They have essentially ignored the passages

they did not like (11:1-2a, 11-12, 25-29). Their argument is untenable; these chapters unmistakably point to God's full acceptance of the Jewish people as Jews.

But this classical view has also manifested itself theologically in the church's tendency to spiritualize what Paul says. In chapter 2 I outlined how theological displacement of the Jewish people became a common position in the church at least as early as 60 C.E. The anti-Jewish polemic in the Gospels themselves is an example. Early gentile Christians reasoned that the new covenant of Christ superseded the old covenant of the law. The church was already thinking of itself as the new Israel, displacing the Jews into the nonstatus of the old Israel.

As I indicated in chapter 4, the spiritualizing of Paul's writings eventually permitted Christians to conclude that Paul's references to "Israel" meant the new Israel—the church. The "remnant" of which Paul speaks came to represent Jews who converted to Christ and assimilated into gentile Christian culture rather than a remnant of Jews faithful to Paul's gospel of inclusiveness who were saved from the purgatory-like wrath to come before their full inclusion.

This subtle rejection of Israel was further validated in the church through the development of a theology of the cross alone. Although this theology was Pauline in content, its failure to recognize important aspects of Paul would haunt the Jewish people for centuries. Paul's discussion of the stumbling stone in Romans 9:30-32, only negative toward Jews if one assumes Torah abrogation, is one of the main passages used to explicate a theology of the cross. "What, then, are we to say? Gentiles, who did not strive for righteousness, have attained it, that is, righteousness through faith; but Israel, who did strive for the righteousness that is based on the law did not succeed in fulfilling that law. Why not? Because they did not strive for it on the basis of faith, but as if it were based on works. They have stumbled over the stumbling stone."

The idea of the stumbling stone is not unique to Romans. "We proclaim Christ crucified, a stumbling block to Jews and foolishness to Gentiles" (1 Cor. 1:23). "But my friends, why am I still being persecuted if I am still preaching circumcision? In that case the offense of the cross has been removed" (Gal. 5:11). The stumbling stone to which Paul refers in these cases is Christ crucified. Thus classical interpreters inferred from what Paul writes in Romans 9 that the Jews have stumbled over

Christ, being unable to accept what he offered, namely, righteousness that comes through faith.[41]

Although this interpretation is close to what Paul intends, if left in this form the theology of the cross ignores two important points. J. Christiaan Beker makes one of these points: "from Augustine to Luther, Calvin, Barth, and Bultmann, the signature of Pauline theology has been 'the cross alone is our theology.' "[42]

Beker is quick to point out that a critical element ignored in the theology of the cross alone is Paul's apocalypticism. He contends that "when the centrality of the cross is divorced from its apocalyptic components, it . . . leads to such an exclusive emphasis on christology that it collapses future apocalyptic into the Christ-event."[43] Beker shows its particular relevance to Romans 9–11:

> Once the Christ-event became defined in such a way that Christ was conceived as the total "fullness of God" (Col. 1:19) rather than as the "first fruits" of the kingdom of God, the fulfillment of God's promises to Israel was now considered to have been actualized in the Messiah, Jesus Christ. This in turn led to the spiritualization of the promises, and their future reference to the new heaven and new earth of God's cosmic triumph was largely ignored.[44]

Until post-Holocaust scholarship emerged, Paul's emphasis on the future fulfillment of God's plan was virtually lost in tradition. The realized eschatology that is exemplified in John's Gospel was transferred onto Paul and the whole of Christianity. For Paul, the present "hardening" of Israel was a temporary phenomenon, "until the full number of the Gentiles come in, [then] all Israel will be saved" (11:25-26). A realized eschatology projected into a situation that Paul saw as temporary twisted Israel's hardening to become a permanent fixture of Christendom. The church essentially took the element of the future out of Paul, and with the future of the cosmos went the future of Israel's full inclusion. What became of the Jews, the people whom God had not rejected? They diminished to Augustine's status of the Witness People, who, according to Augustine, through their "wandering" disposition, testified to the world that they were the "Christ-killers." They were the victims of theological genocide in Christian salvation history.

It is fortunate that contemporary Pauline scholars recognize the apostle's apocalyptic orientation, particularly in Romans 9–11. Linked to this perspective is a growing acceptance that "Paul certainly expected the final events (Rom. 8:18-25; 1 Cor. 14; 1 Thess. 4:13-18) in his own lifetime. When he speaks of . . . Israel's return, he is thinking in terms of years—not even decades, let alone centuries or millennia."[45] These final events are also described in Romans 11. The inclusion of the Gentiles and reentrance of "all Israel" gave impetus to the imminence of a new world where God and all creation are glorified. The eschaton was happening then and was not, in Paul's mind, supposed to be still unresolved some two thousand years later.

Paul's description of how these events were taking place is particularly interesting and is peculiar to him among his contemporaries. He begins with two presuppositions. One is that at the present time only a remnant of Israel is faithful to the gospel of Christ (11:5). The second is that all Israel is elected and will be saved, "for the gifts and the calling of God are irrevocable" (11:26, 28-29). One can understand paradoxical Paul only if one also perceives him as the apocalyptic Paul.

Paul's eschatological argument progresses logically in chapter 11. Before moving into his argument, however, Paul makes clear that his gentile recipients must retain foremost in their minds that God has not rejected God's people (11:1-2). God has not disavowed the Jewish people; they belong to God. Perhaps fearing that his readers might still misunderstand him, Paul repeats this affirmation twice more in chapter 11 (vv. 11 and 28).

Having firmly established this presupposition, he progresses into his argument, which begins with Israel's what he calls unfaithfulness and ends with their full inclusion. He focuses on the present reality (his other presupposition), which is that some Jews have failed in their pursuit of righteousness through Torah, being unfaithful to the claim that God's righteousness can be experienced by Gentiles apart from Torah through Christ (9:31; 10:30). Paul says that Israel's zeal for God is unenlightened (10:2), and they are disobedient (11:30-32). But not all Israel is unenlightened and disobedient—a remnant is faithful to the gospel of Christ.

Realizing that his point may confuse his readers, Paul provides them with a reason for the unenlightened zeal of some Jews. Because Paul assumes that all that happens comes from God, when he states that "a hardening has come upon part of Israel" (11:25; also 11:7-10) he implies that God has hardened Israel. But this explanation only leads to another question: Why would God harden the hearts of God's people? According to Gager, "Paul turns the disobedience of the Jews into the divinely preordained occasion, foretold in scripture, for God to offer salvation to the Gentiles."[46] Yet another question surfaces: What about the Jewish people? Is their purpose in this world to reject the gospel of Christ so that God might offer salvation to the Gentiles? I have already given Augustine's answer. But Paul's response is different. He asserts resoundingly: "So I ask, have they stumbled so as to fall? By no means! But through their stumbling salvation has come to the Gentiles, so as to make Israel jealous. Now if their stumbling means riches for the world, and if their defeat means riches for Gentiles, how much more will their full inclusion mean!" (11:11-12).

Paul never had any question about God's salvation including all Israel. His eschatological framework resolves, for himself, the disparity between the present reality and how things will turn out in the final consummation. Paul knew that a rejection of Israel implies that the gifts and call of God are revocable, which is impossible. Thus God has not rejected the Jewish people.

Christians who continue to say that God has rejected the Jewish people ignore that such an assertion also presupposes that God changes and revokes promises made by God. If Christians understand themselves as beloved, what is to prevent God from revoking the promises made to them through Jesus Christ? Disregarding the apocalyptic Paul and interpreting Romans 9–11 out of a theology of rejection and replacement of Israel not only affects one's understanding of the Jewish people but also makes a statement about God—that one cannot trust God. How can Christians be sure that their spiritual journey will not be cut off?

Does affirming that Paul is indisputably apocalyptic resolve the theological problem of Christian anti-Judaism? It does allow Christians to embrace Jews in the present reality because their acceptance of the gospel of Christ is in the future. But is this enough? Does such a view allow for religious pluralism and open the door for Jewish-Christian dialogue? Perhaps, for Christians, at least those who do not adhere to a Johannine-like understanding of realized eschatology. Would such an understanding be acceptable to Jews? It would not.

Although this view allows for mutual respect and some dialogue, it does not yet go far enough. Its Christ-centered thesis that in the end God will make Jews into Christians is inadequate and unacceptable. It retains an eschatological rejection and replacement theology of the Jews. The conviction that this view is inadequate is reflected in the teachings of an Israeli philosopher, David Hartman: "we cannot live with this kind of bifurcation in religious life. We cannot hold an ultimate theology of superiority and say, but in the interim, in the pre-Messianic times, we indeed will live with a theology of suspension and, therefore, with a theology of pluralism."[47]

Hartman is speaking primarily to Jews, but he believes that Christians and Muslims must also reject any theology of suspension—spiritual monism. John Pawlikowski comments that "Hartman calls for a new pluralistic spirituality rooted in a radical, all-embracing abandonment of previous claims to absolute truth." It is "bad faith," asserts Hartman, "to be pluralistic now, but to be monistic in our eschatological vision."[48] In other words, to claim that Jews should not be theologically excluded in the present, but required to convert to Christianity in some eschatological event, is simply unacceptable to most Jews and should be to Christians as well.

Given that Paul is apocalyptic in orientation and that a theology of suspension is bad faith, can one find any hope in Paul or in the entire New Testament that results in resurrection out of the bleak entombment of anti-Jewish theology? Perhaps the only course is to agree to disagree with Scripture, as E. P. Sanders does. Sanders's hope is that after all the destruction of two thousand years, after all the evil that has been thrust upon Jews in the name of Christ, today Paul would disagree with what he wrote in the first century.[49]

As I have asserted throughout this chapter, Paul can and does provide for Christians and Jews a bridge, if not *the* bridge, of hope in the New Testament. The key lies here: Paul never calls for Jews to be Christians. Rather, Paul summons Jews to accept the gospel of Christ! What does he mean by the gospel of Christ?

> For I tell you that Christ has become a servant of the circumcised on behalf of the truth of God in order that [Christ] might confirm the promises given to the patriarchs, and in order that the Gentiles might glorify God for [God's] mercy. (Rom. 15:8-9a)

"For Paul, the gospel means the extension of the promise beyond Israel to the Gentiles, not the displacement of Israel by the Gentile church."[50] Paul's anguish over the Jewish people is not because they reject Christ as their Messiah. His frustration is that they do not accept Paul's gospel—that God's righteousness is manifested apart from the law

120 Christian Anti-Semitism and Paul's Theology

to the Gentiles (Rom. 3:21). Therefore Romans 9–11, like Paul's discussion of Torah in chapters 1–4, is really about Jewish boasting, the exclusive claim that God's righteousness is imparted only through the law.

Understanding what he meant by gospel changes the whole picture of Paul's struggle in chapters 9–11. This perspective also changes the way Christians approach Jewish-Christian dialogue. Now Christians can see that what Paul calls the Jews' unenlightened zeal (10:2), their ignorance of righteousness (10:3), their "disobedience" (11:30-32), and the "hardening" that has come upon "part of Israel" (11:25) have nothing to do with their not becoming Christians—that is, experiencing by faith "the righteousness of God through the faithfulness of Jesus Christ" (3:22, au. trans.). For Paul, the claim through Christ is for Gentiles only. Thus Paul's use of these terms in chapters 9–11 is merely repeating what he has already said in chapters 1–4. The point again is that some Jews boast of their relation to God (2:17, 23; 3:27).

Out of Paul's struggles with Israel in chapters 9–11, then, emerges his eschatological vision that the "hardened" Jews will soften their exclusive claim on God's righteousness and recognize that through Christ Gentiles may now enjoy authentic existence in relationship with the God of Israel without becoming Jewish. Thus "the particular question addressed here [chaps. 9–11] is, . . . 'Given the constancy of God's righteousness, what are we to make of Israel's refusal to recognize and accept the obvious continuity between God's promise to Abraham and his act of redemption in Christ?'"[51]

Paul never says that Jews are to accept Jesus as *their* Messiah. Christ is their stumbling stone (9:30-32) only because they do not see what for Paul is so obvious—that through God's promise to Abraham the law itself points toward the inclusion of Gentiles as Gentiles (10:3-4). To clarify this point I examine some specific verses.

Chapter 9:1-29 represents Paul's version of Lamentations. Classical interpreters of Paul have rightly judged that 9:3 is important for understanding chapters 9–11, but their interpretation of its meaning is incorrect. "For I could wish that I myself were accursed and cut off from Christ for the sake of my own people, my kindred according to the flesh" (9:3). Traditional Pauline scholars have assumed that Paul's anguish is over Israel's rejection of Christ as the Messiah. They believe that Paul asserts, therefore, that God has cut them off. Yet nothing in the immediate context supports this interpretation. Rather, the context refers to Abraham (v. 7; cf. v. 5). Whenever Paul discusses Abraham he is talking about the Gentiles' inclusion, and, in Romans, the problem of boasting on the part of some Jews.

Paul does allude to those who are cut off in verse 3, but his words do not imply rejection. Paul uses an image here that he expands on in 11:17-24. Thus for him "cut off" refers to a temporary act of God, like "hardening," until all the Gentiles are brought in. Indeed, Christ crucified is so central for Paul that it would be difficult to imagine him referring to being cut off from God more than temporarily. Those who are temporarily cut off or hardened represent, for Paul, only some Jews who are unfaithful to proclaiming God's promise to Abraham that Gentiles are now included.

Paul again uses rhetorical questions in verses 14 and 19 in response to his belief that this temporary hardening is God's will. This response serves as a preface to his eschatological progression in chapter 11. One of the main points he establishes in 9:6-29 is that this hardening is temporary (i.e., "The elder will serve the younger," v. 12; "one vessel for special use and another for ordinary use," v. 21). Paul assures the Gentiles in Rome that this hardening is merciful and that its purpose is for God's glory (v. 23). Lest the Gentiles misunderstand and think that they supersede the Jewish people, Paul makes clear in verse 24 that this call is "not from the Jews only but also from the Gentiles." Again, the message of God's impartiality reverberates.

In verses 30-33 Paul uses the image of the stumbling stone. Its similarity to other references in Paul indicates that the stumbling stone is Christ crucified. Again, Christ crucified is a stumbling stone to Israel not because they refuse to accept Christ as their Messiah but because the Christ-event represents God's inclusion of the Gentiles apart from the law.

> What then are we to say? Gentiles who did not strive for [God's] righteousness have attained it, that is, righteousness through [the] faith[fulness] [of Christ]; but Israel, who did strive for the righteousness [of God] that is based on the law did not succeed in fulfilling that law. Why not? Because they did not strive for it on the basis of faith [of Abraham], but as if it were based on works [of the Law—Moses]. They have stumbled over the stumbling stone. (9:30-32)

Paul does not say that the righteousness of God based upon law is wrong, implying that the righteousness of God associated with the Gentiles is good. He says that the Gentiles did not seek God's righteousness, but that by the faithfulness of God through Christ they have been made aware of God's righteousness. Israel (Paul is generalizing—his argument indicates that he means some of Israel), who pursued God's righteousness through the law, has missed the full meaning of righteousness. This is Paul's clever way of saying that some Jews did not see that righteousness is not only theirs but the Gentiles' as well. When Paul says "the righteousness of God," he is referring to Abraham (cf. chap. 4); God promised righteousness to the nations as well as to Israel. Paul's anguish is that some Jews misunderstood the message of Abraham's faith. These Jews have zeal for God, but it is unenlightened. Although they pursued God's lovingkindness, they stumbled over it. Had they pursued it through faith (their own faith in God and God's faithfulness toward them)— "doing" the law of Moses—instead of basing it on works of the law— "hearing" only—they would not have stumbled. Paul portrays a picture as if they were walking around in pursuit of righteousness and they tripped over it. Some Jews are simply ignorant, Paul reasons, unenlightened of the gospel of Christ, which includes the Gentiles.

Following this argument Paul restates the same point in 10:1-4. Gager is most helpful here.

> If we take "boasting of the law" and "being ignorant of the righteousness that comes from God" as expressions of the same idea, we must conclude that "being ignorant of the righteousness that comes from God" has to do with the exclusivity involved in "boasting in the law." In short, Rom. 10:3 states that the Jews have failed to understand the redemption of the Gentiles in Christ as the expression of God's righteousness, a righteousness revealed as promise in Abraham and as fulfillment in Christ. . . . When Paul speaks of the righteousness of God in this context, he is thinking exclusively of Abraham, Christ, and the salvation of the Gentiles.[52]

Continuing with Paul's progression, one can recognize that in 10:5 Paul refers to faithful Jews, those who are "doers of the law": "Moses writes concerning the righteousness that comes from the law, that 'the [Jewish] person who does these things will live by them.' " In verse 6 he switches attention back to the Gentiles: "But the righteousness that comes from faith. . . ." This language indicates that beginning with verse

6 and concluding with verse 11 Paul speaks only about what is required of Gentiles. This entire section (10:5-11) is Paul's reassertion that God is impartial. This context enables one to understand Paul's meaning in verses 12-13: "For there is no distinction between Jew and Greek; the same Lord is Lord of all and is generous to all who call upon [God]. For, 'Every one who calls on the name of the Lord shall be saved.'" Because Paul has remained theocentric through Romans, one can assume this passage's reference to "Lord" is more inclusive than Christ, although it surely includes God's action through the Christ-event. As a Greek-speaking Jew, *kyrios* would also have been one of the words Paul used for the Hebrew *Yahweh*.

The closing verses of chapter 10 point toward Paul's argument in chapter 11. Verses 14-20 have to do with the Gentiles, while verse 21 is clearly directed toward the Jews who disregard Paul's gospel. As much as this disregard disturbs Paul, he still holds true to his presupposition that God has not rejected God's people (11:1-2).

I have stated, in agreement with David Hartman, that a theology of suspension and a theology of pluralism are incompatible. A theology accepting Jews as Jews now, but with an eschatological vision that accepts Jews only as Christians, is not a credible faith. Genuine pluralistic spirituality is a faith that permits one to maintain the integrity of one's own faith while respecting others in the integrity of their faith. Hartman asserts correctly that an inclusive theology is possible only with a willingness to engage in a "radical all-embracing abandonment of previous claims to absolute truth."[53]

The classical model of a Paul who abrogates Torah is inadequate for this bridge. A theology that rests on Paul as an apocalyptic visionary, embracing Jews in the present only to continue in the hope that they will eventually become Christians, is just another form of the theological rejection and replacement theory. Paul is certainly apocalyptic, but not in the exclusive, christocentric way most Christians have portrayed him.

The portrayal of a Paul who believes in the eschatological vision of the whole world as "Christian" is a betrayal of Paul. The point that differentiates Paul from the dual covenants view is his eschatological formula regarding Jews. His vision was that all Jews will accept Paul's gospel that in Christ "Gentiles no longer needed to become Jews in order to enjoy the advantages once reserved exclusively for Israel."[54] Although Paul was discouraged about Israel's reluctance to embrace such a gospel, nothing about Paul's gospel to and about the Gentiles entails repudiation of the legitimacy of Israel or Torah.[55] Paul is inclusive of Jews without requiring them to have faith through Christ. Their faith is fulfilled by being doers of Torah. For Paul, Jews experience the righteousness of God through faith grounded in living Torah, which includes the Abrahamic promise. Gentiles experience the righteousness of God through the faithfulness of Christ.

Thus Paul never doubts the Jews' inclusion. His problem with the Jews is their boasting in exclusivity over the issue of inclusion of the Gentiles. The absence of christological references in Romans 11, which deals with God's election of Jews, has perplexed scholars. Even more perplexing is that only after the Holocaust did Christians see that Paul had no christology for the Jewish people. Christology is for the Gentiles. Romans 11 is unique, not in its absence of christology, but in its use of Jews and Christ as exclusive terms, under an inclusive promise. Paul's frustration is not with Jews or Gentiles per se but with exclusionism. Romans 11:28-29 are not just an eschatological mystery but a present reality with which one can live: "As regards the gospel [Jews] are enemies of God for your sake; but as regards election they are beloved for the sake of their ancestors. For the gifts and the calling of God are irrevocable."

For Paul, the Jewish people *are* beloved for the sake of their ancestors. Their acceptance as God's elect is a present reality for Paul, whether or not they themselves are inclusive of Paul's gospel. For the gifts and call of God are irrevocable.

Summing up Paul's theology of the Jewish people, I begin with some negatives. Paul abrogates neither Torah nor the Jewish people. He does not insist on an eschatological formula that embraces Jews in the present but insists on their conversion to Christianity in the full realization of the new age. On the positive side, he does believe that Jews are made righteous by faith on the grounds of Torah and that Gentiles are made righteous by faith through Christ. According to Paul, the Gentiles' inclusion in the promises of God has always been the aim of Torah, a hope that has been fully realized by God through the Christ-event. Paul's polemic in Galatians is directed toward gentile troublemakers who are influencing gentile Christians into believing that they must take on Jewish practices in order to be loved by God as Gentiles. Paul's anguish in Romans is over boasting on the part of some Jews who believe that the people of Israel alone are the people who fully access the promise given to Abraham and Sarah. He looks to the eschaton as that time when all boasting mouths will cease and exclusiveness among Jews and Gentiles will end. His eschatological vision, therefore, is not a hope for Jewish salvation. Their salvation has already occurred. Instead, Paul envisions a time when Jews will accept Gentiles as God's righteous children without becoming Jews.

Although Paul is not a systematic theologian, I venture to systematize his understanding of salvation history as follows:

(1) All people (both Jews and Gentiles) have sinned. Humanity is broken and incomplete, cut off from its own blessedness. Therefore humanity is dependent on the covenantal lovingkindness of God in the midst of such a state.

(2) God promises wholeness, reconciliation, and liberation to all humanity and creation itself. A covenant of inclusion has come through the Abrahamic promise, which affirms that Abraham is the forebear of all people, those under the law and those apart from the law.

(3) Jews are grounded in the Abrahamic promise through God's covenant of the Mosaic law. The law is a binding covenant of God's lovingkindness that came to the Jewish people out of the Exodus-Sinai event.

(4) The law is for Jews only. It functions as a curse for Gentiles, serving only to remind them of their inability to fulfill it. Even if Gentiles convert to Judaism (a process encouraged by many Jews in Paul's day), they would never grasp the full intensity and benefits of Torah as Jews do, who have grown up in the traditions and the culture of the law. Jews experience the Exodus-Sinai (law) event as the gift and demand of boundless love. Through faithful adherence to the law Jews discover authentic existence and God's abiding presence.

(5) Therefore the Gentiles' discovery of God's inclusive promise requires looking to an event before God gave the law of Moses to the people of Israel, an event to which Torah witnesses but which precedes Torah—the Abrahamic covenant, a promise of inclusion. Paul understood traditional Judaism as saying that Gentiles are loved by God outside the law but that without becoming Jews, they cannot enjoy the full experience of God's love. He believed such an understanding is exclusive and biased against non-Jews. Their only movement from ignorance to fulfillment of authentic experience would be to convert to Judaism. Thus, because Paul believes that the Jewish people of his day had failed to

witness adequately to Gentiles regarding God's boundless love, the only viable option for non-Jews to discover their blessedness is to look before the law to the inclusive promise of God through Abraham.

(6) In God's good time (Paul believed *now* is that time) God made all things equal for the Gentiles. The Christ-event (Christ crucified and resurrected) is that act of faithfulness in which God re-presents the gift and demand of God's boundless love for those outside the law—the Gentiles. This promise has existed since Abraham, but is now fulfilled for all time in God's eschatological event of Christ's death and resurrection. Through Christ's resurrection God has brought to Gentiles what Jewish witness could not—authentic existence and the knowledge of God's abiding presence.

(7) Paul was convinced that both Jews and Gentiles are called to accept "the gospel of God," which is that in the Christ-event all Gentiles are beloved and accepted unequivocally by God without becoming Jewish. They are now full participants in an enlightened relationship with the God of Abraham while remaining outside the law.

(8) In Romans Paul expressed frustration with "some Jews" who resisted his gospel. This "hardening" to the gospel meant for Paul that at the time of his writing some Jews either did not believe that this event-act of God actually occurred; or, more likely, regardless of the Christ-event claim, found it impossible to affirm that Gentiles have become with Jews enlightened and equal heirs of God without first going through the law (converting to Judaism).

(9) Paul's eschatological hope expounded in Romans 9–11 was that eventually (within his lifetime) all Jews would embrace the gospel, the inclusive claim that Gentiles are beloved children of Abraham outside the law. All Jews, even those who are "hardened," "disobedient," "unfaithful," and have "unenlightened zeal for God," would soon adhere fully to this inclusive promise of God made known through Abraham.

(10) Never did Paul question that God loved and fully accepted the Jews, both presently and eschatologically. "The gifts and the call of God are irrevocable."

(11) Therefore Paul's gospel demanded of the Jews not that they "accept Christ" but that they accept "the gospel of Christ."

(12) The Christ-event is the eschatological act of God that brings all people into full awareness that they are in covenant with God. Distinctions no longer exist. Previously, only Jews knew the good news

(gospel) of God's love through the law, but the good news for Jews had become bad news for Gentiles. Paul claims, however, that since the time of Abraham the good news had been for everyone. Unfortunately, some Jews had failed to proclaim this good news. Now through Christ the good news of the Abrahamic promise is proclaimed to Gentiles, who, like Jews, also now fully experience the good news that they are blessed children of God.

A Tenebrous Irony

It seems ironic to pursue the theology of a man who, roughly two thousand years ago, wrote that "our knowledge is incomplete" (1 Cor. 13:9). Paul recognized his incompleteness, his dimmed vision, and his humanness in the face of the unsearchable and inscrutable acts of God. This Pharisaic writer of Pastoral letters would no doubt be startled to learn that millions of people hail him as "Saint" and regard his letters as "Holy Scripture." He would be even more shocked to discover that the church has twisted his words to substantiate the claim that Christians have replaced the Jewish people as God's elect.

Indeed, if Paul lived today as one of the fortunate Jews to survive the Holocaust, he would have numbers tattooed on his forearm, the memory of a yellow star on his lapel, and an anguished heart from the persecution of his people. What would he witness? Christ crucified? Yes, but in a different way than Christians profess. For he would see through his tear-filled eyes a Torah stripped of its righteousness by the church, nail holes in a door at Wittenberg, "I Found It" bumper stickers, and machines of human design burning Jewish children alive. Paul's dismay that the complete had not yet come would be overshadowed by the daunting reality that the dim mirror is more tenebrous than he perceived.

Recognizing that Paul was a Jew who embraced Jews as Jews is a new way of seeing him. At some early point the church made him a Gentile. Although he did become like the Gentiles that he might win some, in his heart he maintained his Jewishness.

In his Jewishness he knew that God had not nullified the law for Jews. Nor had God rejected the Jewish people. But something new had been fully realized that confirmed what the law had promised all along: the Gentiles are incorporated into the people of God, not by faith grounded in the law, but by the righteousness of God through Jesus Christ. Jews did not have to accept Christ as their Messiah. Gentiles did not have to accept Torah in order to be children of God. God had provided another way for Gentiles to share with Israel the promise to Abraham. In Paul's vision, the gospel embraces Jews as Jews and Gentiles as Gentiles. "For I am not ashamed of the gospel; it is the power of God for salvation to every one who has faith, to the Jew first and also to the Greek. For the righteousness of God is revealed through (God's) faithfulness for faith; as it is written, 'The one who through faithfulness is righteous shall live'" (Rom. 1:16-17, au. trans.).

Thus the core of Paul's gospel is not Christ-centered but God-centered. Christ is the channel through which God imparts the reality of righteousness to the Gentiles.

The church has been looking at Paul in dim reflections for two thousand years, but didn't realize the vision was obscured. The direct correlation between Christian rejection and replacement theology of the Jewish people and the systematic crucifixion of six million Jews is not what Paul had in mind when he spoke of seeing in a mirror dimly.

What about Jewish Christians today? I do not think Paul would understand this concept. "Christianity" is a word used by later authors of New Testament writings. Paul continued to think of himself as a Jew called by God to preach Christ crucified to Gentiles, which meant they could embrace the God of Abraham and Sarah who rendered them as righteous without converting to Judaism. Peter, James, John, and other Jewish apostles are difficult to categorize because historians have no documents authored by them. It is probable, however, that they understood Jesus more in terms of a Jewish Messiah than a Gentile Christ. To call them Jewish Christians or to assume they and Paul had similar understandings of Jesus is based on theological presuppositions that cannot be substantiated in the New Testament. Other than Paul and other Jewish apostles and leaders we have no written material about Jews in the church in the first century. Therefore, from a first-century historical standpoint, "Christians" is a term that should only be used in reference with Gentiles. The theology espoused by such groups as Jews for Jesus would be revolting to him. He would probably not be bothered by the fact that they relate more to God's re-presentation through Christ than through Torah. His frustration with such groups would be that they have taken on Jesus as the Messiah who rejects and replaces Jews as

Jews, calling Jews with Jesus as their messiah as "completed Jews," as if they were not already. Paul would also have difficulties with gentile Christians who participate in particular Jewish practices without being clear about where they stand in their own theology. The example that immediately comes to mind is de-Judaizing and Christianizing the seder meal on Maundy Thursday. Of course, as fellow heirs with Jews of the Hebrew Scriptures, Christians also relate to God's liberative story of the Exodus. The danger occurs when Christians unknowingly use the Ex-odus-Sinai event as another Lenten declaration of the rejection and replacement of the Jewish people. When practiced with an awareness of theologically upholding the integrity of the Jewish people or when as invited guests of Jews, the seder meal can be a powerful experience for Christians.

The word that Paul speaks to Christians today expresses repulsion at Christian boasting in the notion that the only way to God is through Christ. If Romans 1:16-17 is the core process of what Paul means by gospel, then Paul focuses on the eschatological vision of the Jewish people's acceptance of the gospel because their boasting was the issue of the day. Who is boasting now? is the question I think Paul would ask Christians after Auschwitz. The focus of Paul's eschatology is not simply that Jews will embrace Gentiles, along with themselves, as God's people. Paul's vision of God's realm is not just that Jewish boasting and exclu-sionism will end. No, the core of Paul, his eschatology, his gospel, is that the inclusive promise to Abraham embraces the world. "For the creation waits with eager longing for the revealing of the children of God. We know that the whole creation has been groaning in labor pains until now; and not only the creation, but we ourselves" (Rom. 8:19, 22-23). His vision is that there is no exclusionism at all!

My study of Paul reveals one within the New Testament and Christian tradition who embraces Christians as Christians and Jews as Jews. Paul allows Christians to hold to the story of God's re-presentation of un-bounded love in the Christ-event, while also calling them to embrace Israel as they hold to their story of God's re-presentation of unbounded love in Torah.

But my study of Paul has also unearthed the reality that the tables have been turned. What Paul feared might happen has indeed occurred. Christians "claim to be wiser than [they] are" (Rom. 11:25). The branches who have been grafted onto the tree "have become proud" in the grafting

(11:20) and have not continued in the kindness God has shown them (11:22). The tenebrous irony of the church's understanding of Paul is that this apostle of inclusiveness has been misrepresented as the primary textual authority of Christian exclusionism. Paul was aware of the possibility for this misunderstanding when he wrote to the Gentiles, "Note then the kindness and the severity of God: severity toward those who have fallen, but God's kindness to you, provided you continue in his kindness; otherwise you too will be cut off" (11:22). As a Christian it pains me to say, therefore, that the only correct way to read Romans, indeed Paul, in the church today is to see that those who "boast," those "unenlightened in their zeal for God," those who are "hardened"—are many Christians! Those who have ears to hear, listen to Paul's words to the church after Auschwitz: "You that boast in [Christ], do you dishonor God by your boasting? For, as it is written, 'The name of God is blasphemed among the [Jews] because of you'" (cf. 2:23-24).

For Paul, Christianity does not exist without Judaism. Had Hitler been successful, Christianity would have ceased to exist. Out of the embers Paul confronts one with the near destruction not only of the Jewish people but also of Christian faith. His particular claim for Christians is that God is an inclusive God. His God brings resurrection out of the dark entombment of anti-Jewish Christianity. It is a mystery that in the darkness of oven chambers God's light has shown what real faith is not, and thus what faith should be. With God's help, one can bear witness to Paul's gospel today—that faithful Christians are those who embrace Jews as Jews and Christians as Christians. Indeed, faithful Christians are those who embrace God's inclusive promise of authentic existence for all humanity and the cosmos.

> O the depth of the riches and wisdom and knowledge of God!
> How unsearchable are [God's] judgments and how inscrutable [God's] ways!
> "For who has known the mind of the Lord?
> Or who has been [God's] counselor?"
> "Or who has given a gift to [God],
> to receive a gift in return?"
> For from [God] and through [God] and to [God] are all things.
> To [God] be glory forever. Amen. (Rom. 11:33-36)

6

Christology, Liberation, and the Jewish People

Gentile Christianity is certainly not our problem now, as it was for the Jews then; and if Paul were to talk to us today, he would probably have to say exactly the reverse. In his own time he was trying to build a community of Jews and Gentiles. But we Gentile Christians have to try to achieve a community of Gentiles and Jews, if we want to arrive at the same objective. . . . If today the Jews suffer and are isolated, Christians will suffer and be isolated too—or if not they will be guilty. Shall we find the courage to accept the Jews, courage for solidarity with Israel? Or are these merely pious words which will fade away at the next oil crises?

—Jürgen Moltmann[1]

Paul presents to the church and synagogue the opportunity for a theological bridge. But because Paul is an apostle of the Christian faith, the church must instigate the building of this particular bridge. At Auschwitz Jews were murdered for no other reason than being Jewish. The church's indifference to burnt flesh and the reprehensible theology of anti-Judaism in history calls for Christians to take the first step in establishing trust. The church's aim must not be to convert Jews to Christianity nor to persuade Jews to embrace the theology of Paul. The aim is to present to Jews and Christians a Christian theology that respects the integrity of Judaism as a living faith and the Jews as a people called to be fully alive. Christians must listen carefully to the synagogue's response. If the Jewish appraisal is that Christian theology is not credible in the presence of the burning children, then the church must go back to the confessional drawing board and begin again; if need be, go back again, and again, and again.

The synagogue's major obstacle in embracing the church as a trust-worthy friend is Christianity's christology, or doctrine of Christ. Chris-tocentric theology in the church places a wall between Christians and Jews. When christology and theology become doctrinally enmeshed the church's belief system has no room for God to be active in any other faith community outside Christianity. Christians who adhere to this perspective herald, either intentionally or unintentionally, that non-Christian religious communities are theologically dead. This win-lose mentality presents Christianity as the only living faith, a perspective that diminishes the church's life and integrity.

Most Christians engaged in serious dialogue with Jews have become aware of the destructive nature of such a perspective. In efforts to circumvent the christological problem, many Christians sensitized to Jewish distress have adopted revisionist christologies that focus on the historical Jesus—Jesus the faithful Jew. The problem with these chris-tologies is that they fail to take into account the central faith claim of Christianity—as Paul put it, "Christ crucified," or Christ's death and resurrection.

Most scholars adhere to the perspective that the Gospel accounts of Jesus' life were constructed from the back to the front; that is, they began with the faith story of Christ's death and resurrection and de-veloped their account around that faith claim. The absence in Paul's Letters of information about the historical Jesus is a reminder of how focused the early Gentile church was on the Christ of faith, concentrating almost entirely on the Christ-event and saying little about the life of Jesus. Because Paul's writings are the earliest testimony of the Christian faith in the New Testament, the church has a responsibility at least to contend with his christology.

Unfortunately, even Christians engaged in active dialogue with Jews often continue to disregard the possibility of an inclusive Pauline chris-tology because they understand Paul as theologically anti-Jewish. Per-haps as Christians begin to understand Paul as one who accepted Jews as Jews (Jews who do not become Christians), they will be more open to wrestling with Paul's christology. I am convinced that Paul's christology is the only viable inclusive christology in the New Testament that takes seriously the Christ-event as the central faith claim for Christians. To this christology I now turn.

Christology after Auschwitz

What implied christology develops as a result of Paul's assertions? First and primary is that his christology is theocentric, not christocentric. As such, it is not supersessionist toward Judaism. Contrary to traditional understandings of Paul's doctrine of Christ, Paul does not say that Christ is the one who makes the Gentiles righteous but the righteousness of God *through* Christ. Unlike most twentieth-century Christians, Paul never uses God and Christ as synonyms. Christ's death and resurrection are events through which God's gift and demand of boundless love are decisively re-presented for the Gentiles. Thus God's love offers Gentiles "the possibility of authentic existence in faith and returning love."[2]

To take this doctrine to mean that Christ is the only way to experience God's love is exactly the opposite of what Paul is communicating. God's love knows no bounds. Indeed, Paul states that boasting—exclusionism—blasphemes God (Rom. 2:24). Thus the point of God's action through Christ "is not that the Christ is manifest only in Jesus and nowhere else, but that the word addressed to [humanity] *everywhere*, in all the events of their lives, is none other than the word spoken in Jesus and in the preaching and sacraments of the church."[3]

Stated simply, God does not supply Gentiles with *the* track but only with *a* track through Christ. Paul equips Gentiles with a christology that allows Christians—the modern-day heirs of the Gentiles—to experience Christ as *their* decisive re-presentation of God's love, while also allowing Jews, and different faith communities, to experience righteousness through other decisive re-presentations of God's love. Paul's mandate in Romans is that an exclusive claim to God's love is nothing other than unfaithfulness, disobedience, and unenlightened zeal for God. As Schubert Ogden remarks, Paul's christology implies "that authentic existence can be realized apart from faith in Jesus Christ or in the Christian proclamation."[4] Rosemary Ruether contends similarly that "the cross and resurrection are contextual to a particular historical community. These are breakthrough experiences which found *our* people, that mediate hope in the midst of adversity *for us*."[5] Of Paul, Ogden comments that "the underlying intention of all his christological formulations is to affirm that the history of Jesus of Nazareth is the decisive re-presentation to all [humankind] of the same promise and demand re-presented by the Old Testament revelation (cf. Rom. 3:21)—and, beyond that, also attested by the whole of creation and [humanity's] conscience as well."[6]

The first precept for a Christian theology after Auschwitz, then, is that Paul's christology is not Christ-centered but God-centered.

Paul's emphasis on the Christ-event, as opposed to the historical Jesus, is the second presupposition for a Christian theology after Auschwitz. If only Paul's writings had survived, today one would know little about Jesus of Nazareth except that he was crucified. For Paul, the day-to-day activities of the man Jesus are not primary for faith. What is primary is Christ crucified and resurrected.

Traditional and revisionist christologies have put much emphasis on the historical Jesus. As previously mentioned, a common approach to Jewish-Christian dialogue is to rediscover Jesus the Jew as opposed to the Jesus of tradition who stood in conflict with first-century Judaism. Indeed, such a quest is essential for reading the Gospels informatively and for embracing a historical understanding of Jesus and his culture. The work of Jewish scholars like Ellis Rivkin, Jacob Neusner, and Pinchas Lapide has contributed greatly to the picture of the historical Jesus. This information has resulted in breaking down walls of hostility, allowing both Christians and Jews to enter the world behind the anti-Jewish polemic of the Gospels and to rediscover Jesus' message. Christians are finally admitting that Jewish tradition, interpreted by Jewish scholars, is perhaps the best resource of information available about Jesus the Jew. Nonetheless, emphasizing the historical Jesus alone does not go far enough in providing an acceptable christology after Auschwitz.

Such an emphasis ultimately breaks down because it is impossible to rediscover completely the historical Jesus. Although from the Gospels and other available literature one can reasonably infer the implicit testimony that Jesus exemplified in his life and message "the gift and demand of boundless love and thus . . . the possibility of authentic existence in faith,"[7] one cannot decisively conclude that Jesus made such a claim. "Consequently, if one assumes it to be necessary theologically to establish that a christology has support in what Jesus himself actually said and did before it can be judged to be appropriate, one places oneself in an impossible position."[8]

Even if one could prove that Jesus made such a claim, one must recognize that for Paul and the earliest apostles the importance of telling the story was the "witness of faith to Jesus, not historical report about him."[9] Similarly, a Jew might say that the importance of the Exodus-Sinai event is not the historical facts of the event but its liberative significance in the life of the Jewish people now. Thus, according to Ogden, in God's re-presentation through Christ, "the significant thing is not that Jesus at least implicitly claimed to be the Christ . . . ; rather, the significant thing is that what the apostolic community understood by Jesus—the Jesus to whom they themselves bore witness, implicitly if not explicitly, as the Christ—was the one through whom they had experienced, and who, through their own witness, was still to be experienced as implying, just such a claim."[10] In other words, the testimony of Christians has always been and continues to be "that *Jesus means love*—not that Jesus *meant* love."[11]

The essence of Paul's christology rests on the centrality of the Christ-event, not on the historical Jesus. Through Christ crucified and resurrected God confronted Gentiles, and confronts their Christian heirs today, with the gift and demand of boundless love and the possibility of authentic existence in faith. If as Ruether suggests, "theologically, anti-Judaism developed as the left hand of christology,"[12] then the church has misunderstood or chosen to ignore the christology of Paul, which allows for the coexistence of other re-presentations of God in other communities of faith outside the church.

The third precept of a christology after Auschwitz is that the work of God that occurs in the Christ-event results in liberation for those who are oppressed. In Christ, the gift and demand of God's love are decisively re-presented for those who understand themselves or are regarded by others as excluded from the possibility of authentic existence. These are what Gustavo Gutiérrez calls the world's "non-persons"—those people "being excluded from active participation in the existing social and cultural order."[13]

Specifically, Paul envisioned the death and resurrection of Christ as the event that brings the world's nonpersons into personhood. He understood his world as one where the claim for authentic existence has belonged exclusively to the Jew, the male, and the free. Paul asserted the radical claim that through the event of Christ, God has made known to the world that God loves all persons as they are. The promise to Abraham was intended for all persons. Indeed, there are no distinctions between Jew or Gentile, free or slave, male or female (Gal. 3:28; Rom. 10:12). Thus the christology of Paul is one of freedom.

Paul's understanding of the crucifixion and resurrection of Christ as God's act of liberation is not a surprising claim from a first-century Jewish

Pharisee. After all, Paul was raised hearing the Exodus-Sinai story, the paradigmatic Jewish story of liberation that hails God as the great Liberator. For Paul the Jew, and for Jews today, the deliverance of the Hebrew people out of the land of Egypt is more than an historical narrative. It is the story of a God who transformed a motley group of captives into God's chosen people. It is the story of God's liberative and reconciling love that makes Jews free, now. Like Jews for thousands of years, Paul embraced God as the one who brings authentic existence to people who did not formerly exist in the eyes of the establishment. (They had always existed in God's eyes.) Paul understood God as the one who, after making all creation, said, "It is very good" (Gen. 1:31). Paul would say that Christ is God's instrument of grace for those still outside—the Gentiles, women, and slaves. His vision was one that realigned people with themselves and all creation as God's original blessings—gifts to one another and to creation.

Although Paul's christology of liberation for Gentiles centers explicitly on God's act of love through the Christ-event, one can infer that he must have understood this event to be consistent with whatever knowledge he had of the historical Jesus. I have already stated that the ministry of Jesus is impossible to reconstruct apart from the largely anti-Jewish depiction of Jesus in the Gospels and Acts. But if one separates the parables of Jesus, the stories about Jesus, and some teachings attributed to Jesus from the historical commentary of the early church, one implicit and consistent theme surfaces throughout—inclusiveness. The parable of the Good Samaritan, Jesus' encounter with the woman at the well, sayings such as "the first shall be last and the last shall be first"—all these point to an historical Jesus whose mission, at least implicitly, appears to have been the inclusion of the excluded and the calling into question of the status quo. Luke records Jesus as echoing the prophet Isaiah: "The Spirit of the Lord is upon me, because he has appointed me to bring good news to the poor. He has sent me to proclaim release to the captives and recovery of sight to the blind, to let the oppressed go free, to proclaim the year of the Lord's favor" (Luke 4:18-19).

Thus Paul, and probably Jesus, espoused a theology of hope grounded in Israel's paradigmatic principle of liberation. A theology of freedom cannot be credible if it is concerned only with one's own or one's own people's freedom; it must entail the freedom of others as well. Although self-determination is always an essential ingredient of liberation, embracing the interrelatedness of one's own freedom with the freedom of others should always be a tenet of liberation. If one's freedom means oppression for another or one's particular claim of freedom does not logically progress in universal fashion toward freedom for all, one is still bound by exclusivist claims.

> To accept God's love through faith is to be freed from oneself and everything else as in any way a necessary condition of a meaningful life. But for the very same reason, the acceptance of God's love through faith establishes one's freedom *for* all things as well as one's freedom *from* them. . . . One can be thus free for [others] as the proper object of one's love only by promoting their own freedom to be and to become fully themselves—active subjects of their own self-creation, instead of merely passive objects of the self-creations of others.[14]

Therefore the picture that emerges from Paul's christology is one of universal hope and liberation. It is theocentric rather than christocentric. Yet Christ's death and resurrection is the event by which God enables Gentiles to have authentic existence—what Paul referred to as experiencing the righteousness of God. God's liberating love in Christ is intended to include those who are excluded, not to replace the included with a new exclusive group. One is not free who boasts of exclusive righteousness.

Although Paul believed that God's judgment (which is not synonymous with "exclusion") fell against some boastful Jews, God's wrath now descends on many Christians who adhere to a rejection and replacement theology toward Jews. Christians who accept God's liberating righteousness by faith through Christ only to become exclusionists themselves thrust the church into a different kind of captivity. Instead of being captive by others' exclusionism, the church is captive to itself, that is, theologically and anthropologically bound in its own exclusionism. Liberation theologians acknowledge what Paul has been saying to the church for some two thousand years: Only when one recognizes that God sets others free does one discover freedom oneself. How long will the church insist on a theology of anti-Judaism? Is such a position not also anti-Christian?

The near destruction of the Jewish people in the Holocaust embodies the captivity of the church in its own oppressive exclusionism. Indeed, a Christian theology that embraces Jews without requiring them to convert to Christianity can only result in a Christian theology that liberates Christians. God's righteousness, which comes as both gift and demand, does not distinguish between Jew and Greek, female and male, slave and free. The practical theology that springs from Paul's christology liberates not just people within the church who know authentic existence through Christ but Gentiles the world over. In summary, to embrace an inclusive Christian theology after Auschwitz means adhering to a theocentric christology of God's liberating and cosmic love.

Liberation in an Interfaith Context

Although Paul's understanding of the Christ-event clearly calls for liberation of the oppressed, one cannot properly call it a liberation theology, either in Paul's time or today. Liberation theology's primary, distinctive characteristic is the freedom principle of self-determination. Justo and Catherine González reflect this conviction: Liberation theology is "theology done from the perspective of those who have been traditionally powerless in society and voiceless in the church."[15] Simply stated, theologies of liberation differ from the traditional interpretation of the Christian message in their refusal to leave the gospel in the hands of the powerful.[16] Thus, even though Paul sought to proclaim an impartial and inclusive gospel, he wrote from the perspective and out of the experience of a free male Jew about the inclusive promise of Gentiles, women, and slaves. The theology of the cross that he espoused did not emerge from slaves, women, or Gentiles—those whom Paul regarded as the powerless and voiceless of his society. Therefore one could label Paul as a liberation theologian only in the remote sense that Paul believed that the powerful discovered new inner freedom by encouraging the liberation of the world's powerless.

Another dimension to the discussion of Paul and liberation is that since its modern birth in 1968 at Medellin, Columbia, liberation theology has been couched almost entirely within an inter-Christian framework and has ignored an interfaith contextualization. If, for example, Anglo Christians in North America adhered to the principle of self-determination, they would know that a policy of noninterference is required of them in relation to the theology and moral practices of Latino Christians in Central America—no matter how much the Christians from the north differ from their southern neighbors. The same might be said in the church of Anglo Americans in relation to African Americans, men to women, straights to gays, or any other groups who have a voice in relation to groups who have been silenced. When one turns to groups outside the Christian framework—such as the Jewish people, or people of other religions—however, liberation theology in the church has been for the most part inoperative.

This impasse on the part of the church is primarily the result of christocentric as opposed to theocentric liberation theologies among Christians. It is one thing for Christians who have been traditionally powerless prophetically to rake over the coals fellow Christians in positions of power; even if the powerful react defensively, they rarely question the destabilizing position from the underside as non-Christian. But when the prophetic voice comes from outside the Christian framework, saying, for instance, that the logical movement of Christian theology ends with the burning children, the church more readily disregards the position, reasoning that non-Christians cannot instruct Christians on how to formulate Christian theology. How can a Christian gospel message emerge out of the voiceless and powerless if these people are not even Christian?

The answer goes back to the principle of self-determination. Jews can no more formulate Christian theology than Christians can Jewish theology. Even if, through consciousness-raising from another group, I significantly alter my theology and my life-style to show solidarity with the other group, my theology is not a liberation theology because I am not of the oppressed group myself. Thus, at least under the current understanding of liberation theology, as a white male I cannot be a Christian feminist theologian, even though my theology and actions alter considerably as I seek to align myself with women actively striving for liberation in a largely patriarchal society. Likewise, as a Christian I cannot call myself a Jewish liberation theologian or even call the perspective portrayed in this book a Christian liberation theology of the Jewish people. Jews are the only people who can have a liberation theology of the Jewish people. Thus one might properly label Paul's writings as a liberating and inclusive Jewish theology of the gentile people. Furthermore, with gentile or Christian exclusionism as the focus in this book, my own position based on Paul's writings is more accurately called a liberating and inclusive Christian theology of the Jewish people—a position confessionally developed out of the cries of dead Jewish children, yet Christian position nonetheless.

Having stated that by definition Christians cannot hold a liberation theology of the Jewish people, I must add that I am by no means suggesting that Christians should not speak in judgment to Jews when the situation calls for it. For example, in the present situation between Palestinians and Israelis in the Middle East, one must recognize that the problems are complex, and that Christians who are critical of Israeli policies risk being labeled as anti-Semitic. Nevertheless, Christians and Jews must speak out against injustices everywhere in the world or risk abrogating the implications of Irving Greenberg's standard of authority—credibility before the burning children. Whether these children are Jewish, Palestinian, Cambodian, black South African, or lesbian, their oppression, torture, or killing is always an atrocity that people who love mercy and seek justice and mercy must actively seek to eliminate.

A prophetic voice from the outside may not be entitled to be called a liberation theology, but it can still be a call for liberation and justice. The ambiguity of the modern world is a reminder that one cannot easily distinguish the oppressor and the oppressed. The embrace of human nature requires all people to recognize that a person or group may simultaneously be the oppressed in one aspect of life and the oppressor in another aspect of life.

Christians' formulating an inclusive theology of the Jewish people need to be aware that the liberation of the Jewish people and Jewish theology is the work of Jews, not Christians. They should, however, continue to struggle with what it means to have a Christian inclusive theology of the Jewish people. In this century, radicalism sometimes emerges out of bourgeois roots; the oppressor class can become empathetic unto death, even if the oppressor still cannot know in fullness the plight of the oppressed. Dietrich Bonhoeffer reflects such empathy:

> There remains an experience of incomparable value. We have for once learnt to see the great events of world history from below, from the perspective of the outcast, the suspects, the maltreated, the powerless, the oppressed, the reviled—in short, from the perspective of those who suffer. . . . We have to learn that personal suffering is a more effective key, a more rewarding principle for exploring the world in thought and action than personal good fortune.[17]

Echoing Bonhoeffer, Gustavo Gutiérrez asserts that such a theology "is a reflection which makes a start with the historical praxis of people. It seeks to rethink the faith from the perspective of that historical praxis, and it is based on the experience of the faith derived from the liberating commitment. For this reason, this theology comes only after that involvement, the theology is always a *second act.*"[18]

Therefore, the radical theology of freedom does not advocate the abandonment of the traditional disciplines of biblical, historical, systematic, and moral theologies. Rather, such a theology assumes that wrestling with these disciplines is the second act. The starting place is the suffering of the oppressed. In the case of this book, the oppressed are the Jewish people. If the oppressed target Christians as the oppressor, the first act of Christians is to listen to the Jewish judgment against them. The second act is to construct a theology that is particular to one's own faith claim but that also results in an inclusive, universal relationship to people of other faith communities.

When Christians assert traditional theologies without first examining their practical implications (praxis), the logical progression often results in suffering instead of freedom. The cries of the suffering call one to look at tradition's fringes and reexamine one's own interpretation of the Christian message. Does one's theology imply oppression and exclusionism of particular people and groups? If so, is not the claim of authentic existence a lie? One hopes that the result of such wrestling is not the abandonment of the traditional disciplines but a reworking and revitalizing of their content.

It would be presumptuous to claim that such wrestling results in a theology of absolute truth. But when its logical conclusion is freedom rather than oppression, it convicts one of the untruth in the traditional approach. If nothing else, one is at least moving toward a theology that points in the direction of authentic existence for all people and for all of creation. The logical digression of a Christian theology that leads to murdered children in oven chambers cannot be true even if it is orthodox or standardized.

The particular tragedy of the Holocaust challenges the basic understanding of Christian biblical interpretation, tradition, ethics, and doctrines. When put into action traditional doctrines often work out differently from the way scholars and church officials initially presented them. The death of innocent Jewish children must be an event that helps determine the character of particular doctrines of the Christian faith after Auschwitz.

One doctrine affected by a theology of freedom and inclusion is the doctrine or study of God (theology). Is God really the unchangeable and static God of tradition? Or is God a living, dynamic, changing, and creating God who effects transformation in the hearts of people and brings liberation from the oppressive order of society? Many theologians suggest that God is dynamic and is on the side of the broken. This is the gospel of grace. To those who do the breaking, the gospel of God comes as judgment. Does this imply that God is partial? To echo Paul in Romans, by no means! Rather, to say that God sides with the suffering is to acknowledge that life is often unjust. The good news of the Christ-event is that "God's justice is equalizing!"[19] In the witness of Scripture God is impartial. In order for justice to be accomplished, one must also recognize that God never straddles the fence, but sides with the broken and oppressed.

Inclusive Christian theology that is conscious of suffering also changes the common perspective of the doctrine or study of humanity (anthropology). The established church's position toward humanity is that "God is best served by our self-abasement."[20] Yet theologians have pointed out that this self-abasing view has more to do with the influence of Gnostic dualism in early Christian theology than with how God relates to human beings in Scripture. Patristic theologians such as Origen, and later, Augustine, claimed that the flesh is evil and the spirit is good and negatively influenced much in Christianity, from the church's views on sexuality to death and dying. In preoccupation with the inner self and shame, Christians have mortified the flesh by exalting asceticism, celibacy, and intellectualism. The result has been the sacrifice of pleasure, sexuality, and feelings. This fall-redemption-centered spirituality has more in common with Augustine than with the God of Abraham and Paul.

The Yahwist tradition in the Hebrew Scriptures makes a different claim: all creation, including human beings, is very good (Gen. 1:31). According to Milton Steinberg, for the Jew "life is good. Wherefore a [person] should treasure it, not despise it; affirm and not deny it; have faith in it and never despair of its possibilities. For behind it is God."[21] This understanding of humanity stems from the Genesis creation stories, which affirm that humanity is created by God in God's image. Thus the priestly creation account concludes: "And God saw everything that [God] had made, and behold, it was very good" (v. 31).

To be human, that is, to be created in the image of God, is as much a responsibility as it is a privilege. David Blumenthal reflects on this declaration in Genesis: "the presence of the image of God in humanity implies the imitation of that image. . . . The burden of being human, in the sense of molding oneself to the personhood of God, is enormous. . . . As Abraham Joshua Heschel put it, 'A Jew must strive to be Torah incarnate,' to embody the very presence of the divine."[22]

In this light the sin of humanity is not pride—claiming to be God— as traditional Christianity has asserted. Rather, humanity's sin is the failure to recognize that human beings are created as beloved—what Matthew Fox calls "original blessing." In other words, sin occurs when one fails to recognize authentic existence both for oneself and for others. This perspective does not belong to Judaism alone. It is also evident in the stories about Jesus, in the teachings of Paul, and in most indigenous spiritualities around the world. Advocating the recovery of this holistic picture in the New Testament, Adolf Hansen contends that Christians must engage in the intentional work of "re-Judaizing and de-Hellenizing the Christian faith."[23]

God's creative and liberative work claims the earth's beauty and humanity's personhood, not their debasement. If any group suggests that others are nonpersons because they are of a different race, gender, creed, sexual orientation, economic station, or political party, that group blasphemes God's freeing love in creation. A liberating theology claims that all creation is made in God's image.

The doctrine or study of last things (eschatology) is also profoundly affected by listening to the voice of the oppressed. Important to this doctrine is that history is dynamic. Although theologians of freedom admit that the Bible speaks occasionally about eternal life as life after death, they recognize also that the dominant emphasis in both the Hebrew Scriptures and the New Testament is on a new age, the reign of God, the kingdom of heaven. Even the biblical references to eternal life are in the context of a new heaven and earth. Jesus' declaration that the reign of God is at hand does not refer merely to a peaceful reordering of souls. Such a pronouncement calls for the recognition that God has ordered the universe for peace with justice.

Eternal life does not consist in being plucked out of history, but in being a participant in its culmination. In the present life, therefore, our task is to move toward that new order, to work for it, to announce it, and to train for it. . . . Thus, at every point of Christian doctrine, liberation theology asks two basic questions: What does it really mean when we see it from the clearer vantage point of the oppressed? And, what is the hidden agenda in the interpretation which has been handed down to us?[24]

Confessional awareness of Christianity's exclusionism is important in developing a theology after Auschwitz. Regarding Christianity's relationship to the Holocaust, Clark Williamson writes that "confession is necessary to a life committed to creative transformation, because it removes the blockages, particularly the commitments to past ways of thinking, acting, and valuing, which hinder the working of creative transformation."[25]

Becoming aware of Christian responsibility in the destruction of the Jewish people during the Holocaust prevents one from slipping into a posture of pity. But awareness of responsibility is not enough. Even when it is appropriate, guilt paralyzes; it serves no constructive purpose if one cannot move beyond its debilitating restraints. One must stride past awareness to authentic empathy. Thus Williamson asserts that "confession—it is a way of assuming responsibility for the future, for how we preach and teach—especially on those passages in which the anti-Jewish argument is present. Will we decide to take responsibility for what we say? Or must we continue to fertilize the soil in which negative attitudes toward Jews and Judaism grow?"[26]

Empathy differs significantly from feeling guilt over exclusionism. Instead of focusing on the oppressor, empathy focuses on the oppressed. Robert McAfee Brown makes the point as follows:

One of Elie Wiesel's characters comments, "When a Jew says he is suffering, one must believe him, and when he is afraid, one must assume his fear is justified. In neither case does one have the right to doubt his word. Even if one cannot help him, one must at least believe him."

This provides an excellent starting point for a new theology: When we hear the cry, "I'm hurting," we must take it seriously. And when we discover that the cry really means, "You are hurting me," we must hear it with utmost seriousness.[27]

Brown calls this movement of listening the "Abrahamic venture." It seems naive to think that people who know comfort and security would be willing to be in genuine solidarity with those who have no comfort or security. Who is going to engage in the "self-emptying" that such a decision would involve? Brown suggests that this kind of listening requires the kind of faith that Abraham had—hope against hope, the willingness to give up that which is familiar and venture into insecurity. Creativity and transformation do not occur without significant risk—risk of change, risk of ambiguity, and risk of losing power and control. To engage in the Abrahamic venture

> is a matter of willingness to subject oneself, at risk, to the power of the gospel—a gospel that emphasizes turning around, "conversion," a fresh start, a letting-go, and a recognition that this finally comes by grace—not to be attained but only received. . . . Something of the Abrahamic quality will have to invest the lives of those who take on the task of liberation today. The degree of our ability to respond will not finally rest on the soundness of our analysis, though that is important, but on the extent of our willingness to risk our security on behalf of the insecurities of others.[28]

The most effective way to risk and to eradicate the church's oppression of those excluded in the church and the church's theology is through what Juan Luis Segundo calls the "hermeneutic circle."

> *Firstly,* there is our way of experiencing reality, which leads us to ideological suspicion. *Secondly,* there is the application of our ideological suspicion to the whole ideological superstructure in general and to theology in particular. *Thirdly,* there comes a new way of experiencing theological reality that leads us to exegetical suspicion, that is, to the suspicion that the prevailing interpretation of the Bible has not taken important pieces of data into account. *Fourthly,* we have our new hermeneutic, that is, our new way of interpreting the fountainhead of our faith (i.e., Scripture) with the new elements at our disposal.[29]

According to the Gonzálezes, "To put those ideas in less terse language, one could say that most of us began with a theological naiveté. We believed, not only that what the Bible said was true, but also that the Bible actually said what our mentors and the tradition before them told us that it said."[30] Then Christians heard the cry of the oppressed— children burned alive in oven chambers. They listened intently, but were told not to worry, that those who suffer will find comfort. When some questioned why people kill in the name of Christ, they were told that "blessed are the peacemakers" refers to inner contentment, not an end to gas chambers.

At this point answers were no longer adequate, and some became suspicious that something had gone terribly wrong. Is the church the institution that wages peace or wages war? Is God on the side of the oppressed or the oppressor? In disillusionment, some left the church for secular or nontraditional alternatives. But some stayed. Driven from credulity into turmoil, those who stayed began questioning what they had so freely accepted before. In searching through Scripture, they discovered on the fringes of tradition that much of what the Bible says liberates those who are oppressed. Scripture and tradition had been "so closely intertwined that to doubt the traditional interpretation was to doubt the authority of both Bible and tradition," and enough doubt was raised to assert that much of what we had been told it said was simply not true.[31] The process had started. A new way of experiencing reality had begun. It was not the Bible that had changed, but people's understanding of the Bible. Indeed, some saw that God was bringing beginnings into their own existence and into the existence of others and the belly of the earth itself.

The hermeneutic circle, or something similar, prompts transformation for people politically, existentially, and historically. Politically, one becomes aware that governments, churches, and all bureaucratic systems have the possibility for both good and evil. Jews were systematically murdered in concentration camps. Engaging in the hermeneutic circle by facing the tragedy of the Holocaust means that the Christian perspective on history takes a quantum leap. In the face of dying Jews, particularly when theological justification is given for their dying, one must be suspicious of the oppressive ways the Jesus proclamation has been interpreted and search out a new paradigm of hope. The tendency to categorize in black and white compels one to rediscover a paradigm from the beginning of Christianity—one about a Paul who spoke in shades of gray. One must beware of the interpretations of Scripture that conclude logically in Egypt instead of in the land of milk and honey, in a darkened tomb instead of in an open cave with the stone rolled away, in oven chambers instead of in the land of freedom. Exclusive biases appear in the way lectionaries are divided, in translations, and especially in commentaries. If these biases do not point toward an inclusive God, they do not point to the God hailed by Abraham and Sarah, Paul and Priscilla.

What then can one say about the suffering of the Jews, the heirs of Paul, the survivors of the death camps, the dead of Auschwitz? Is it enough to say that Israel became a state, that the matter is finished? It is not. The church will continue to be haunted by cremated corpses as long as it ignores the destruction of the Jews.

For the most part, Christianity has not known what to do with this oppressed group. Jews can not be conveniently classified under "Christ crucified," except when Christians erroneously blame Jews for Pilate's crime. Jewish liberation is conspicuously missing from most accounts of Christian liberation theology today. But Irving Greenberg's words, quoted at the beginning of this book, compel Christians to be accountable to God for their exclusionist position toward the Jews. Indeed, if Christian theology ignores the Holocaust in its new hermeneutic, then it is anti-Jewish.

Paul is an advocate of hope by insisting that Jews exist under the law as Jews, and Gentiles exist through Christ as Gentiles. Both are made righteous by God in Abraham's promise through different paths and are called to embrace each other. Paul chastens Jews who could not embrace Gentiles apart from the law. But he also believes that the church cannot exist without God's chosen—the people called Israel. A branch withers and dies without the root. If the church's theology is anti-Jewish, then it is also anti-Christian.

After the Holocaust the church's integrity and moral fabric is at stake in what it includes and excludes in its theology regarding the Jews. J. B. Metz affirms this perspective: "faced with Auschwitz, I consider as blasphemy every Christian theodicy (i.e., every attempt at a so-called 'justification of God') and all language about 'meaning' when these are initiated outside this catastrophe."[32]

Perhaps the greatest fear among Christians is that the proclamation of a Christian theology of Judaism will somehow abrogate the church's particular faith claim through Christ. But such a proclamation affirms the particular claim and announces the universal claim that God is love for both Christians and Jews.

The task of an inclusive Christian theology resulting in liberation after Auschwitz is not to focus only on the liberation of the Jewish people. The goal is to listen to the silent cries of dead Jews as one hears the cries of dead Christians in the Third World. The freedom from the church's own exclusivist claims against people of other faiths and people within the Christian faith will mean that the church too will be set free. The crucifixion of God occurs every time any of God's children is killed or diminished. Are Christians so naive to think that God's face is seen only on the face of Christians who hurt or the face of those Christians who think and act alike?

J. B. Metz issues this summons: "it is our primary duty as Christians to listen—*for once to begin really listening*—to what Jews are saying of themselves and about themselves."[33] Here, perhaps, is a Christian hermeneutic with which Jews can live—literally. As Jesus must have stared at Peter while the Romans murdered him, with sunken cheeks and glazed eyes the Jews of Auschwitz can look at Christians today and cry. They do not merely say "I'm hurting." They cry "You are hurting me." But now, instead of turning away, Christians look into their eyes and say, "Please forgive me, for I have hurt you. Take my hand and together we shall walk. I will never forget your suffering."

7

No Chimneys!

> Then Nebuchadnezzar was so filled with rage
> against Shadrach, Meshach, and Abednego that
> his face was distorted. He ordered the furnace
> heated up seven times more than was
> customary. So the men were bound, still
> wearing their tunics, their trousers, their hats,
> and their other garments, and they were thrown
> into the furnace of blazing fire.
> Then King Nebuchadnezzar was astonished
> and rose up quickly. He said to his counselors,
> "Was it not three men that we threw bound into
> the fire?" They answered the king, "True, O
> king." He replied, "But I see four men
> unbound, walking in the middle of the fire, and
> they are not hurt; and the fourth has the
> appearance of a god."
> —Daniel 3:19, 21, 24-25

The apocalyptic book of Daniel is a story about the suffering of Jews and the triumph of God. It is a story of hope set in the midst of the Babylonian exile of the Jewish people in the sixth century B.C.E., but was probably written around 167–164 B.C.E. during the Jewish persecutions and forced hellenization of Judaea under Antiochus IV (Epiphanes), who reigned from 175 to 163 B.C.E.[1]

The pervading focus through Daniel is that God is present when the people of God suffer. From this perspective the prophet Daniel wrote of the presence of a fourth figure in the fiery furnace where three of God's faithful were condemned to die. The prophet of Israel wanted his readers to know that this one who appeared to be like a god was the one God of Abraham who enters the fiery furnaces with God's people. This word of comfort assured many Jews persecuted by the Seleucid dynasty of Syria that God will be triumphant in the end.

But Jews murdered in the fiery furnaces of Auschwitz had no word of comfort. Unlike Daniel's hope, the hope of dying Jews at Auschwitz went up in smoke. No fourth figure appeared in the fire—only the smoke of chimneys and the overshadowing presence of ashes. "Where is God now?" asked the prisoner of death next to Wiesel. God could not have abandoned the beloved of Israel in their dying.

Perhaps God was just as present with the Jews at Auschwitz as with the Jews in Babylon. But at Auschwitz God took the shape of ashes along with six million Jews and the other five million non-Jewish victims. The perplexing question after the Holocaust is not whether God was present with the Jewish people. Rather, the most puzzling question is why the voice of God was largely absent from the church.

Some Christians did choose to stand with suffering Jews in the Holocaust. These righteous Gentiles understood the cross of Christ as the event of faith that compels humans to stand in solidarity with the oppressed, even unto death. Many more Christians, however, chose to stare silently away from the flames while embracing twenty centuries of anti-Jewish theology.

The Christian exclusionism of Scripture and tradition, which logically digressed to the genocide of the Jewish people, illumines a significant truth that the church can no longer ignore: Anti-Judaism is anti-God. Anti-Jewish theology and the faithful worship of God are mutually exclusive. Some post-Holocaust scholars have asserted that anti-Judaism is at the very core of Christian theology. They claim that every book and letter in the New Testament is either explicitly or implicitly polemical toward the Jews. But, as I have maintained throughout this book, Paul is an exception to this rule.

As a Jew, Paul's theology was a Jewish theology of the Gentiles. Gentiles must have thought his gospel a radical one: God extends the promise of Abraham to Gentiles apart from the law through Christ. Gentiles now experience the gift and demand of God's boundless love by faith through Christ. They do not have to become Jews to share in God's covenant. But contrary to classical interpretation, Paul never said that God had rejected the Jewish people or that the Gentiles had replaced the Jewish people as God's children. Jews experience the gift and demand of God's covenantal love by faith grounded in the law.

Several considerations are important for the church as Christians adopt a more liberative and inclusive theology of the Jewish people. Each requires risk and careful scrutiny.

The first consideration regards the meaning of "liberative." Today Christians frequently toss about the word "liberation," but it can suggest different things to different groups. Liberation's primary social contexts in Western society have been in the African American struggle for freedom, women's suffrage, gay and lesbian rights, and freedom among the poor and oppressed in Latin America. When some Christian groups speak of liberation they are calling for a radical redistribution of power and wealth, sometimes even advocating violent measures when peaceful measures do not get desired results. Some advocates of freedom, such as Desmond Tutu and Martin Luther King, Jr., have also believed that the gospel has profound implications for the structures of society, yet they have held fast to the principle that nonviolence is essential to any credible theology of freedom. Whether liberation advocates are pacifists or believe in taking up arms to achieve their ends, liberation at its core means freedom—freedom from paternalism, parochialism, sexism, classism, racism, ageism, or homophobia, from anything or any thought that restricts or deprives the vibrancy of human beings and the earth itself.

The second consideration is that a liberative and inclusive Christian theology has a different meaning for Jews than for Christians. Jews are wise to suspect any Christian theology. The church's progress report for the last two thousand years has demonstrated a Christianity that is destructively anti-Jewish. Anti-Judaism in Christian theology is usually subconscious on the part of Christians, but it subtly persists nevertheless. I offer two examples of this persistence.

One is in the lack of awareness Christians exemplify in God-talk. Christian feminists have helped Christians see the narrowness in using only male metaphors for God and sexist language in general. As a result, many Christians now use male-female inclusive language. In the interfaith context, however, most Christian inclusivists have not yet grasped the exclusive language evident in their failure to distinguish among God, Christ, and Jesus. As a consequence, Christian theology tends to be christocentric and triumphalist. A christocentric church has no theological room for God's love to triumph outside the bounds of the Christ-event or the Jesus proclamation. In their efforts to use inclusive language by focusing only on racial minorities, women, and the broken *within* the church, Christian theologians have bypassed the issue of inclusivism *outside* the church. To this extent, most discussions of inclusion among Christians today do not wrestle with one-world paradigms and interfaith contextualizations, and have inadequately dealt specifically with anti-Semitism, anti-Jewish theology, and the destruction of the Jewish people in the Holocaust.

Another way anti-Judaism exclusively perseveres in Christian theology is by removing the Exodus-Sinai event from the context of salvation history for the Jewish people and into an abstraction for Christians today. I do not suggest that the Exodus-Sinai event should cease to be an important story of God's boundless love for Christians. This story is part of the church's story also. For instance, the language and emotion of African American spirituals illustrate how at times "Go Down, Moses" may have provided the only glimmer of hope for American slaves fortunate enough to survive the Middle Passage, the deadly boat trips from Africa to the new world, but left enslaved in a seemingly hopeless existence. I do suggest, however, that when the Exodus-Sinai event becomes for Christians only the church's story of faith, the law and the Jewish people cease to exist theologically and become abstractions—a subtle form of theological genocide.

In addition to the meaning of Christian theology and its frequent anti-Jewishness, a third consideration for Christians should be the specific meaning of a Christian theology of the Jewish people. Because this theology embraces a group outside the church, it is unlike most other Christian theologies. Credibility is therefore measured differently than in traditional theologies of inclusion.

An important principle to traditional theology in the church is that the genesis and credibility of a theology of the oppressed can come only from the oppressed group, not from the oppressing group. Therefore Christians must realize that they are not called to develop a Jewish theology. Christians are responsible for Christian theology. Jewish theology can be born and evolve only out of Judaism itself. Yet because of the profoundly anti-Jewish element in Christianity and the church's tendency to be theologically exclusive, the church must embark on the journey of constructing a theology of the Jewish people.

Developing such a theology in the church is a great risk. The theology is Christian, and Christians, as the historical oppressors of the Jewish people, are incapable of measuring whether a Christian theology of the Jewish people is credible for Jews. Thus Christians must wrestle with theology and present it to the Jewish survivors of the Holocaust and their heirs today. Christians must ask all Jews everywhere, Is this theology credible in the presence of burning children? Then, with utmost seriousness, Christians must listen and willfully wrestle again and again until they hear that their theology is credible. The Christian task, then, is not to persuade Jews to accept Paul's understanding of gospel. Rather, the Christian task is to ask the Jewish people if they could live (literally) with a Christian who accepts an Inclusive Promise understanding of Paul's gospel.

Finally, Christians must be aware that after Auschwitz the Jewish people suspect Christians as well as Christian theology. Jews have two thousand years of documented history on the danger of trusting Christians. It is important for Christians to understand that anytime a Christian makes a statement about the Jewish people, Jews must listen carefully and ask if they can trust this Christian. Nothing is more representative of this issue than when Christians make critical remarks about the State of Israel. Theologically, for Jews, the State of Israel is to the Holocaust as, for Christians, the resurrection of Christ is to the cross of Jesus. To the Jewish people Israel represents fulfillment of the promises of God and the security of belonging in a world of people who have convincingly tried to tell Jews they do not belong.

Robert McAfee Brown, a strong proponent of casting off all anti-Jewish theology from the church, suggests that dialogue between Christians and Jews will have come a great distance when Christians can criticize particular policies or actions of Israel without Jews calling them anti-Semitic.[2] The thrust of Brown's statement is not that Jews are wrong in making this claim, but that most Christians simply do not grasp the distress Jews have about the Holocaust. It is a matter of trust. Christians concerned with liberation and inclusiveness should be concerned about the liberation of all people, including Palestinians. But Christians' trustworthiness for Jews will have to be proved over time and on an individual basis. This trustworthiness will be seen in non-Jews' efforts to understand the complexities of the Middle East situation, in the church's work to eradicate anti-Jewish theology among Christians, and in demonstrations that any criticism of Israel is grounded on the unequivocal support of Israel's right to statehood and self-determination.

In drawing near to conclusion, it seems appropriate to let one who has walked through the Valley of dark places to define hope. If there is any possibility for hope—hope that the Holocaust will never happen again, hope that God is still alive, hope that humaneness is alive—it is best expressed by one who survived: Elie Wiesel.

> When you live on the edge of a mountain, you see very far. You see the abyss, but you also see very far. And so, because never in human history have people had more reasons to despair, and to give up on man, and God, and themselves, hope is now stronger than ever before. It's irrational; it's absurd, of course. But it may be a way of achieving a certain victory. Not absolute victory. A small measure of victory.[3]

Paul implores Christians to be inclusive and provides for them a way to be bearers of a good news that honors the God whose promises are irrevocable. He did believe that God's event of Christ affected Jews, but not that Jews should become Christians. Instead, Paul held his ground for the hope that Jews would embrace his conviction that Gentiles are children of Abraham outside the law—through the Christ-event. The history of Christian genocide of Jews through the ages calls into question for the faithful Jew whether Christians' anti-Jewish God could be the same God Jews worship. Therefore, reading him today, Christians must recognize a Paul who entreats the church to embrace a theology that is distinctively Christian yet universally inclusive of the Jewish people and people of other faiths. It is difficult to know what impact inclusive theology could have in today's divided and groaning world. Even a small measure of victory makes a difference. Perhaps this understanding of Christian faith is credible in the presence of the burning children. This is the world's hope—no chimneys, forever, for anyone.

Notes

Preface

1. J. B. Metz, *The Emergent Church: The Future of Christianity in a Postbourgeois World*, trans. Peter Mann (New York: Crossroad, 1981), 21.

2. Bailey Smith as quoted in "It Is Interesting: Baptist Leader Insists He Is 'Pro-Jew,'" *The Washington Post*, 18 Sept. 1980.

3. Ibid., 355.

4. See Raul Hilberg, *The Destruction of the European Jews* (Chicago: Quadrangle, 1961), 3–4, and Clark Williamson, *Has God Rejected His People? Anti-Judaism in the Christian Church* (Nashville: Abingdon, 1982), 122.

5. Kenneth L. Woodward, "How to Read Paul, 2,000 Years Later: Theologian or Pastor?" *Newsweek*, Feb. 29, 1988, 65.

6. Juan Luis Segundo, S.J., *The Liberation of Theology*, trans. John Drury (Maryknoll, N.Y.: Orbis, 1976), 9.

7. Robert McAfee Brown, "Liberation Theology: Paralyzing Threat or Creative Challenge?" in *Mission Trends No. 4: Liberation Theologies in North America and Europe*, ed. Gerald H. Anderson and Thomas F. Stransky (New York: Paulist, Grand Rapids: Eerdmans, 1979), 20.

8. Irving Greenberg, "Cloud of Smoke, Pillar of Fire: Judaism, Christianity, and Modernity after the Holocaust," in *Auschwitz: Beginning of a New Era? Reflections on the Holocaust*, ed. Eva Fleischner (New York: KTAV, 1977), 23.

Chapter 1: Into the Fire

1. Haiku by Mark E. Lett, May 1991. Previously unpublished; printed by permission of the author.

2. Filip Muller, "Eyewitness Auschwitz," in *A Holocaust Commemoration for Days of Remembrance*, compiled by the Committee for Jewish-Christian Dialogue—Austin Presbyterian Theological Seminary, B'nai B'rith Hillel Foundation of the University of Texas, and Episcopal Theological Seminary of the Southwest (Austin, Tex: Worley, 1984), 9.

3. Clark Williamson, *Has God Rejected His People? Anti-Judaism in the Christian Church* (Nashville: Abingdon, 1982), 125.

4. William L. Shirer, *The Rise and Fall of the Third Reich*, as quoted by Abba Eban, *Heritage: Civilization and the Jews* (New York: Summit, 1984), 302.

5. George H. Stein, ed., *Hitler, Great Lives Observed* (Englewood Cliffs, N.J.: Prentice-Hall, 1968), 26.

6. Adolf Hitler, *Mein Kampf*, trans. Ralph Manheim (Boston: Houghton Mifflin Company, 1943), 623.

7. Edward H. Flannery, *The Anguish of the Jews: Twenty-Three Centuries of Antisemitism*, rev. ed. (New York: Paulist, 1985), 208.

8. Eban, *Heritage*, 294.

9. Ibid., 298.

10. Ibid., 296–97.

11. The distinction between the terms "anti-Jewish" and "anti-Semitic" is particularly important not only for this study but for this entire subject. Unfortunately, even prominent scholars often fail to make this distinction. The term "anti-Semitic" is a misnomer that was first used in the late nineteenth century to signify *racial* antipathy toward Jews. "Semite" is a term denoting a particular race or racial group, Caucasian, comprising chiefly Jews and Arabs but in ancient times also others of the eastern Mediterranean area. Many Jews in Europe and the United States have blond hair and blue eyes, clearly non-Semitic in racial background. Ethiopian Jews are black in racial background. Therefore, "Semitic" is more inclusive than "Jewish" but also exclusive of many Jews of different racial backgrounds. Nevertheless, because of its incorrect use in literature since the early 1900s, I use it in this book to mean racial hatred toward the Jewish people. I use the terms "anti-Jewish" and "anti-Judaic" to refer to a theological construct connoting *religious* discrimination. Anti-Semitism is inclusive of anti-Judaism because anti-Judaism preceded and was instrumental in the birth of anti-Semitism, but anti-Judaism is exclusive of racial distinction. For further discussion, see Flannery, *Anguish*, 4–5; David Blumenthal and Michael McGarry, "Antisemitism," in *A Dictionary of the Jewish-Christian Dialogue*, ed. Leon Klenicki and Geoffrey Wigoder (New York: Paulist, 1984), 9–15.

12. Flannery, *Anguish*, 185–89.

13. Ibid., 185.

14. Nathan C. Belth, *A Promise to Keep: A Narrative of the American Encounter with Anti-Semitism* (New York: Times Books, 1979), 144.

15. Ibid., 58–68.

16. Ibid., 67.

17. Jonathan D. Sarna, "American Anti-Semitism," in *History and Hate*, ed. David Berger (Philadelphia: Jewish Publication Society, 1986), 121. See also idem, "The 'Mythical Jew' and the 'Jew Next Door' in Nineteenth-Century

America," in *Anti-Semitism in American History*, ed. David A. Gerber (Urbana: Univ. of Illinois Press, 1986), 57–78.

18. Belth, *Promise*, 77–78.

19. Gerald L. K. Smith, "Introduction," in Henry Ford, Sr., *The International Jew: The World's Foremost Problem* (Los Angeles: Christian Nationalist Crusade, n.d.), 6.

20. See Ellis Rivkin, *What Crucified Jesus?* (Nashville: Abingdon, 1984).

21. Ibid., 16–37, 111–24.

22. Williamson makes a good argument for the irony between Bonhoeffer's actions and theology in *Has God Rejected*, 103–4.

23. Ibid., 135–36. See also Alexander Donat, *The Holocaust Kingdom: A Memoir* (New York: Holocaust Library, 1978), 355–61.

24. Williamson, *Has God Rejected*, 136.

25. G. B. Ginzel, ed., *Auschwitz als Herausforderung für Juden und Christen* (Heidelberg: Verlag Lambert Schneider, 1980), 176.

26. J. B. Metz, *The Emergent Church: The Future of Christianity in a Postbourgeois World*, trans. Peter Mann (New York: Crossroad, 1981), 18.

27. The cross, or "Christ crucified and resurrected," is a central and guiding concept in Paul's theology. Chapters 3–5 deal extensively with this concept.

28. Gustaf Aulen, *Christus Victor: An Historical Study of the Three Main Types of the Idea of Atonement*, trans. A. G. Herbert (New York: Macmillan, 1979), 1–15.

29. Elie Wiesel, *Night*, trans. Stella Rodway (New York: Avon, 1969), 75–76.

30. Peter von der Osten-Sacken, *Christian-Jewish Dialogue: Theological Foundations*, trans. Margaret Kohl (Philadelphia: Fortress, 1986), 101–17.

31. John G. Gager, *The Origins of Anti-Semitism: Attitudes Toward Judaism in Pagan and Christian Antiquity* (New York: Oxford Univ. Press, 1985), 202.

32. "Letter from Birmingham City Jail," in *A Testament of Hope: The Essential Writings of Martin Luther King, Jr.*, ed. James Melvin Washington (San Francisco: Harper & Row, 1986), 290.

Chapter 2: A Revised Standard Version

1. Norman A. Beck, *Mature Christianity: The Recognition and Repudiation of the Anti-Jewish Polemic of the New Testament* (Cranbury, N.J.: Associated University Presses, 1985), 21, 35.

2. Ken Wilber, *No Boundary: Eastern and Western Approaches to Personal Growth* (Boulder, Colo.: Shambhala Publications, 1979), 85.

3. Abraham J. Heschel, "On Prayer," *Conservative Judaism* 25, no. 1 (1970): 6.

4. Charles Y. Glock and Rodney Stark, *Christian Beliefs and Anti-Semitism* (New York: Harper & Row, 1966).

5. Ibid., 51–53.

6. Ibid., 59.

7. Ibid., 62–64.

8. Rodney Stark et al., *Wayward Shepherds* (New York: Harper & Row, 1971), 50.

9. Ibid., 42.

10. "Ministering Within the Congregation and to the World," para. 439, no. 1, *The Book of Discipline of the United Methodist Church: 1984* (Nashville: United Methodist Publishing House, 1984), 222–23.

11. See Eric M. Meyers and James F. Strange, *Archaeology, the Rabbis, and Early Christianity* (Nashville: Abingdon, 1981). Of particular interest for this subject are chapters 6–9, which focus on archaeological data that suggest Jewish Christianity survived the destruction of the second temple. The irony is that around the time that Emperor Constantine declared Christianity (i.e., the remnant of gentile Christianity) the official religion of the empire evidence of such a sect within Judaism ceases to exist.

12. Krister Stendahl, *Paul Among Jews and Gentiles: And Other Essays* (Philadelphia: Fortress, 1976), 70.

13. This is my own paraphrase of a statement made by Ellis Rivkin in a personal conversation in his office at Hebrew Union College–Jewish Institute of Religion, Cincinnati, on Nov. 30, 1987.

14. Joachim Jeremias, *New Testament Theology*, Part 1: *The Proclamation of Jesus*, trans. J. Bowden (New York: Scribner's, 1971), 147; quoted in Clark Williamson, *Has God Rejected His People? Anti-Judaism in the Christian Church* (Nashville: Abingdon, 1982), 64.

15. Ellis Rivkin, "Pharisees," *Interpreter's Dictionary of the Bible, Supplementary Volume*, ed. Keith Crim et al. (Nashville: Abingdon, 1976), 657–63.

16. For a detailed discussion, comparison, and synthetic picture of the Pharisees in Josephus, the Gospels, and the tannaitic literature of the early rabbinic period see Ellis Rivkin, *A Hidden Revolution: The Pharisees' Search for the Kingdom Within* (Nashville: Abingdon, 1978); Jacob Neusner, *First-Century Judaism in Crisis: Yohanan ben Zakkai and the Renaissance of Torah* (Abingdon: Nashville, 1975); idem, "The Pharisees: Jesus' Competition," and "The Figure of Hillel: A Counterpart to the Problem of the Historical Jesus," in *Judaism in the Beginning of Christianity* (Philadelphia: Fortress, 1984), 45–61, 63–88.

17. See Rivkin, *Hidden Revolution*, 211–51.

18. Clark Williamson, "The New Testament Reconsidered: Recent Post-Holocaust Scholarship," *Quarterly Review* 4, no. 4 (1984): 42. For a detailed comparison and contrast between the traditions of Hillel and the traditions of Jesus, see Neusner, "Figure of Hillel"; and Williamson, *Has God Rejected*, 23–28.

19. John T. Pawlikowski, "Jews and Christians," *Quarterly Review* 4, no. 4 (1984): 28.

20. For a detailed analysis of the Jewish groups attacked in the Gospels see Williamson, *Has God Rejected*, 67–70. "Scribes" are frequently targeted with the Pharisees and probably represent the same group in the generalizing minds of the Gospel writers. Rivkin (*Hidden Revolution*, 104–24) suggests that the Gospel writers use the terms "Pharisees," "scribes," "lawyers," "teachers of the law," and "hypocrites" synonymously; they are portrayed with "identical characteristics, functions, doctrines, and teachings but enjoy separate and distinct embodiments" (124). Rivkin refers primarily to the Pharisees, not the scribes, because (1) they are the group most frequently marked as the warring faction against Jesus; (2) they are the group that most influenced the teachings of Rabbinic Judaism after the second temple period; and (3) their name remains the most common biblical term used metaphorically today by Christians to describe that which is un-Christian.

21. Albert Friedlander, *Leo Baeck: Teacher of Theresienstadt* (New York: Holt, Rinehart and Winston, 1968), 58; quoted by Williamson, "New Testament Reconsidered," 43.

22. Franklin H. Littell, *The Crucifixion of the Jews: The Failure of Christians to Understand the Jewish Experience* (New York: Harper & Row, 1975), 6.

23. Emil Schürer, *A History of the Jewish People in the Time of Jesus*, ed. N. Glatzer (New York: Schocken, 1961), 198.

24. Leo Trepp, *A History of the Jewish Experience* (New York: Behrman House, 1973), 44. See also *The Loeb Classical Library* (Boston: Harvard University Press, 1927, 1928) s.v.v. "Josephus' works," and "Jewish War II," 169–77.

25. Ellis Rivkin, *What Crucified Jesus?* (Nashville: Abingdon, 1984), 117.

26. Ibid., 70–89.

27. Jules Isaac, *The Teaching of Contempt* (New York: Holt, Rinehart and Winston, 1964), 128.

28. Not until the last half of the first century C.E. were "the Writings" added to "the Law" and "the Prophets" to form the canon of the Hebrew Scriptures. Likewise, the canonical New Testament was not officially agreed upon until well into the fourth century C.E. "Jesus kerygma," then, refers to

much of the canonical New Testament, but may include other documents being circulated from the fourth century.

29.   More comprehensive work on this subject is available in the books I have found the most resourceful, *Elder and Younger Brothers* by A. Roy Eckardt, *The Anguish of the Jews* by Edward H. Flannery, *The Crucifixion of the Jews* by Franklin H. Littell, and *Has God Rejected His People?* by Clark M. Williamson.

30.   Irving Greenberg, "The Relationship of Judaism and Christianity," *Quarterly Review* 4, no. 4 (1984): 10–11.

31.   Ibid., 11.

32.   Williamson, *Has God Rejected*, 122.

33.   Ibid.

34.   A. Roy Eckardt, *Elder and Younger Brothers: The Encounter of Jews and Christians* (New York: Schocken, 1973), 7.

35.   Ibid., 91.

36.   *The Ante-Nicene Fathers*, ed. A. Roberts and J. Donaldson (Grand Rapids: Eerdmans Publishing Co., 1885), 1:146–47.

37.   Ibid., 203.

38.   Williamson, *Has God Rejected*, 96.

39.   Norman Perrin, *New Testament: An Introduction* (New York: Harcourt Brace Jovanovich, 1974), 331.

40.   Pawlikowski, "Jews and Christians," *Quarterly Review* 4, no. 4 (1984): 24.

41.   Samuel Sandmel, *Anti-Semitism in the New Testament?* (Philadelphia: Fortress, 1978), 148; Williamson, *Has God Rejected*, 98.

42.   Edward H. Flannery, *The Anguish of the Jews: Twenty-Three Centuries of Antisemitism* (New York: Paulist, 1985), 52–53.

43.   Williamson, *Has God Rejected*, 98–99.

44.   Flannery, *Anguish*, 50.

45.   Ibid., 50–51.

46.   Clemens Thoma, *A Christian Theology of Judaism*, trans. Helga Croner (New York: Paulist, 1980), 151.

47.   Williamson, *Has God Rejected*, 106.

48.   Sandmel, *Anti-Semitism*, 155.

49.   Raul Hilberg, *The Destruction of the European Jews* (Chicago: Quadrangle, 1961), 5–6, and Eckardt, *Elder and Younger Brothers*, 12–14.

50.   For a more detailed discussion of Hilberg's listing, see also Eckardt, *Elder and Younger Brothers*, 12–15; Flannery, *Anguish*, 55ff.; and Williamson, *Has God Rejected*, 107–12.

51. Flannery, *Anguish*, 82.

52. Williamson, *Has God Rejected*, 113.

53. Morris Bishop, *The Middle Ages* (New York: American Heritage, 1970), 216.

54. Ibid., 92.

55. Flannery, *Anguish*, 92–93.

56. Jacob Marcus, ed., *The Jew in the Medieval World: A Source Book* (New York: Atheneum, 1974), 115–20.

57. Flannery, *Anguish*, 93.

58. Nicholas Berdyaev, *Christianity and Anti-Semitism*, trans. Alan A. Spears (Kent, England: Hand & Flower Press, 1952), 12; quoted by Williamson, *Has God Rejected*, 114.

59. Williamson, *Has God Rejected*, 117.

60. Ibid., 116–17.

61. Flannery, *Anguish*, 96–98.

62. Ibid., 143.

63. Martin Luther, *That Jesus Christ Was Born a Jew* (1523), in *Luther's Works*, ed. I. Brandt, 55 vols. (Philadelphia: Muhlenberg Press, 1962), 25: 200–201.

64. Abba Eban, *Heritage: Civilization and the Jews* (New York: Summit, 1984), 199.

65. Ibid., 199–200.

66. Williamson, *Has God Rejected*, 102.

67. See Flannery, "The Age of the Ghetto," in *Anguish*, 145–59; and Eban, *Heritage*, 189–91.

68. Eban, *Heritage*, 200.

69. Williamson, *Has God Rejected*, 102–3.

70. Flannery, *Anguish*, 175–78. See also 329 n. 18: "The term 'rationalism' in this work does not connote the use or rule of reason but that philosophy which erects reason as the sole source and arbiter of truth to the exclusion of faith or religious experience as well as other non-rational sources of truth."

71. Ibid.

72. William Harry Montgomery, *Jesus Was Not Jew* (Poughkeepsie, N.Y.: Research Co., 1935).

73. Williamson, *Has God Rejected*, 103–5.

74. By "rational faith" I mean a faith that can be explicated by rational criteria. This definition differs from the "rationalism" of the nineteenth century

and the "blind faith" embraced by modern fundamentalism, which discourages
rational explication.

75. Dietrich Bonhoeffer, *No Rusty Swords*, trans. Edwin H. Robertson and
John Bowden, ed. Edwin H. Robertson (New York: Harper & Row, 1965), 226;
quoted by Williamson, *Has God Rejected*, 103.

76. Williamson, *Has God Rejected*, 103.

77. Karl Barth, *Church Dogmatics*, II/2, trans. G. W. Bromiley et al., ed.
G. W. Bromiley and T. W. Torrance (Edinburgh: T. & T. Clark, 1957), 208–9;
see Williamson, *Has God Rejected*, 104–5.

78. See Markus Barth, "Was Paul an Anti-Semite?" *Journal of Ecumenical
Studies*, 511.

79. Karl Barth, *Dogmatics in Outline*, trans. G. T. Thomson (New York:
Philosophical Library, 1947), 75–76; quoted in *A Holocaust Commemoration
For Days of Remembrance*, the Committee for Jewish-Christian Dialogue (Aus-
tin, Tex.: Worley, 1984), 11.

80. Robert McAfee Brown, *Elie Wiesel: Messenger to All Humanity* (Notre
Dame, Ind.: Univ. of Notre Dame Press, 1983), 3.

81. Ibid., 5.

Chapter 3: In a Mirror Dimly

1. Elie Wiesel, "Then and Now: The Experience of a Teacher," *Social
Education*, 42 (1978): 271.

2. Elie Wiesel, "Why I Write," in *Confronting the Holocaust: The Impact
of Elie Wiesel*, ed. Alvin H. Rosenfeld and Irving Greenberg (Bloomington,
Ind.: Indiana Univ. Press, 1978), 203.

3. A. Roy Eckardt, "The Recantation of the Covenant?" in *Confronting the
Holocaust: The Impact of Elie Wiesel*, ed. Alvin H. Rosenfeld and Irving Greenberg (Bloomington, Ind.: Indiana Univ. Press, 1978), 163.

4. Krister Stendahl, *Paul Among Jews and Gentiles: And Other Essays*
(Philadelphia: Fortress, 1976), 16.

5. Ibid., 17.

6. Ibid., 86.

7. Ibid., 12–13.

8. Ibid.

9. J. Christiaan Beker, *Paul the Apostle: The Triumph of God in Life and
Thought* (Philadelphia: Fortress, 1984), 340.

10. Ernst Käsemann, *Perspectives on Paul*, trans. Margaret Kohl (Philadelphia: Fortress, 1971), 70.

11. Stendahl, *Paul Among Jews*, 130.

12. Matthew Black comments: "The key to an understanding of Paul's essential thesis is his conviction of the total bankruptcy of contemporary Pharisaic 'scholasticism.'. . . This was 'legalistic righteousness,' . . . losing sight entirely of the gracious personal will of a holy and good God" (*Romans*, New Century Bible Commentary, 2d ed. [Grand Rapids: Eerdmans; London: Marshall, Morgan & Scott, 1989], 37). See Clark Williamson, "The New Testament Reconsidered: Recent Post-Holocaust Scholarship," *Quarterly Review* 4, no. 4 (1984): 44.

13. Ibid., 340.

14. E. P. Sanders, *Paul, the Law, and the Jewish People* (Philadelphia: Fortress, 1983), 199.

15. Emil Brunner, *The Letter to the Romans*, trans. H. A. Kennedy (Philadelphia: Fortress, 1959), 93; cited in A. Roy Eckardt, *Elder and Younger Brothers: The Encounter of Jews and Christians* (New York: Schocken, 1973), 67.

16. Stendahl, *Paul Among Jews*, 1.

17. John G. Gager, *The Origins of Anti-Semitism: Attitudes Toward Judaism in Pagan and Christian Antiquity* (New York: Oxford Univ. Press, 1985), 193.

18. Rosemary R. Ruether, *Faith and Fratricide: The Theological Roots of Anti-Semitism* (New York: Seabury, 1974), 96, 98.

19. Samuel Sandmel, *Anti-Semitism in the New Testament?* (Philadelphia: Fortress, 1978), 8.

20. I am specifically referring here to two problem texts in the undisputed Pauline corpus of letters (Romans, 1 and 2 Corinthians, Galatians, Philippians, 1 Thessalonians, and Philemon): 2 Cor. 11:24 and 1 Thess. 2:14-15.

(1) 2 Corinthians 11:24: "Five times I have received at the hands of the Jews the forty lashes less one." This text is problematic because it speaks of "the Jews" so harshly. The immediate context reveals that the subject is boasting. Paul is apparently upset by the boasting of his Jewish brethren, who were possibly threatening Paul's gospel by proselytizing Gentiles. Verse 25 is peculiar in that it uses a generalized designation, "the Jews," the only place it appears in this section. Also, it is the only verse that moves from the general to the particular regarding the hardships he has encountered. This verse is a later textual variant placed into Paul's argument by a gentile church that interpreted this context as a polemic against the Jewish people. In John's Gospel the use of "the Jews" reveals a generalized picture of Jesus' life. The reference to the lashes reveals a projection of Jesus' persecution in the gospel tradition at the hands of the Romans by the cat-o'-nine-tails. Although Paul tends to exaggerate, this blatant depiction reveals a tradition later than Paul.

(2) 1 Thessalonians 2:14-15: "the Jews, who killed both the Lord Jesus and the prophets, and drove us out, and displease God and oppose all men." This is the worst vindictive against the Jews in the undisputed letters of Paul. "On

virtually every ground—language, ideas, structure, presumed dates—the passage is inconsistent with the Paul of the other letters" (Gager, *Anti-Semitism*, 255). This is clearly not Paul (Ernst Best, John Gager, Victor Paul Furnish, F. F. Bruce) and flagrantly expresses a later variant added to the text from a gentile church that had blamed the crucifixion of Jesus on the Jews. If this verse is deleted the passage is more consistent and reads more smoothly. The picture that emerges is one of a Paul who is upset about the Jewish reluctance to receive the gospel, which is a primary theme in Romans.

21.   From Barry Cytron, "Jews and Judaism in the Writings of Paul (Focus on Romans, Chs. 9–11)," a paper given at the Tenth National Workshop on Christian-Jewish Relations, Minneapolis, Nov. 8–11, 1987.

22.   Ibid.

23.   The RSV reads "enemies of God" here. "Enemies" is too strong a translation for what Paul means by the word ἐχθροί. "Of God" does not appear in the Greek text. Its inclusion in various translations may come from its use in the last part of v. 29, but it presumes an anti-Jewish understanding of "hostile" to the gospel.

24.   Clark M. Williamson, *Has God Rejected His People? Anti-Judaism in the Christian Church* (Nashville: Abingdon, 1982), 58.

25.   Stendahl, *Paul Among Jews*, 76.

26.   Peter von der Osten-Sacken, *Christian-Jewish Dialogue: Theological Foundations*, trans. Margaret Kohl (Philadelphia: Fortress, 1986), 72.

27.   Sanders, *Paul, the Law*, 172; see also 171.

28.   Ibid., 48.

29.   Sanders, *Paul, the Law*, 131. "Righteoused" is not an English word but Pauline commentators frequently prefer it as more accurate than "justified." I prefer the Middle English term "rightwise" or simply "made righteous."

30.   Gager, *Anti-Semitism*, 225.

31.   Sanders, *Paul, the Law*, 131.

32.   Ibid., 197.

33.   Sanders, "Paul's Attitude toward the Jewish People," *Union Seminary Quarterly Review* 33 (1978): 185.

34.   Sanders, *Paul, the Law*, 197.

35.   Gager, *Anti-Semitism*, 191.

36.   Beker, *Paul*, 342.

37.   Erwin R. Goodenough with A. T. Kraabel, "Paul and the Hellenization of Christianity," in *Religions in Antiquity*, ed. Jacob Neusner, Studies in the History of Religions 14 (Leiden: Brill, 1968), 33.

38.   Ibid., 34.

39.   Beker, *Paul*, 205.

40.   Gager, *Anti-Semitism*, 205. See Gaston, "Paul and the Torah," in *Antisemitism and the Foundations of Christianity*, ed. Alan Davies (New York: Paulist, 1979), 54–56.

41.   John A. T. Robinson, *Wrestling with Romans* (Philadelphia: Westminster, 1979), 7.

42.   Sanders, *Paul, the Law*, 183.

43.   Ibid., 182.

Chapter 4: Galatians: Before Moses Was Abraham

1.   Samuel Sandmel, *Philo's Place in Judaism: A Study of Conceptions of Abraham in Jewish Literature*. Augmented Ed. (New York: KTAV, 1971), 107.

2.   Samuel Sandmel, *Philo of Alexandria: An Introduction* (New York: Oxford Univ. Press, 1979), 57.

3.   Ibid., 151.

4.   Sandmel, *Philo's Place*, 107.

5.   Charles B. Cousar, *Galatians*, Interpretation: A Bible Commentary for Teaching and Preaching (Atlanta: John Knox, 1982), 104.

6.   John G. Gager, *The Origins of Anti-Semitism: Attitudes Toward Judaism in Pagan and Christian Antiquity* (New York: Oxford Univ. Press, 1985), 231.

7.   Cousar, *Galatians*, 5–6, 20.

8.   Clark M. Williamson, *Has God Rejected His People? Anti-Judaism in the Christian Church* (Nashville: Abingdon, 1982), 53.

9.   Gager, *Anti-Semitism*, 231.

10.   Ibid., 235.

11.   Ibid., 234.

12.   It is doubtful that Paul ever understood himself as an apostate to Judaism, even though he had given up the practice of Torah for the sake of the gospel of Christ to the Gentiles. It is important to note in his writings that he never expected his fellow Jews to revoke Torah for themselves.

13.   Gager, *Anti-Semitism*, 234.

14.   Ibid.

15.   Ibid., 235.

16.   Ibid., 233.

17.   Lloyd Gaston, "Paul and the Torah," in Alan T. Davies, ed., *Anti-Semitism and the Foundations of Christianity* (New York: Paulist, 1979), 58.

18.   Markus Barth, *Ephesians*, Anchor Bible, 2 vols. (Garden City, N.Y.: Doubleday, 1974), 1:246; see Gager, *Anti-Semitism*, 233.

19.   Williamson, "New Testament Reconsidered," 47.

20.   Gager, *Anti-Semitism*, 236–37. I disagree slightly with Gager's assessment that Paul was never outside the law. Although Paul never viewed himself as outside the law, his call to preach the gospel among the Gentiles placed him outside the *practice* of Torah. Such a commitment distinguished Paul from other Jews, but he probably never saw this distinction himself. Even though Paul stands outside the law in practice, he grounds his standing through use of the Law (the Pentateuch—the Abraham story) and the Prophets.

21.   Also Paul, who became like the Gentiles for the sake of the gospel.

22.   See Gager, *Anti-Semitism*, 240.

23.   Ibid.

24.   RSV excludes "and," but the Greek text has *kai*.

25.   Ernst Käsemann, *Perspectives on Paul* (Philadelphia: Fortress, 1971), 140–41.

26.   Cousar, *Galatians*, 149; Hans Dieter Betz, *Galatians: A Commentary on Paul's Letter to the Churches in Galatia*, Hermeneia (Philadelphia: Fortress, 1979), 312ff.

27.   Cousar, *Galatians*, 149.

28.   Carl R. Holladay, *Preaching the New Common Lectionary*, Year C, After Pentecost (Nashville: Abingdon, 1986), 75.

29.   The text according to Willy Staerk, *Altjüdische liturgische Gebete* (KIT 58; Berlin: de Gruyter, 1930), 19. On the Shemoneh Esreh, see Elbogen, *Gottesdienst*, 27ff, 232ff; Kaufmann Kohler, "The Origin and Composition of the Eighteen Benedictions with a Transition of the Corresponding Essene Prayers in the Apostolic Constitutions," HUCA 1 (1924), 387–425.

30.   Staerck, 30–32.

31.   Betz, *Galatians*, 322.

32.   Holladay, *Lectionary*, Year C, Pentecost, 75.

33.   Betz, *Galatians*, 323.

34.   Cousar, *Galatians*, 150.

35.   E. D. Burton, *A Critical and Exegetical Commentary on the Epistle to the Galatians*, International Critical Commentary (New York: Charles Scribner's Sons, 1920), 358. See Gager, *Anti-Semitism*, 228.

36.   Peter Richardson, *Israel in the Apostolic Church* (Cambridge: Cambridge Univ. Press, 1969), 79–80. See Gager, *Anti-Semitism*, 229.

37.   Gager, *Anti-Semitism*, 229.

Chapter 5: Romans: The Inclusive Promise of God

1.   Victor Paul Furnish, *Theology and Ethics in Paul* (Nashville: Abingdon, 1982), 162.

2. *The Romans Debate*, ed. Karl P. Donfried (Minneapolis: Augsburg, 1977), x. This book gives an excellent depiction of the complexities involved in establishing the context of Romans. Nine essays are offered by different scholars regarding the nature, purpose, and background of Paul's Letter to the Romans. Much of the current dialogue regarding Romans has moved in the direction of Donfried's own essay, challenging Bultmann's doctoral dissertation, *Der Stil der paulinischen Predigt und die Kynisch Stoische Diatribe*, of 1910 and illuminating anew chaps. 9–11 as the primary emphasis of Romans.

3. See esp. Wolfgang Wiefell, "The Jewish Community in Ancient Rome and the Origins of Roman Christianity," in ibid., 100–119.

4. John G. Gager, *The Origins of Anti-Semitism: Attitudes Toward Judaism in Pagan and Christian Antiquity* (New York: Oxford Univ. Press, 1985), 230.

5. Ibid.

6. Sam K. Williams, "The 'Righteousness of God' in Romans," *Journal of Biblical Literature* 99, no. 2 (1980): 289.

7. J. Christiaan Beker, *Paul the Apostle: The Triumph of God in Life and Thought* (Philadelphia: Fortress, 1984), 344.

8. The issue of "call" has been important in most discussions about Paul since the early 1960s. Of particular importance is whether he converted from Judaism to Christianity. Paul's Damascus road experience (Gal. 1:11-17; Acts 9:1-19; 22:4-16; 26:9-19) is often referred to in Christian circles as Paul's "conversion." Unfortunately, such an understanding of Paul is packed with images of Augustine's Paul of Western introspective conscience and Luther's tormented and guilt-ridden Paul, but is not the Paul of the New Testament.

W. D. Davies correctly asserts that for many in Christendom conversion implies abandonment, and as such, should not be applied to the Jews ("Paul and the People of Israel," *New Testament Studies* 24 [1977]: 24). In Paul's time, Christianity and Judaism did not exist apart from each other, at least in theory. "Followers of 'the Way' (Acts 9:2) constituted a movement *within Judaism*. Paul did not become a Christian" (Clark M. Williamson, *Has God Rejected His People? Anti-Judaism in the Christian Church* [Nashville: Abingdon, 1982], 56).

Paul was converted in the sense of "transformed" or "changed." Although it sounds inconsistent with Paul himself, he did give up his former life in Judaism for the sake of the Gentiles. But Paul's change was not a conversion in the sense of forsaking Judaism.

Krister Stendahl remarks that "call" is more descriptive of Paul's experience than "conversion." "Serving the one and the same God, Paul receives a new and special calling in God's service. God's Messiah asks him as a Jew to bring God's message to the Gentiles" (*Paul among Jews and Gentiles: and Other Essays* [Philadelphia: Fortress, 1976], 7).

The four accounts of Paul's experience on the road affirm, to some extent, Stendahl's explanation. Acts 9:15 states, "But the Lord said to [Ananias], 'Go, for he is an instrument whom I have chosen to bring my name before Gentiles and kings and the people of Israel." Then in Acts 22:15 Ananias said to Paul, "You will be [God's] witness to all the world of what you have seen and heard." In Acts 26:17-18 the Lord appointed Paul to go to the Gentiles, the ones "to whom I am sending you to open their eyes, that they may turn from darkness to light and from the power of Satan to God, so that they may receive forgiveness of sins and a place among those who are sanctified by faith in me" (see Williamson, *Has God Rejected*, 56).

Luke's account in Acts and Paul's own account in Galatians show parallels to the understanding of call portrayed in Isaiah and Jeremiah, perhaps conveying that Paul saw himself as a prophet of Israel. In Galatians he indicates that he has been set apart in the womb, is called through grace, and set apart to preach to the Gentiles. Isaiah writes, "The Lord called me from the womb, from the body of my mother [God] named my name" (Isa. 49:1), and "I will give you as a light to the nations, that my salvation may reach to the ends of the earth" (Isa. 49:6). Similarly, Paul echoes Jer. 1:15, "Before I formed you in the womb I knew you, and before you were born I consecrated you; I appointed you a prophet to the nations [i.e., the Gentiles, *goyim*]" (see Stendahl, *Paul Among Jews*, 81).

Paul understood himself as an "apostle" of Israel, not as an "apostate" apart from Israel. The debate of where Paul stood in relation to Israel is not new. Because of his unique message, it is not difficult to see how some of those with whom he came in contact—Jews, Jewish followers of the Way, and gentile Christians—must have believed that he stood outside Judaism. But Paul answers his opposition within the Corinthian church: "Are they Hebrews? So am I. Are they Israelites? So am I. Are they descendants of Abraham? So am I" (2 Cor. 11:22).

Elsewhere Paul writes, "I advanced in Judaism beyond many among my people of the same age, for I was far more zealous for the traditions of my ancestors" (Gal. 1:14). Paul hardly sounds ashamed of his past or his people. Those in Judaism are "my people," he boasts proudly. Again in his letter to the Philippians he exclaims, "If anyone else has reason to be confident in the flesh, I have more: circumcised on the eighth day, a member of the people of Israel, of the tribe of Benjamin, a Hebrew born of Hebrews; as to the law, a Pharisee; as to zeal, a persecutor of the church; as to righteousness under the law, blameless" (3:46).

Finally, with passionate conviction, he shares with the Romans his love for and link to the Jewish people when he says, "I ask, then, has God rejected [God's] people? By no means! I myself am an Israelite, a descendant of Abraham, a member of the tribe of Benjamin. God has not rejected [God's] people whom [God] foreknew" (11:1-2).

Like Paul's own writings, Luke recognized the Jewishness of Paul. Luke attributes this statement to Paul: "I am a Jew, born at Tarsus in Cilicia, but brought up in this city at the feet of Gamaliel, educated strictly according to our ancestral law, being zealous for God just as all of you are today" (Acts 22:3). Rabban Gamaliel, a well-known scholar, legal authority, and Pharisee, ran a noted rabbinical school (see Williamson, *Has God Rejected,* 49; and Ellis Rivkin, *A Hidden Revolution: The Pharisees' Search for the Kingdom Within* [Nashville: Abingdon, 1978], 26–27; see also index in Rivkin for more about Rabban Gamaliel).

On Paul's refusal to see himself or his gospel apart from Israel, Calvin Roetzel comments: "And while the messianism through which Paul viewed the traditions, scriptures and established symbols of Israel intensely focused his message, generated new symbols and destabilized patterns judged secure, to say that Paul placed himself outside Judaism is going too far. He was convinced that he was a part of God's people now blessed with God's final visitation. To become a part of that people he did not need to go through a conversion which triggered the repudiation of one religion for another" (Calvin J. Roetzel, "Paul's Burden," a paper presented at the Tenth National Workshop on Christian-Jewish Relations, Minneapolis, Nov. 8–11, 1987).

Perhaps the most accurate picture is that Paul experienced some kind of conversion, but because he himself describes his experience more in terms of "call," the latter term is more helpful in explicating Paul's gospel.

9. Schubert M. Ogden, *Christ without Myth* (New York: Harper & Brothers, 1961), 156.

10. Paul J. Achtemeier, *Romans* Interpretation: A Bible Commentary for Teaching and Preaching (Atlanta: John Knox, 1985), 50.

11. Gager, *Anti-Semitism,* 248.

12. Ibid., 249. Jews never denied Gentiles the right to convert to Judaism. In fact, proselytizing Gentiles was especially encouraged in Paul's day. But most Jews considered Gentiles *as* Gentiles to be outside God's enlightened promises even though God loved them. Later (Rom. 4) Paul argues that Gentiles are not bound by the Exodus-Sinai covenant (Torah) like Jews. Rather, he points toward God's covenant with Abraham, a promise that Abraham would be the father not only of Israel but of many nations. Paul broke from his Pharisaic roots not by abrogating the mitzvah system of salvation for Jews but by extending its principles of lovingkindness and mercy to include Gentiles as well as Jews.

13. See the argument divisions in the table of contents in Achtemeier, *Romans.*

14. Ibid., 216.

15. Gager, *Anti-Semitism,* 249.

16. Ibid., 215.

17. Paul could hardly be speaking of Jews since all Jews had their sins relinquished on the Day of Atonement each year.

18. Williams, "Righteousness of God," 274.

19. Ibid., 273.

20. Achtemeier, *Romans,* 78.

21. Carl R. Holladay, *Preaching the New Common Lectionary, Year B, Lent, Holy Week, Easter* (Nashville: Abingdon, 1984), 40.

22. Ernst Käsemann, *Commentary on Romans*, trans. and ed. Geoffrey W. Bromiley (Grand Rapids: Eerdmans, 1980), 119.

23. Achtemeier, *Romans*, 78.

24. Käsemann, *Romans*, 121.

25. Stendahl, *Paul Among Jews*, 87.

26. Ibid., 92.

27. Gager, *Anti-Semitism*, 220.

28. Stendahl, *Paul Among Jews*, 92.

29. See Gager, *Anti-Semitism*, 221.

30. Lloyd Gaston, "Paul and the Torah," in *Antisemitism and the Foundations of Christianity*, ed. Alan Davies (New York: Paulist, 1979), 62–67; cf. Gager, *Anti-Semitism*, 221.

31. See Gager, *Anti-Semitism*, 221–22.

32. Stendahl, *Paul Among Jews*, 94–95.

33. Charles Ernest Burland Cranfield, "Romans 9:30—10:4" *Interpretation* 34 (January, 1980): 72–73; Gager, *Anti-Semitism*, 224.

34. Käsemann, *Romans*, 282.

35. G. E. Howard, "Christ the End of the Law: The Meaning of Rom. 10:4ff.," *Journal of Biblical Literature* 88 (1969): 336.

36. Gager, *Anti-Semitism*, 249.

37. Ibid., 224.

38. Ibid., 224–25.

39. Stendahl, *Paul Among Jews*, 4.

40. From a lecture in the seminary class on Romans taught by Calvin Porter at Christian Theological Seminary in Indianapolis (Fall, 1980).

41. John Knox, "Romans," *Interpreter's Bible*, ed. G. A. Buttrick et al., 12 vols. (Nashville: Abingdon, 1954), 9:540.

42. J. Christiaan Beker, *Paul's Apocalyptic Gospel: The Coming Triumph of God* (Philadelphia: Fortress, 1982), 72.

43. Ibid., 73.

44. Ibid., 108.

45. Gager, *Anti-Semitism*, 260.

46. Ibid., 257.

47. John T. Pawlikowski, "The Challenge of Jesus the Christ for the Synagogue," *Proceedings of the Center for Jewish-Christian Learning: College of St. Thomas, 1987 Lecture Series*, vol. 2 (Spring, 1987), 30.

48. Ibid.

49. E. P. Sanders, *Paul, the Law, and the Jewish People* (Philadelphia: Fortress, 1983), 197.

50. Beker, *Paul the Apostle*, 344.

51. Gager, *Anti-Semitism*, 223.

52. Ibid., 250.

53. Pawlikowski, "Challenge of Christ," 30.

54. Gager, *Anti-Semitism*, 263.

55. Ibid., 260.

Chapter 6: Christology, Liberation, and the Jewish People

1. Jürgen Moltmann, *The Power of the Powerless: The Word of Liberation for Today* (San Francisco: Harper & Row, 1983), 99.

2. Schubert M. Ogden, *The Point of Christology* (San Francisco: Harper & Row, 1982), 122. I have found Ogden's writings particularly helpful in constructing a post-Holocaust christology. Unlike other christologies, Ogden's is both distinctively Christian for the church and theologically inclusive of other faith communities outside the church.

3. Schubert M. Ogden, *Christ without Myth* (New York: Harper & Brothers, 1961), 156.

4. Ibid., 144.

5. Rosemary R. Ruether, "Christology and Jewish-Christian Relations," in *To Change the World: Christology and Cultural Criticism* (New York: Crossroad, 1981), 43.

6. Schubert M. Ogden, *The Reality of God and Other Essays* (New York: Harper & Row, 1963), 202.

7. Ogden, *Point of Christology*, 120.

8. Ibid., 111.

9. Ibid., 121.

10. Ibid.

11. Ibid., 122.

12. Ruether, *Change the World*, 31.

13. Gustavo Gutiérrez, "Faith as Freedom: Solidarity with the Alienated and Confidence in the Future," in *Living with Change, Experiencing Faith*, ed. Francis A. Eigo (Villanova, Pa.: Villanova University Press, 1976), 37.

14. Ogden, *Point of Christology*, 123.

15. Justo L. González and Catherine G. González, *Liberation Preaching: The Pulpit and the Oppressed* (Nashville: Abingdon, 1980), 11.

16. Ibid., 13.

17. Dietrich Bonhoeffer, *Letters and Papers from Prison*, ed. Eberhard Bethge, enlarged ed. (New York: Macmillan, 1972), 17.

18. Gustavo Gutiérrez, "Freedom and Salvation: A Political Problem," in *Liberation and Change*, ed. Ronald H. Stone (Atlanta: John Knox, 1977), 83.

19. Ibid., 22.

20. González and González, *Liberation Preaching*, 23.

21. Milton Steinberg, *Basic Judaism* (New York: Harcourt Brace Jovanovich, 1975), 59.

22. David Blumenthal, "Personhood: The Jewish View," in *A Dictionary of the Jewish-Christian Dialogue*, ed. Leon Klenicki and Geoffrey Wigoder (Ramsey, N.J.: Paulist, 1984), 144.

23. Lecture notes from Adolf Hansen's Greek language and literature course at the University of Indianapolis (Fall, 1976). Hansen, now a vice president of Garrett-Evangelical Theological Seminary in Evanston, Illinois, believes that the recovery of the Jewishness of the Christian message would allow for a much more holistic understanding of sexuality, death and dying, the human condition, and theology. I am greatly indebted to his constructive influence in the formation of my own theology.

24. González and González, *Liberation Preaching*, 24.

25. Clark M. Williamson, *Has God Rejected His People? Anti-Judaism in the Christian Church* (Nashville: Abingdon, 1982), 138.

26. Ibid., 140.

27. Robert McAfee Brown, "Liberation Theology: Paralyzing Threat or Creative Challenge," in *Mission Trends No. 4: Liberation Theologies in North America and Europe*, ed. Gerald H. Anderson and Thomas F. Stransky (New York: Paulist; Grand Rapids: Eerdmans, 1979), 20.

28. Ibid., 22–23.

29. Juan Luis Segundo, *The Liberation of Theology* (Maryknoll, N.Y.: Orbis, 1976), 9.

30. González and González, *Liberation Preaching*, 31–32.

31. Ibid., 30.

32. Metz, "Christians and Jews after Auschwitz: Being a Meditation also on the End of Bourgeois Religion," in *The Emergent Church: The Future of Christianity in a Postbourgeois World*, trans. Peter Mann (New York: Crossroad, 1981), 19.

33. Ibid., 20.

Chapter 7: No Chimneys

1. See commentary notes in The *New Oxford Annotated Bible with the Apocrypha: RSV*, ed. Herbert G. May and Bruce M. Metzger, expanded ed. (New York: Oxford Univ. Press, 1977), 1067.

2. Robert McAfee Brown, "Darkness and Light in Jewish-Christian Relations," a lecture given at the Tenth National Workshop on Christian-Jewish Relations, Minneapolis, Nov. 8–11, 1987.

3. Elie Wiesel, "A Small Measure of Victory," in *An Interview with Elie Wiesel* by Gene Koppell and Henry Kaufman (Univ. of Arizona Press, 1974), 5.

Bibliography

Achtemeier, Paul J. *Romans*. Interpretation: A Bible Commentary for Teaching and Preaching. Atlanta: John Knox, 1985.

Anderson, Gerald H., and Stransky, Thomas F., eds. *Mission Trends No. 4: Liberation Theologies in North America and Europe*. New York: Paulist; Grand Rapids, Mich.: Eerdmans, 1979.

Aulen, Gustaf. *Christus Victor: A Historical Study of the Three Main Types of the Idea of the Atonement*, translated by A. G. Herbert. New York: Macmillan, 1979.

Beck, Norman A. *Mature Christianity: The Recognition and Repudiation of the Anti-Jewish Polemic of the New Testament*. Cranbury, N.J.: Associated University Presses, 1985.

Beker, J. Christiaan. *Paul the Apostle: The Triumph of God in Life and Thought*. Philadelphia: Fortress, 1980.

————. *Paul's Apocalyptic Gospel: The Coming Triumph of God*. Philadelphia: Fortress, 1982.

————. *Suffering and Hope: The Biblical Vision and the Human Predicament*. Philadelphia: Fortress, 1987.

Belth, Nathan C. *A Promise to Keep: A Narrative of the American Encounter with Anti-Semitism*. New York: Times Books, 1979.

Berdyaev, Nicholas. *Christianity and Anti-Semitism*. Translated by Alan A. Spears. Kent, England: Hand & Flower Press, 1952.

Betz, Hans Dieter. *Galatians: A Commentary on Paul's Letter to the Churches in Galatia*. Hermeneia: A Critical and Historical Commentary on the Bible. Philadelphia: Fortress, 1979.

Bishop, Morris. *The Middle Ages*. New York: American Heritage, 1970.

Bonhoeffer, Dietrich. *Letters and Papers From Prison*. Edited by Eberhard Bethge. Enlarged edition. New York: Macmillan, 1972.

————. *No Rusty Swords*. Translated by Edwin H. Robertson and John Bowden. Edited by Edwin H. Robertson. New York: Harper & Row, 1965.

The Book of Discipline of the United Methodist Church: 1984. Nashville: The United Methodist Publishing House, 1984.

Brown, Robert McAfee. *Elie Wiesel: Messenger to All Humanity.* Notre Dame, Ind.: Univ. of Notre Dame Press, 1983.

Brown, Robert McAfee, and Sydney Thompson Brown, eds. *A Cry for Justice: The Churches and Synagogues Speak.* Mahwah, N.J.: Paulist, 1989.

Brunner, Emil. *The Letter to the Romans.* Translated by H. A. Kennedy. Philadelphia: Fortress, 1959.

Cousar, Charles B. *Galatians.* Interpretation: A Bible Commentary for Teaching and Preaching. Atlanta: John Knox, 1982.

Craddock, Fred B. *Philippians.* Interpretation: A Bible Commentary for Teaching and Preaching. Atlanta: John Knox, 1985.

Cranfield, Charles Ernest Burland. "Romans 9:30—10:4. *Interpretation* 34 (January 1980): 70–74.

Cytron, Barry. "Jews and Judaism in the Writings of Paul (Focus on Romans, Ch. 9–11)." Paper read at the Tenth National Workshop on Christian-Jewish Relations, Minneapolis, November 8–11, 1987.

Davies, W. D. "Paul and the People of Israel." *New Testament Studies* 24 (1977): 4–39.

Donat, Alexander. *The Holocaust Kingdom: A Memoir.* New York: Holt, Rinehart and Winston, 1965.

Donfried, Karl P., ed. *The Romans Debate.* Minneapolis: Augsburg, 1977.

Eban, Abba. *Heritage: Civilization and the Jews.* New York: Summit, 1984.

Eckardt, A. Roy. *Elder and Younger Brothers: The Encounter of Jews and Christians.* New York: Schocken, 1973.

Ellis, Marc H. *Beyond Innocence and Redemption: Confronting the Holocaust and Israeli Power: Creating a Moral Future for the Jewish People.* San Francisco: Harper & Row, 1990.

Flannery, Edward H. *The Anguish of the Jews: Twenty-Three Centuries of Antisemitism.* Mahwah, N.J.: Paulist, 1985.

Fleischner, Eva. "Heschel's Significance for Jewish-Christian Relations." *Quarterly Review* 4, no. 4 (1984): 64–81.

Ford, Henry, Sr. *The International Jew: The World's Foremost Problem.* Los Angeles: Christian Nationalist Crusade, n.d.

Friedlander, Albert. *Leo Baeck: Teacher of Theresienstadt.* New York: Holt, Rinehart and Winston, 1968.

Furnish, Victor Paul. *II Corinthians: A New Translation with Introduction and Commentary.* Anchor Bible. Garden City, N.Y.: Doubleday, 1984.

———. *The Moral Teaching of Paul.* Nashville: Abingdon, 1979.

———. *Theology and Ethics in Paul.* Nashville: Abingdon, 1968.

Gager, John G. *The Origins of Anti-Semitism: Attitudes Toward Judaism in Pagan and Christian Antiquity.* New York: Oxford Univ. Press, 1985.

Gaston, Lloyd. "Paul and the Torah." In *Anti-Semitism and the Foundations of Christianity,* edited by Alan T. Davies, 48–71. New York: Paulist, 1979.

Ginzel, G. B., ed. *Auschwitz als Herausforderung für Juden und Christen.* Heidelberg: Verlag Lambert Schneider, 1980.

Glock, Charles Y., and Rodney Stark. *Christian Beliefs and Anti-Semitism.* New York: Harper & Row, 1966.

González, Justo L., and Catherine G. González. *Liberation Preaching: The Pulpit and the Oppressed.* Edited by W. D. Thompson. Nashville: Abingdon, 1980.

Greenberg, Irving. "Cloud of Smoke, Pillar of Fire: Judaism, Christianity, and Modernity after the Holocaust." In *Auschwitz: Beginning of a New Era? Reflections on the Holocaust.* Edited by Eva Fleischner. New York: KTAV, 1977.

————. "The Relationship of Judaism and Christianity: Toward a New Organic Model." *Quarterly Review* 4, no. 4 (1984): 4–22.

Gutiérrez, Gustavo. "Faith as Freedom: Solidarity with the Alienated and Confidence in the Future." In *Living with Change, Experience, Faith.* Edited by Francis A. Eigo, Villanova, Pa.: Villanova University Press, 1976.

Gutiérrez, Gustavo, and Richard Shaull. *Liberation and Change.* Atlanta: John Knox, 1977.

Heschel, Abraham Joshua. "On Prayer." *Conservative Judaism* 25, no. 1 (1970): 1–12.

Hilberg, Raul. *The Destruction of the European Jews.* Chicago: Quadrangle, 1961.

Holladay, Carl R., et al. *Preaching the New Common Lectionary: Year B (Lent, Holy Week, Easter).* Nashville: Abingdon, 1984.

————. *Preaching the New Common Lectionary: Year C (After Pentecost).* Nashville: Abingdon, 1986.

A Holocaust Commemoration for Days of Remembrance. The Committee for Jewish-Christian Dialogue—Austin Presbyterian Theological Seminary, B'nai B'rith Hillel Foundation of the University of Texas in Austin, and Episcopal Theological Seminary of the Southwest. Austin, Tex.: Worley, 1984.

Howard, G. E. "Christ the End of the Law: The Meaning of Romans 10:4ff." *Journal of Biblical Literature* 88 (1969): 331–37.

Käsemann, Ernst. *Commentary on Romans.* Edited and translated by Geoffrey W. Bromiley. Grand Rapids: Eerdmans, 1980.

————. *Perspectives on Paul.* Translated by Margaret Kohl. Philadelphia: Fortress, 1971.

Klenicki, Leon, and Geoffrey Wigoder, eds. *A Dictionary of the Jewish-Christian Dialogue.* New York: Paulist, 1984.

Knox, John. "Romans." In *Interpreter's Bible Commentary.* Edited by G. A. Buttrick et al. Vol. 9. Nashville: Abingdon, 1954: 355–668.

Lapide, Pinchas. *The Resurrection of Jesus: A Jewish Perspective.* Translated by Wilhelm C. Linss. Minneapolis: Augsburg, 1983.

Lapide, Pinchas, and Ulrich Luz. *Jesus in Two Perspectives: A Jewish-Christian Dialogue.* Translated by Lawrence W. Denef. Minneapolis: Augsburg, 1985.

Lapide, Pinchas, and Peter Stuhlmacher. *Paul: Rabbi and Apostle.* Translated by Lawrence W. Denef. Minneapolis: Augsburg, 1984.

Littell, Franklin H. *The German Phoenix: Men and Movements in the Church in Germany.* Garden City, N.Y.: Doubleday, 1960.

————. *The Crucifixion of the Jews: The Failure of Christians to Understand the Jewish Experience.* San Francisco: Harper & Row, 1975.

Marxsen, Willi. *The Resurrection of Jesus of Nazareth.* Translated by Margaret Kohl. Philadelphia: Fortress, 1975.

May, Herbert G., and Bruce M. Metzger, eds. *The New Oxford Annotated Bible with the Apocrypha: Revised Standard Version.* New York: Oxford Univ. Press, 1977.

Metz, Johann Baptist. *The Emergent Church: The Future of Christianity in a Postbourgeois World.* Translated by Peter Mann. New York: Crossroad, 1981.

Meyers, Eric M., and James F. Strange. *Archaeology, the Rabbis, and Early Christianity.* Nashville: Abingdon, 1981.

Moltmann, Jürgen. *The Power of the Powerless: The Word of Liberation for Today.* Translated by Margaret Kohl. San Francisco: Harper & Row, 1983.

Montgomery, W. H. *Jesus Was Not Jew.* Poughkeepsie, N.Y.: Research Company, 1935.

Neusner, Jacob. *First-Century Judaism in Crisis: Yohanan ben Zakkai and the Renaissance of Torah.* Nashville: Abingdon, 1975.

————. *Judaism in the Beginning of Christianity.* Philadelphia: Fortress, 1984.

————, ed., *Religions in Antiquity: Essays in Memory of Erwin Ramsdell Goodenough. (Studies in the History of Religions 14. Leiden: Brill, 1968.*

Ogden, Schubert M. *Christ without Myth.* New York: Harper & Brothers, 1961.

————. *The Point of Christology.* San Francisco: Harper & Row, 1982.

————. *The Reality of God and Other Essays.* New York: Harper & Row, 1963.

Osten-Sacken, Peter von der. *Christian-Jewish Dialogue: Theological Foundations.* Translated by Margaret Kohl. Philadelphia: Fortress, 1986.

Pawlikowski, John T. "The Challenge of Jesus the Christ for the Synagogue." In *Proceedings of the Center for Jewish-Christian Learning: 1987 Lecture Series, College of St. Thomas,* Vol. 2 (Spring, 1987).

————. "Jews and Christians: The Contemporary Dialogue." *Quarterly Review* 4, no. 4 (1984): 23–36.

Perrin, Norman. *New Testament: An Introduction.* New York: Harcourt Brace Jovanovich, 1974.

Power, W. J. A. "The Book of Genesis: A Folk Theology." *Perkins Journal* 37, no. 2 (1984): 1–56.

Rivkin, Ellis. *A Hidden Revolution: The Pharisees' Search for the Kingdom Within.* Nashville: Abingdon, 1978.

————. "Pharisees." In *The Interpreter's Dictionary of the Bible, Supplementary Volume.* Edited by Keith Crim et al. Nashville: Abingdon, 1976.

————. *What Crucified Jesus?* Nashville: Abingdon, 1984.

Robinson, John A. T. *Wrestling With Romans.* Philadelphia: Westminster, 1979.

Roetzel, Calvin. "Paul's Burden—Jews and Judaism in the Writings of Paul (Focus on Romans, Ch. 9–11)." Paper read at the Tenth National Workshop on Christian-Jewish Relations, Minneapolis, Nov. 8–11, 1987.

Ruether, Rosemary Radford. *Faith and Fratricide: The Theological Roots of Anti-Semitism.* New York: Seabury, 1974.

————. *To Change the World: Christology and Cultural Criticism.* New York: Crossroad, 1981.

Sachs, Nelly. *O the Chimneys.* Translated by Michael Hamburger. New York: Farrar, Straus & Giroux, 1967.

Sanders, E. P. *Paul and Palestinian Judaism: A Comparison of Patterns of Religion.* Philadelphia: Fortress, 1977.

————. *Paul, the Law, and the Jewish People.* Philadelphia: Fortress, 1983.

————, ed. *Jewish and Christian Self-Definition.* Vol. 1, *The Shaping of Christianity in the Second and Third Centuries.* Philadelphia: Fortress, 1980.

Sanders, E. P., A. I. Baumgarten, and Alan Mendelson, eds. *Jewish and Christian Self-Definition.* Vol. 2, *Aspects of Judaism in the Graeco-Roman Period.* Philadelphia: Fortress, 1981.

Sanders, E. P., and Ben F. Meyer, eds. *Jewish and Christian Self-Definition.* Vol. 3, *Self-Definition in the Greco-Roman World.* Philadelphia: Fortress, 1982.

Sandmel, Samuel. *Anti-Semitism in the New Testament?* Philadelphia: Fortress, 1978.

————. *Philo of Alexandria: An Introduction.* New York: Oxford Univ. Press, 1979.

————. *Philo's Place in Judaism: A Study of Conceptions of Abraham in Jewish Literature.* Augmented ed. New York: KTAV, 1971.

Sarna, Jonathan D. "American Anti-Semitism." In *History and Hate.* Edited by David Berger. Philadelphia: Jewish Publication Society, 1986.

————. "The 'Mythical Jew' and the 'Jew Next Door' in Nineteenth-Century America." In *Anti-Semitism in American History.* Edited by David A. Gerber. Urbana and Chicago: Univ. of Illinois Press, 1986.

Schoneveld, J. (Coos). "The Jewish 'No' to Jesus and the Christian 'Yes' to Jews." *Quarterly Review* 4, no. 4 (1984): 52–63.

Schürer, Emil. *A History of the Jewish People in the Time of Jesus.* Edited by N. Glatzer. New York: Schocken, 1961.

Segundo, Juan Luis. *The Hidden Motives of Pastoral Action: Latin American Reflections.* Translated by John Drury. Maryknoll, N.Y.: Orbis, 1978.

————. *The Liberation of Theology.* Maryknoll, N.Y.: Orbis, 1976.

Silberman, Charles E. *A Certain People: American Jews and Their Lives Today.* New York: Summit, 1985.

Simon, Ulrich. *A Theology of Auschwitz: The Christian Faith and the Problem of Evil.* Atlanta: John Knox, 1967.

Stein, George H., ed. *Hitler* Great Lives Observed. Englewood Cliffs, N.J.: Prentice-Hall, 1968.

Steinberg, Milton. *Basic Judaism.* New York: Harcourt Brace Jovanovich, 1975.

Stendahl, Krister. *Paul Among Jews and Gentiles: And Other Essays.* Philadelphia: Fortress, 1976.

Thoma, Clemens. *A Christian Theology of Judaism.* Translated by Helga Croner. Ramsey, N.Y.: Paulist, 1980.

Trepp, Leo. *The Loeb Classical Library.* Boston: Harvard University Press, 1927, 1928, s.v.v. "Josephus' Works" and "Jewish War II": 169–77.

Van Buren, Paul M. *A Theology of the Jewish-Christian Reality.* Part 2, *A Christian Theology of the People Israel.* New York: Seabury, 1983.

Washington, James Melvin, ed. *A Testament of Hope: The Essential Writings of Martin Luther King, Jr.* San Francisco: Harper & Row, 1986.

Wiesel, Elie. *Night.* Translated by Stella Rodway. New York: Avon, 1969.

————. *The Oath.* Translated by Marion Weisel. New York: Random House, 1973.

————. "Then and Now: The Experience of a Teacher." *Social Education* 42 (1978): 266–71.

Wilber, Ken. *No Boundary: Eastern and Western Approaches to Personal Growth.* Boulder, Colo.: Shambhala Publications, 1979.

Williams, Sam K. "The 'Righteousness of God' in Romans." *Journal of Biblical Literature* 99, no. 2 (1980): 241–91.

Williamson, Clark M. "Anti-Judaism in Process Christologies?" *Process Studies* 10, nos. 3–4 (1980): 73–92.

———. *Has God Rejected His People? Anti-Judaism in the Christian Church.* Nashville: Abingdon, 1982.

———. "The New Testament Reconsidered: Recent Post-Holocaust Scholarship." *Quarterly Review* 4, no. 4 (1984): 37–51.

Woodward, Kenneth L. "How to Read Paul, 2,000 Years Later." *Newsweek*, Feb. 29, 1988: 65.

Yaseen, Leonard C. *The Jesus Connection: The Triumph Over Anti-Semitism.* New York: Crossroad, 1985.

Name and Subject Index

Pharisees 26, 27, 28, 29, 30, 31, 32, 67, 95, 136, 159
Philo of Alexandria 33, 66, 68, 69
Physically impaired 2
Picquart 6
Pilate, Pontius 11-12, 25, 33, 34, 147
Pogroms 36, 39, 40, 41
Poland 5
Polemic(s) 36, 44, 55, 56, 57, 98, 100, 105, 115, 124, 134
Polish 2
Polytheism 79
Pope Clement VI 43
Pope John XXIII x
Pope Urban II 42
Populist party 8
Porter, Calvin 170
Portugal 43
Practical theology xi, 138
Priscilla 147
Process theology 15
Promise 69, 102
Prophets 67, 112, 159, 166
Proselytiz(ing) 35, 45, 66
Protestants 12, 25, 45

Rabbinic Judaism 29
Racism ix, x, xii, 5, 6, 8, 11, 24, 47, 151, 156
Railcars 2, 3, 53
Rathenau, Walter 5
Rational Anti-Semitism 47
Rational liberalism 48
Rationalism 161
Reagan, Ronald 11
Re-Judaizing 143
Reconstructionist Judaism 95
Reform Judaism 95
Reformation 36, 44, 45, 46, 48
Rejection theology x, xi, 12, 20, 28, 45, 48, 58, 62, 63, 83, 91, 114, 118, 123, 128, 129, 137, 150
Remnant 115, 117
Renaissance 47
Replacement theology x, 45, 48, 58, 62, 63, 83, 91, 118, 123, 127, 128, 129, 137, 150
Resurrection 32, 109, 119, 126, 130, 132, 133, 135, 153

Revisionist christologies 132, 134 (See Christology)
Richardson, Peter 83, 166
Rivkin, Ellis 28, 29, 30, 34, 134, 157, 158, 159
Roberts, A. 160
Robinson, John A. T. 65, 165
Roetzel, Calvin 169
Roman Empire 11-12, 25, 34, 79, 148
Roman law 79
Roosevelt Administration 7
Rousseau, Jean Jacques 47
Ruether, Rosemary R. 56, 57, 58, 133, 135, 163, 171
Rumania 5
Russians 2

Sacraments 91, 133
Sadducees 30, 31, 95
Salvation history 68, 69, 88, 116, 125
Sanders, E. P. x, 57, 61, 63, 65, 66, 81, 92, 119, 163, 164, 165, 171
Sandmel, Samuel 39, 56, 57, 58, 66, 68, 160, 163, 165
Sanhedrin 34
Sarah 69-70, 79, 84, 85, 98, 103, 109, 125, 128, 147
Sarna, Jonathan D. 9, 156
Saxony 46
Schleiermacher, Friedrich 47
Schoeps, Hans Joachim 56
Schurer, Emil 159
Scripture 13, 14, 19, 25, 26, 35, 46, 50, 54, 56, 66, 76, 112, 114, 127, 142, 145, 150
Second Isaiah 18
Second temple 28
Seder meal 129
Segundo, Juan Luis xi, 145, 155, 172
Seleucid dynasty of Syria 149 (See Hasmonian Revolt/Antiochus IV)
Self-determination 138, 139
Sexism 151
Shadrach 149
Shammai 31
Shemoneh Esreh 82, 83 (Babylonian recension) (See Birkat ha-Shalom)
Shirer, William L. 156
Silberman, Charles ix

Scripture Index